21st Century Common Sense

(Fourth Edition)

21st Century Common Sense

(Fourth Edition)

A Bold Reform Agenda for our Broken, Gridlocked, Dysfunctional, and Boring Politics

Dr. Bob Spear

Printed in the United States of America

Fourth Edition, 2022

ISBN 13: 978-1-7330976-7-3

21CommonSense LLC

190 South Shore Road

Swanton, Maryland 21561, USA

Acknowledgments

Thanks to all those who advised, critiqued, edited, and otherwise contributed to the creation of this book. Some of you agreed with me, some disagreed in whole or in part, but all offered useful advice and suggestions. The most important contributor throughout was my advisor and editor Steve Herman. In addition to Steve, this list includes Susan Mezey, Michael Mezey, Kevin Faley, Jessica Josephson, Patrick Hunt, and Mark Stutzman. The list also includes several members of my family, especially my mother Idamae Spear, my brother-in-law Michael Fargione, and my wife Mary Helen Spear.

This book benefits greatly from the contributions of Carrie Tazbir, my illustrator. Please visit her portfolio at www.wix.com/carrietazbir.

Mary Helen was not only a valuable critic of various drafts but also the long-suffering spouse who put up with my preoccupation with this work for the last several years. I thank her forever and from the bottom of my heart.

Note: All of the many state and county maps, as well as maps of existing and previous Congressional Districts (CDs), are taken from official state sources in Maryland, Pennsylvania, North Carolina, Minnesota, and Louisiana. Maps showing proposed CDs were drawn by the author and are superimposed on official state maps.

Notes on the Fourth Edition

Based on feedback from readers and additional research, most especially the monograph *Every Vote Equal* by J.R. Koza *et al.* (2013), this version reflects a better understanding of the national popular vote to elect the President. Clearly the best solution is a constitutional amendment to provide for the direct election of the President. The National Popular Vote Interstate Compact (NPVIC) is preferred only if we are unable to pass the constitutional amendment Either way (NPVIC or constitutional amendment) the candidate with the most votes should win.

I replaced the three rounds of Presidential primaries proposed in the first edition of this book with a single National Primary Election. Ditto for the Chancellor primary. The Presidential/Chancellor primary is now combined with all Congressional primaries into one National Primary Election. Each primary election has three winners, determined through Ranked Choice Voting. The three primary winners then compete in the general election.

In the Fourth Edition, I am basing the revised Congressional redistricting proposal on county boundaries supplemented by Zip Code Tabulation Areas (ZCTAs) when it becomes necessary to partition a county. I eliminated multi-seat Congressional Districts as well as the procedure for counting ballots in multi-seat elections.

I have deleted or shortened explanations and caveats in the proposed Constitution II, recognizing the advantages of simplicity and asperity in language, as the Framers modeled for us all in the 1787 Constitution.

The Chancellor makes all judicial appointments, which are for 16-year terms. The Associate Justices of the Supreme Court select the Chief Justice from among themselves, again for a 16-year term.

Finally, I greatly shortened the detailed directions for redistricting, which now appear in Appendix 1.

Table of Contents

Executive Summary

THIS BOOK IN FIVE MINUTES

Full realization of democracy in America is a work in progress. We've come a long way, but still have a long way to go. This book discusses 21st century challenges to our democracy and proposes fixes to meet those challenges.

Part I. Challenges

1. Presidential Selection Challenge: The Presidential campaigns are way too long, the candidate selection process is overly complex and undemocratic, Vice Presidents (our likely future Presidents) are appointed rather than elected, and the electoral college is obsolete.

2. U.S. Senate Challenge: The Senate is not representative of the people. Each voter in the least populous state has 66 times more power to choose their Senator than each voter in the most populous state. That is hardly a democracy.

3. Gerrymander Challenge: Both major parties have become quite sophisticated and effective at drawing legislative districts that unfairly favor themselves.

4. Other Election System Challenges: First-Past-The-Post (FTPT) voting; the entrenched two-party system; caucuses, conventions, and closed primaries; interminable electioneering; voting rights restrictions; unlimited money in political campaigns; and lack of transparency and financial disclosures by candidates and officeholders all detract from the proper functioning of our democracy.

Part II. Fixes

1. Ranked Choice Voting (RCV)
   a. After selecting their 1st choice for each office, voters may also select a 2nd and a 3rd choice.
   b. If the top candidate has less than a majority of the 1st choice votes, then the candidate with the fewest votes is eliminated, and votes for

that candidate are reassigned to each voter's next highest choice. This process continues until someone has a majority of the total vote.

2. Two-Party System

    a. Open primaries are mandated for all federal elected offices. In an open primary, all candidates compete against each other, and all voters select among all candidates for that office regardless of party affiliation. All voters can vote in every primary. Open primaries replace all closed primaries, caucuses, and conventions. Every primary election has three winners, who go on to the general election.
    b. Eliminate legal preferences for the two-party system. Repeal all laws which mention or favor political parties.
    c. Political parties will still exist. They can hold meetings, caucuses, and conventions at their own expense. They can endorse candidates and adopt platforms. But no party has a legal advantage over any other party or independent candidate.

3. Empower Citizens to Amend the Constitution

    a. Citizens and states can propose a constitutional amendment. (Congress can also propose a constitutional amendment, as at present.)

    b. Voters have the final say: Voters must approve a constitutional amendment in two general elections separated by another general election and a new President. In both of these amendment ratification votes, ratification requires approval by a majority of all votes cast, including a majority of the votes cast in 60% of the states containing 60% of the U.S. population.

4. Presidential Selection Fix

    a. Shorten, simplify, and democratize the process of choosing Presidential candidates:

        i.   Hold a single National Primary Election for President, ending on October 15,

        ii. Apply the RCV procedure on a nationwide basis to determine the top three candidates who qualify for the general election, which concludes on December 15.

        iii. The three finalists for President must each announce their Vice Presidential running mate by October 22.

    b. Preferred alternative: Replace the position of Vice President with a new Chancellor of the Senate. Elect the Chancellor for a four-year term of office in even-numbered years not evenly divisible by 4 (that is, the years when we currently have mid-term elections). The Chancellor presides over the Senate, is first in line to succeed the President, and makes all judicial appointments.

    c. Provide for the direct election of the President and Vice President/Chancellor.

5. U.S. Senate Fix: Reconstitute the US Senate as a representative body. Each state gets one Senator for every five seats in the House, but every state gets at least one Senator, and no state gets more than six.

6. U.S. House of Representatives Fix: Mandate a rule-governed process for drawing congressional districts based solely on equalizing populations and keeping neighbors together. Except to resolve anomalies, this process must function without human decisions concerning any CD boundary, eliminating the gerrymander forever.

7. Other Election System Fixes

    a. Compress the political campaign season to run from Independence Day to the general election in December.

    b. Automatically register all voters at age 18. Establish a National Voter Registration Authority to maintain all voter rolls.

    c. The National Primary Election runs from October 1 to 15, and the National General Election runs from December 1 to 15. Voters mail their paper allots or drop them off at collection boxes so as to arrive by the final day of each election. Announce 1st-choice vote totals for each candidate daily.

    d. Campaign finance reform: Limit who can contribute, how much, and when. Limit fund-raising by candidates. Provide public financing for all general election campaigns.

e. For candidates and elected officials, require transparency and full financial disclosure, and prohibit nepotism.

Part III. A Revised Constitution

The proposed Constitution II would replace the existing 1787 Constitution. This new constitution incorporates all previous amendments to the 1787 Constitution, all the fixes proposed in Part II, and additional fixes that ought to be considered as long as we are rewriting the whole document. Part III also includes a procedure for ratification and transitioning to Constitution II.

The additional challenges and fixes included in Constitution II include these:

1. Congressional Rules Challenges and Fixes:

    a. Challenges: Congress follows rules which promote gridlock, preventing necessary legislative action. Presidents step into the resulting power vacuum, creating the imperial presidency.

    b. Fixes

        i. Limit or eliminate the filibuster. Reestablish majority rule in both chambers of Congress.

        ii. Reform the Senate's "advise and consent" procedure. Allow the President to make appointments if the Senate fails to act within 60 calendar days following a nomination.

        iii. Give Congress both advance notice and veto power over Presidential executive orders.

2. Bill of Rights Challenges and Fixes:

    a. Challenges: The Bill of Rights in the Constitution is incomplete. Some implied rights lack specificity or clarity. Some citizen rights and some states' rights are missing entirely.

    b. Fixes:

        i. Some implied rights should be clarified, such as privacy; freedom from discrimination and torture; the right to bear arms; and the rights to life, liberty, and the pursuit of happiness.

        ii. Some citizen rights missing from the Constitution should be included, such as the definition of citizens, voting rights, initiative and referendum, and approval of constitutional amendments.

iii. Some states' rights should also be included, such as the right of states to work in concert with each other without ceding power to the federal government, a limited right of states to supersede federal law, and a limited right to secede from the Union (with concurrence by both the state and the Union).

I offer Constitution II as a starting point for debate, not as the final solution. I am raising issues that Americans should discuss; others will certainly offer different and perhaps better solutions. I only ask that we judge each proposed solution by these measures: Will it make us more free? Will it make our democracy more representative, more democratic? Will it unify us or better bring us to consensus? Will it help us govern ourselves?

21st Century Common Sense
A Bold Reform Agenda for our Broken, Gridlocked, Dysfunctional, and Boring Politics

Preface

Democracy Works Best When We All Participate

Underlying Principle of Democracy:

"All men are created equal."

Every citizen is born with the same rights and responsibilities, fully equal before the law with every other citizen; and every citizen has the same power to participate in the public debate, voice his/her opinion, recommend a course of action, and influence the outcome.

If we can point to one underlying principle of democracy, it is the bold statement in the Declaration of Independence: "All men are created equal." This single principle informs all our democratic institutions and every form of democratic government. In a pure democracy like ancient Athens, all citizens come together in a huge meeting place to make all public decisions together. In a representative democracy, people freely select their representatives who in turn come together to make decisions for the common good. Whichever form of democracy the people choose, the underlying principle remains the same. No single citizen should have an advantage in the public square over any other citizen based on financial assets, social position, inheritance, educational attainment, race, gender, sexual orientation, religion, political affiliation, zip code or city or state where he/she happens to reside, or any other irrelevant factor.

In practice, this pure, underlying principle often gets compromised for two main reasons. Honest brokers don't always agree on how to implement the underlying principle in the fairest way, or the competing parties do not enter the political discussion as equals.

In the American system of government, we have instituted a number of practices that undermine the all-men-are-created-equal principle, that is, practices which effectively make some citizens more equal than others. Some citizens have a built-in and unfair advantage over their compatriots. For example, in the original Constitution, a slave was counted as 3/5 of a person for purposes of determining the population of each state and therefore the number of seats that each state would have in the House of Representatives. Similarly, each state was awarded two seats in the Senate, regardless of the number of persons in that state. Both of these constitutional provisions contradict the notion that all of us are created equal. Though not directly stated in the Constitution, the Supreme Court has enshrined the notion that corporations have the same rights as people, which means that corporations have a voice in public debates. We tolerate many practices in the public domain that make some people more equal than others, especially the outsized influence of corporate lobbyists and of the political donor class. When it comes to drafting laws, selecting candidates for public office, or getting the attention of elected officials, lobbyists and major contributors have an inside track. Joe citizen may try to compete, but he does so at a considerable disadvantage.

The major purpose of *21st Century Common Sense* (21CommonSense.org) is to examine the practices that give some Americans an unfair advantage and to recommend adjustments that would tend to level the playing field. There is no perfect system, nor will any set of laws or constitutional amendments make for an ideal system. The fixes that we will discuss are imperfect, of course, but they could help make the existing system better.

From the outset, let me state that I accept without qualification or argument the underlying principle that all of us are created equal. Someone who rejects that principle might find little of merit in *21st Century Common Sense*. We will examine those practices which give some citizens an inherent advantage over others to see whether we can realize greater opportunity for all.

Unfair or unequal practices include provisions of the federal or state constitutions, federal or state laws (or the lack of applicable laws), judicial decisions, or just common or accepted or traditional social or cultural practices. Regardless of the provenance of the practice or the reason for its continuance, we will examine it with a view to making our public business more fair, open, and equal for all.

This mission is not pie-in-the-sky rhetoric. Rather, it is exactly what our Founding Fathers undertook when they signed the Declaration of Independence, when they adopted the Articles of Confederation, and when they adopted the US Constitution. Our project will be a reappraisal of how we can better govern ourselves so as to make ours a more perfect union.

The Original Common Sense

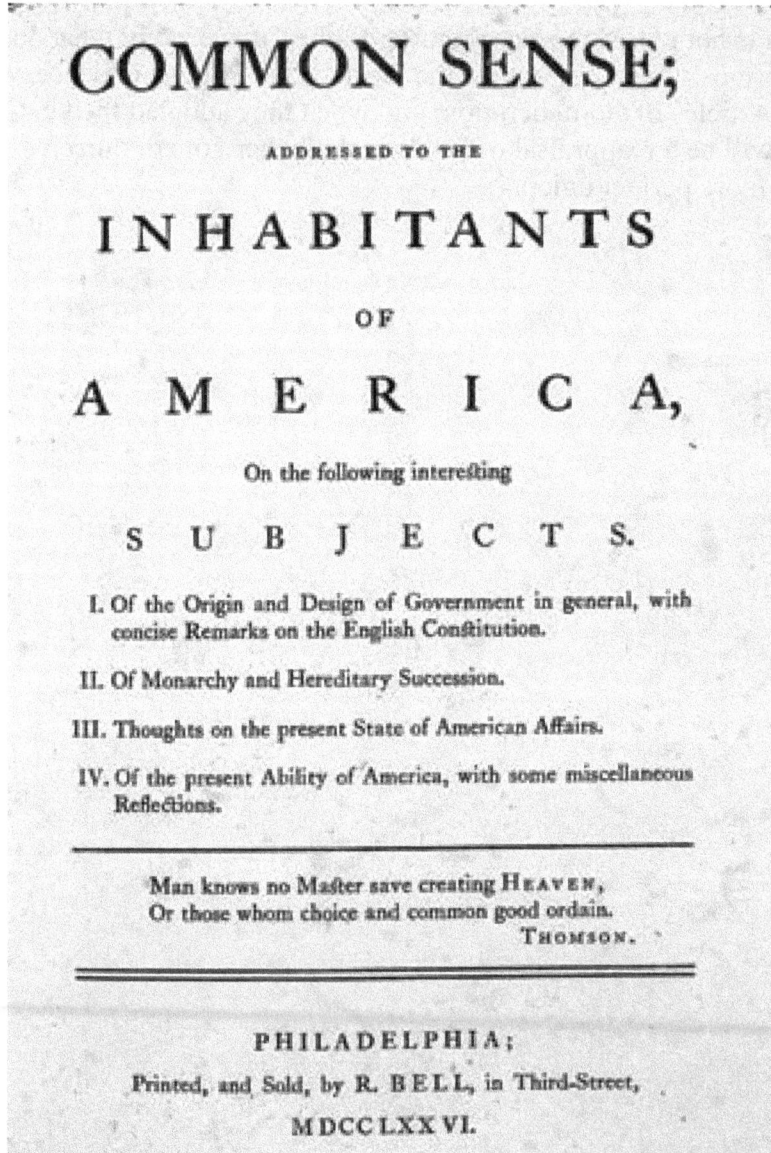

COMMON SENSE;

ADDRESSED TO THE

INHABITANTS

OF

A M E R I C A,

On the following interesting

S U B J E C T S.

I. Of the Origin and Design of Government in general, with concise Remarks on the English Constitution.

II. Of Monarchy and Hereditary Succession.

III. Thoughts on the present State of American Affairs.

IV. Of the present Ability of America, with some miscellaneous Reflections.

Man knows no Master save creating HEAVEN,
Or those whom choice and common good ordain.
THOMSON.

PHILADELPHIA;
Printed, and Sold, by R. BELL, in Third-Street,
MDCCLXXVI.

Thomas Paine's *Common Sense*, published in January 1776, inspired American colonists to adopt, by July of that same year, a completely radical idea: revolution against the government of King George III and establishment of a new and independent country based on the principles of liberty and self-government.

You can read Thomas Paine's original pamphlet, often called the most influential political tract of all time, at https://archive.org/details/commonsense00painrich

Common Sense for the 21st Century

21st Century Common Sense is a 21st century version of the same thing: bold proposals for reforming the American Government based on the principles of liberty and self-government. Unlike Thomas Paine's revolutionary tract, my ideas are bold rather than radical: Thomas Paine and his fellow revolutionists wanted to throw out the British Monarchy and everything associated with it; I on the other hand want to build on what we have achieved, preserve all that is good and valuable in our existing political structures, but boldly transform the broken pieces into something more democratic, more representative, more of a perfect union.

Let me briefly comment on my purpose, assumptions, and intended audience:

- My **Purpose** is to spark discussion, debate, and action. I am tired of hearing Americans grousing about our broken politics. We need to begin the kind of national conversation that leads to real political reform. Such reforms may include new federal and state laws and constitutional amendments, new political customs, and new social norms.

- **Assumptions**: As you peruse this volume, I assume that you will recognize and concur with the litany of ills we face. I am less sanguine about the prospects for general acceptance of the solutions I am proposing. These are all draft proposals – the best that this author is able to offer at the time of writing, but not necessarily the best you or all of us together can devise. Our political dysfunction today is analogous to the economic dysfunction this nation faced in the Great Depression. When FDR was campaigning for President in 1932, he famously stated, "The country needs and, unless I mistake its temper, the country demands bold, persistent experimentation. It is common sense to take a method and try it. If it fails, admit it frankly and try something else. But above all try something."[1]

---

[1] Franklin Roosevelt, Commencement Address at Oglethorpe University, May 22, 1932. *The Atlanta Constitution*, May 23, 1932.

Perhaps that is a prescription worth remembering when we try to reform our politics.

- **Audience**: While political scientists and students of American government may find something of interest here, I do not offer my commentary as a formal academic work, building on the last two centuries of academic political science research. Rather, this book is directed at laymen, reasonably informed American voters, and anyone interested in improving the American political system.

21st Century Common Sense is presented as a series of interrelated essays:

- *Part I. Challenges* provides some historical context on how we got to our current democracy and on the challenges we face in maintaining and improving it.
- *Part II. Fixes* lays out the constitutional amendments, federal and state laws, and cultural/social behaviors needed to meet those challenges.
- *Part III: A Revised Constitution* incorporates all previous amendments to the 1787 Constitution, all the fixes proposed in Part II, and several other provisions that may as well be updated if we are going to create a whole new document. Part III also suggests a procedure for proposing Constitution II to the people and states for ratification and for transitioning to Constitution II.

In addition to this printed version, you can view a set of PowerPoint presentations summarizing the main points at 21CommonSense.org.

Part I. Challenges

Ship of State

Introduction to Part I

How We Got Here

American democracy has been under development since Colonial times as settlements, villages, town, cities, and colonies experimented with various forms of self-government. They paid little more than lip service to what was going on in Europe. It's true that the King of England appointed royal governors for each colony. But England was months away by ship. An emissary had to cross the Atlantic twice to get a message or decision over and back, and so governors usually depended on the colonists themselves to implement the functions of government. Each colony had an elected legislative body (lower chamber) and a privy Senate (upper chamber) appointed by the governor but made up of colonists. Purely local matters were largely left in the hands of those localities.

In the mid-18th century, relations between England and their American colonies became increasingly bitter as the English King and Parliament began to intervene more directly and forcefully into Colonial affairs over the colonists' objections.

England believed that it was only exercising its God-given right to rule, the colonists thought that England was usurping their rights of self-government that they had enjoyed for two centuries.

Hence a movement began among the Colonies to separate themselves from England, to declare independence, and to form a new nation.

Bitter argument between loyalists (or Tories) and separatists came to a head in 1776. In January of that year, Thomas Paine published *Common Sense,* his 48-page pamphlet excoriating the King and Parliament and indeed all autocratic governments. His essay was a forceful polemic in favor of American independence. Then, at a meeting of all the colonies in Philadelphia in July 1776, the American Colonies issued their *Declaration of Independence* from England. Before that meeting *Common Sense* had gone through multiple printings and reprintings, making it the single most successful political pamphlet in history. Before Independence, historians estimate that about a third of the colonists supported separation from England, a third wanted to remain a part of England, and a third were undecided. But Thomas Paine's pamphlet helped swing opinion in favor of independence.

To become and remain a new nation, America first had to fight and win a war against England, the American Revolutionary War (1776-1783). Then America had to set up the mechanics of a new government. The colonies cooperated marginally well during the war, motivated by the urgency of facing a common enemy. But that cooperation was certain to falter once the war was over. For that reason, discussions/meetings/conventions took place from 1777 to 1781. Their purpose was to establish the post-war American Government, uniting the thirteen original states in perpetuity. These meetings finally produced the Articles of Confederation, which lasted as America's foundational document from 1781 to 1787.

While perhaps a good first step in creating a constitutional democracy, the Articles of Confederation was flawed in many serious ways. Because its authors mistrusted the kind of strong central government epitomized by England, they designed an exceedingly weak national government. The Articles of Confederation gave most powers to the states and gave the central government no enforcement mechanism to ensure that every state lived up to its obligations. The Articles created Congress, a unicameral national legislature that also exercised executive and judicial functions. The Articles of Confederation did not provide for the election of any federal official directly by the people. Rather, each state legislature appointed two to seven Delegates to Congress. All votes in Congress were taken by state with each state having one vote. Major decisions required the concurrence of nine states; lesser matters could be decided by a simple majority. Further, the Articles required unanimous consent of every state legislature in order to adopt any amendments to the Articles themselves.

Recognizing that the Articles of Confederation was not working, leaders throughout the states called for a Constitutional Convention, which convened in Philadelphia in 1787. Every state was invited to send a delegation to help write a new foundational document or to at least amend the original Articles. Every state except Rhode Island sent a delegation. That convention produced the 1787 Constitution of the United States, and ultimately all 13 states ratified it. Interestingly, the 1787 Constitution required only nine states to ratify it, after which it came into full force and effect among those states that had ratified it. The authors knew going in that they would probably not be successful if they required unanimous consent, so they decided to ignore that requirement of the Articles. (In this respect the Framers set a very good precedent for the solution to our current challenges presented in Part III of this work.)

While the 1787 Constitution corrected many of the faults of the Articles of Confederation, American democratic government remained then (and still remains) a work in progress. Among the most significant improvements of the 1787 Constitution over the Articles of Confederation are the following:

- A far stronger federal government with the power and authority to carry out its duties throughout the United States.
- Separation of the powers of the federal government into three co-equal branches – legislative, executive, and judicial.
- A federal system of governments, composed of a federal government separate and distinct from the several state governments, which remain sovereign within their own jurisdictions.
- A careful system of checks and balances, both between the federal government and the states and among the co-equal branches of the federal government.
- A bicameral legislature, the Congress, consisting of a more numerous lower chamber, the House of Representatives, and an upper chamber, the Senate. The people elect the House of Representatives directly, with the number of Representatives from each state proportional to the population in each state. Originally, state legislatures appointed the members of the Senate, with two senators per state.

- Election of the President by electors appointed by each state, with the number of electors from each state equaling the total number of senators and representatives from that state. (We now refer to the collection of electors from all states as the electoral college, even though the term "electoral college" does not appear in the Constitution.) Quite interestingly, the 1787 Constitution does not require that the people choose the electors from each state, though that is the case today. (In the first Presidential election, held from December 1788 through January 1789, only six states held a popular vote.)
- The Senate's "advice and consent" role in confirming Presidential executive and judicial appointments and in ratifying treaties as well as other limitations on the power of the President.
- A fairly detailed list of the powers of Congress, limitations on the powers of Congress, powers of the states, and limitations on the powers of the states.
- Jurisdiction of the federal courts.

While ratification of the Constitution was being debated, many critics thought the role of the federal government would be too powerful vis-à-vis both the states and the individual citizen. Therefore, a series of amendments were proposed to make the rights of the people and of the states more secure. These amendments would then be submitted to the states for their approval as soon as the Constitution itself was adopted. Ten of these amendments were ratified in 1791 and became known as the Bill of Rights. Many of our most precious rights as American citizens derive directly from the Bill of Rights. These first ten amendments are as follows:

Amendment 1: Freedom of religion, speech, the press, and assembly

Amendment 2: Right to bear arms

Amendment 3: Limits on the quartering of soldiers in private houses

Amendment 4: Limits on searches and seizures without a warrant

Amendment 5: Rights of defendants in criminal cases: indictment by a grand-jury; protection against double-jeopardy and self-incrimination; prohibition against the loss of life, liberty, or property without due process of law; limits on eminent domain

Amendment 6: More rights of defendants in criminal cases: speedy trial by an impartial jury, access to information concerning the accusations against them, confrontation of witnesses, compulsory evidence for the defense, and the assistance of counsel

Amendment 7: Right to a trial by jury in civil cases

Amendment 8: Prohibition of excessive bail, excessive fines, and cruel and unusual punishments

Amendment 9: Rights of the people beyond those enumerated in the Constitution

Amendment 10: Powers not given to the federal government by the Constitution are reserved to the states and to the people.

The original 1787 Constitution was less than perfect from the outset, and it did not create a most perfect union. Even the Framers themselves, or many of them, recognized that their work was incomplete – hence the insistence on the Bill of Rights, adopted as amendments to the Constitution during George Washington's first term as President.

Progress in Democracy

After 1791, the long course of American history bends in favor of the expansion of democracy, enfranchisement of wider segments of the populace, and giving more power to the people. Though some of these changes remain controversial, all of them expand citizen rights, empower individuals and groups, and/or ensure equality before the law. We have made major improvements through constitutional amendments, judicial decisions, laws, and customs. Examples in each category follow:

Expansion of democracy through constitutional amendments

- Abolition of slavery (13th Amendment, 1865)
- Citizenship rights (14th Amendment, 1868)
- Right to vote regardless of race (15th Amendment, 1870)
- Direct election of Senators by the people (17th Amendment, 1913)
- Women's right to vote (19th Amendment, 1920)
- Limit of President to two terms of office (22nd Amendment, 1951)

- Right to vote for President extended to the District of Columbia (23rd Amendment, 1961)
- Elimination of poll tax or other impediments to voting (24th Amendment, 1964)
- Right of all citizens to vote at age 18 (26th Amendment, 1971)

Expansion of rights through Supreme Court decisions

- Brown v. the Board of Education of Topeka, Kansas (1954): Made school segregation illegal
- Miranda v. Arizona (1966): Requires law enforcement to advise suspects in custody of their right to remain silent (right against self-incrimination) and of their right to an attorney
- Loving v. Virginia (1967): Banned laws which forbade interracial marriage
- Roe v. Wade (1973): Established a woman's right to an abortion before the third trimester of pregnancy
- District of Columbia v. Heller (2008): Established the Second Amendment right of an individual citizen to own a firearm for traditionally lawful purposes, such as self-defense within the home

Expansion of rights through federal laws

- Social Security Act
- Voting Rights Act
- Freedom of Information Act
- Right to organize unions
- Child labor laws, minimum wage laws, and laws concerning workplace health and safety
- Equal access to education for women, the disabled, minorities, and the poor
- Expanding access to healthcare: Medicare, Medicaid, Veterans Health Administration, and the Affordable Care Act
- Environmental protection laws – the EPA, clean water, and clean air
- Right to privacy

Remaining Electoral Challenges

Although we have made progress toward the achievement of "a more perfect union", much remains to be done. The balance of Part I of this paper discusses the principal election-related challenges we face today. Part II proposes constitutional amendments, laws, and procedures which would go a long way toward meeting those challenges. Finally, Part III proposes a rewrite of the 1787 Constitution, titled Constitution II, an easier and more straightforward path to meeting all these challenges at once, empowering citizens, making our country more democratic and more representative of its citizens, and "forming a more perfect union".

The principal electoral challenges are these:

1. Deficiencies in the manner of choosing the President and Vice President
2. The Non-Representative U.S. Senate
3. Gerrymandering of Congressional Districts
4. Other counterproductive characteristics of current federal election practices

Challenge 1. Presidential Selection

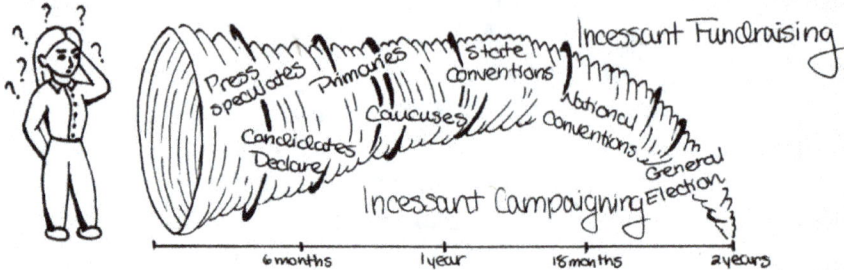

Most Americans agree that our Presidential elections last too long and are unnecessarily complicated and unrepresentative. Vice Presidential candidates are appointed rather than elected, and the electoral college is obsolete.

...Too Long

1. In the last several Presidential election cycles, we have been evolving into a perpetual Presidential campaign season. No sooner do we complete a Presidential election than parties and candidates begin jockeying for position in anticipation of the next election, four years hence. Since many of the potential Presidential candidates already hold elective office, they have limited time or patience for the mundane task of governance (for which they supposedly were elected to their current positions) and instead become focused almost exclusively on the next Presidential election.

2. Right now, the period of active campaigning extends at least two years. In January 2015, fully 21 months before the 2016 general election, pundits, insiders, and experts agreed that it was becoming almost too late for any additional candidates to get into the race. (Of course, the ultimate winner did not enter the fray until June, although lots of speculation about his potential candidacy surrounded him before he

officially announced.) For the 2020 presidential election cycle, the same timeframes ensued: Potential candidates were campaigning by the time of the 2018 midterm elections.

3. These interminable campaigns are endurance contests, exhausting for both the candidates and the public. They do not necessarily show which candidates might have the requisite qualifications, experience, character, temperament, and wisdom to serve as Chief Executive. Rather, they show which candidates can survive the grueling schedule while committing the fewest public gaffes.

4. Interminable campaigning and lack of attention to actually governing frustrates the public and turns them off to serious political discourse. We hear sound bites and talking points *ad nauseam*. Rarely do we hear serious proposals or debates about real issues.

...Too Complicated

1. In addition to going on way too long, the process involves procedures and schedules established by each state, with no rhyme or reason for each state's choices (at least none discernible to the public) and certainly no national plan.

2. Some states have a primary, while others have a caucus. Why?

3. In most states, the primary or caucus is held on the same day for all, while in other states the Republicans hold their primary or caucus on one day while the Democrats hold theirs on a different day. Why?

4. Several states have both a primary and a caucus. Why?

5. In some states, voters may choose which party's primary/caucus to vote in on election day; in other states, voters must be a registered member of a particular party in order to vote in that party's primary; and in a third group of states, Democrats vote in the Democratic primary, Republicans vote in the Republican primary, and independents can vote in either; and finally, at least in Nevada, Independents can vote in both the Republican and the Democratic primaries. Why?

6. Some states award delegates to winning candidates proportionally while other states have a winner-take-all rule. Why?
7. Caucuses are unrepresentative and basically unfair, contributing to the general perception that the whole process is rigged.
8. After all the primaries and caucuses and state conventions, national party conventions can still thwart the will of the electorate.

Conclusion: Presidential primaries should be simplified and standardized among all states. If this were done, public apathy would abate, enthusiasm engendered, voter participation increased, and confidence in the results restored.

...Undemocratic

How many times have you heard voters and pundits decry the choices available to them? Citizens are unhappy and frustrated with the process, which results, in their view, in two major party candidates neither of whom reflect the interests of the citizens these candidates purport to represent. Part of the problem here is that, during the primary season, candidates must appeal to the most radical, entrenched, vocal, diehard elements of their own political party – after all, that is usually the best way to win the party's nomination. The public be damned. Candidates who appeal to the majority of the electorate, rather than the majority of their own party, rarely succeed. As a result, we often end up with two major party candidates who are disliked by most of the voters who will choose between them on the day of the general election.

This might not be the only time that we need to remember the caution the Founding Fathers, especially George Washington, gave us against the formation of "factions", that is, political parties. Factions divide us; factions make it difficult for us to agree on a common agenda, a common solution, or a common candidate.

We do have political parties, and they are powerful, entrenched, and resilient against reform. Any effort to do away with political parties is probably doomed to failure. The two-party system is entrenched in every state, hallowed by tradition, and protected by myriad laws. It has served us well in many cases. For example, political parties make it possible for Congress to pass laws by insisting on some degree of party discipline in voting for a legislative agenda.

Yet we need to find a way to allow citizens to select candidates for President without respect to party labels. It's fine for citizens who agree on a common agenda to coalesce in order to elect candidates who agree with them – that is, it's fine for citizens to unite as members of a political party. Nevertheless, citizens in a true democracy should be able to select Presidential candidates who appeal to the nation writ large rather than to limit our choices to those who have won the allegiance of only their own political party.

VP Candidates Appointed

We leave the selection of Vice President entirely in the hands of one person, the Presidential candidate of each political party. How often have we witnessed this charade? The party's candidate for President, facing the camera with serious demeanor, announces solemnly that his choice of Vice President is not only his first important decision but also that he takes this responsibility very seriously. Further, the candidate states that he is choosing the one person most capable of fulfilling the duties of Vice President and also, if necessary (gulp and sigh), President.

Yet we know from long experience that these statements are poppycock. More likely, the person chosen as the Vice Presidential candidate is one who may unify the party, help the party win one or more key states in the general election, provide geographic balance to the ticket, or shore up some perceived shortcomings in the Presidential candidate.

Rarely is the Vice Presidential candidate the only or the best person to carry out the duties of that office: 1) serve as President of the Senate, 2) cast the tie-breaking vote in the Senate when the votes are evenly divided, 3) count the ballots for President and Vice President following the next Presidential election, and 4) inquire daily at the White House as to the President's health. It's this last responsibility, of course, which should be our primary concern.

Presidents sometimes use their V.P.'s in other ways as well, such as performing ceremonial functions as an adjunct to or substitute for the President, joining the President's cabinet, or serving as a Presidential advisor.

The Vice President occupies the second-highest position in our democracy and has a clear advantage when it comes to choosing a successor. Fourteen of our nation's Vice Presidents later became President, either through the death or resignation of the President or by a subsequent election. Think about that: 14 of our 46 Presidents to date (nearly a third) served earlier as Vice President. Only two Vice Presidents wanted the job of President but never got elected. So why should we leave the selection of Vice President solely in the hands of one person?

One can make an argument for the current custom: After their election, the President and Vice President should work together as a team, and for this reason the team captain should be able to choose his/her running mate. But that argument seems less persuasive than the argument that the voters should choose the Vice Presidential candidate, especially in light of the fact that V.P.'s so often later become Presidents.

We should not pretend that the voters get to choose the Vice President in the general election. Voters almost never make their selection for President based on who is running for VP. At best, that is a secondary consideration.

To summarize the argument: Presidential candidates select our Vice Presidents; we do not really elect them. Vice Presidents become Presidents (14 did so, and only two who wanted to, failed in that attempt). This outcome is hardly democratic. Hence we need a more democratic system of choosing our Vice Presidents.

We do have some leeway here: the constitution is completely silent on the question of how we go about selecting candidates for Vice President. Recall that in the original 1787 Constitution, the electors (members of what we now call the electoral college) were required to vote for two people. The person receiving the most votes would become the next President, and the person with the second-most votes would become the next Vice President. With George Washington on the ballot in the first two Presidential elections, this procedure was not a problem: Washington was the unanimous choice for President while a plethora of candidates split the vote for second place. After Washington's tenure, political parties formed and began fielding a ticket consisting of a Presidential candidate running alongside his Vice Presidential candidate. If electors chose the party's ticket, the likely result would be a tie between the Presidential and Vice Presidential candidates. Indeed, the likelihood of a tie was a major issue following the elections of 1796 and 1800.

The 12th Amendment to the Constitution, ratified in 1804, solved this problem since it requires members of the electoral college to fill out two ballots, one for President and another for Vice President. Since 1804, political parties have contested every Presidential election. Each party nominates a ticket consisting of a Presidential and a Vice Presidential nominee, and voters in the general election are asked to choose among the tickets.

However, the Constitution does not mandate candidates for President and Vice President running together as a "ticket". If we choose to do so, could we not move away from Presidential and Vice Presidential elections controlled by two major political parties? Since the selection of Vice President is so momentous, shouldn't we let voters determine the nominees? Democracy is all about choice and especially about who gets to make the choices. When we think about improving the way we choose our next President, we should also consider ways of democratizing the selection of Vice President. Shouldn't we insist on a primary election for Vice President?

[Interesting sidebar: Election of 1788]

Only 10 of the 13 original states submitted electoral votes in the first Presidential election. Rhode Island and North Carolina could not participate because they had not yet ratified the Constitution. Only six states held a popular election to choose electors. Five states opted to let the state legislature choose electors, but New York's legislature became deadlocked and so it cast no electoral votes. George Washington was unanimously elected President with 69 electoral votes. Everyone knew that Washington would win, but after that all bets were off. John Adams, with 34 electoral votes, came in second and became our first Vice President.

The Framers expected most elections to end up in the House of Representatives. That actually happened in 1801 and 1825, but we have avoided any subsequent occurrences. Because most Americans now believe that the people should select the Chief Executive, we would consider the notion of throwing the Presidential election into the House as a constitutional crisis.[2]

Obsolete Electoral College

The US Constitution established the electoral college system, which gives each state a number of Presidential electors equal to the states' representation in Congress – that is, the number of its Representatives in the House plus its two Senators. We currently have 538 electors (based on 435 seats in the House of Representatives, 100 Senators, plus 3 from the District of Columbia). The Presidential candidate that wins a majority of the electoral college votes (270) is declared the winner. The Constitution also provides that state legislatures have the power to determine how those electors will be selected, and the Supreme Court has adjudged that this power belongs exclusively to the state legislatures. The Constitution does not require participation by the people in any way: Although we have a public election for President in all 50 states and in Washington, DC, such an election is not constitutionally required. The legislature of Alaska or Maryland or

---

[2] United States Presidential Election, 1788–89. https://en.wikipedia.org/wiki/United_States_Presidential_election,_1788-89 [accessed on June 6, 2017.]

(you name it state) could decide tomorrow that they will no longer hold a Presidential election, but rather, that state's Presidential electors (members of the electoral college) will be chosen by lot, or randomly by zip code, or by a committee of the legislature, or by any other means the legislature so chooses. About the only restriction placed on state legislatures is that they cannot appoint a member of Congress or any other federal officer to serve as a Presidential elector.

The Framers' Objectives

In 21st century America, it's easy to criticize the Framers of the Constitution for creating the electoral college and for not considering a role for the citizenry at large. But remember again that the Framers, while fearful of too much power in the hands of an autocrat or for those already in power, were also fearful of too much power in the hands of a mob. Hence they created this indirect Presidential selection method.

The Framers had three main objectives when they created the electoral college system, but those objectives have not panned out in reality:

1. Ensure the indirect selection of the President and Vice President – that is, allow states to choose the electors but then allow those electors to choose whomever they want for President. Nothing in the Constitution suggests or requires that the electors will be pledged to support a particular candidate. In fact every four years we face the prospect of "faithless electors", that is, members of the electoral college who threaten to vote or who actually vote for a different candidate than the one to whom they are nominally pledged. "Faithless electors" have never altered the outcome of an election; yet by way of contrast, the Founders' original intent of independent electors making the Presidential selection has never worked in practice. [Note: If the system of indirect election of the President has never worked as intended, you might ask why, after two centuries, do we still have it? Why indeed!]

    a. Reality check: Today the last thing anyone wants or expects of Presidential electors is independent judgment. Meanwhile, polling over many decades demonstrates that the overwhelming majority of Americans much prefer direct election of the President.

2. Balance large states versus small states and give an outsized influence to small states. This is why the number of electors in the electoral college assigned to each state equals the total number of Senators and Representatives for that state. Had the Framers not been persuaded by the fear of the small states being engulfed by the large states, then the electoral college might very well have been designed with only the number of seats in the House assigned to each state, rather than the total of the Senators and the Representatives. Including the number of Senators (two per state) gives an advantage to states with smaller populations.

   a. Reality check: In *Every Vote Equal,* the authors demonstrate how badly the small states have been served by the current system. The only small state with a meaningful role in Presidential elections is New Hampshire, because of its first-in-the-nation primary. Presidential campaigns totally ignore all the other small jurisdictions (defined as those with only one or two House seats -- AK, DC, DE, HI, ID, ME, MT, ND, RI, SD, VT, and WY), though together these 12 states + DC have 40 electoral votes. Meanwhile, Ohio alone, with 18 electoral votes, gets tons more attention than all the small states combined.[3] The simple reality is that large versus small states has never been an election issue, so perhaps we could safely dispense with the inherent advantage to those states with small populations.

3. Encourage the selection of candidates who have a wide geographic following. The electoral college system was supposed to make it difficult for a candidate wildly popular in one state or region of the country to be elected President if that candidate had little or no support elsewhere.

   a. Reality check: This design has not always worked perfectly: We elected Abraham Lincoln in 1860 with support from only the Northern states. Further, since at least 41 states + DC have not

---

[3] Koza, J.R. et al. (2013). *Every Vote Equal,* p.54f.

been competitive for years, the current system results in meaningful Presidential campaigns in only a handful of competitive states. Nationwide appeal is irrelevant.

The Constitution also provides a procedure for choosing the President when no candidate receives a majority of electoral votes. In that case, the House of Representatives chooses the President, but every state gets only one vote. Just about all Americans agree that letting the House pick the President would be a disaster for our democracy, making it exceedingly difficult for the ultimate winner to govern, especially if the House chose a candidate without a plurality of either the electoral vote or the popular vote.

Current Practice

At present, in every state except two (Nebraska and Maine), the candidate receiving the most popular votes in that state is awarded all the electoral votes in that state. Since most states are not competitive, Presidential campaigns ignore them. For example, in the general election campaign in 2016, what candidate bothered to campaign in Massachusetts (which Hillary Clinton won 61% to 34%) or Kansas (which Donald Trump won 57% to 36%)? Answer: no one. Campaigns ignore voters in all but a handful of states. Many analyses of Presidential campaigns have been published, showing that the 8 or 9 swing states receive all or nearly all of the campaign visits by the Presidential candidates themselves during the last two months of the campaign, meaning that the other 41 states are ignored. This focus continues post-election: In their first year in office, the new President visits these same swing states most often.

The ultimate results of Presidential elections sometimes appear perverse: In five of our Presidential elections, the candidate who won the popular vote failed to win the Presidency.

After the 2016 election, a Pennsylvania political activist opined that the current electoral college system is just fine, observing that both major party candidates paid attention to Scranton and Harrisburg in the waning days of the campaign, and that they would not have done so if we had a system where the winner is the one receiving the most popular votes. The observation about the candidates paying attention to Scranton and Harrisburg is true, but the logic is backward: How about the citizens of Los Angeles, who received no visits or attention from either party in the run-up to the election? Don't those citizens also merit some attention?

The motivation to change the electoral college system is to make every vote count and to encourage candidates to attend to the concerns of voters in every state.

National polls indicate that 58% of American voters would prefer a system in which the candidate for President receiving the most popular votes would be the winner of the election[4].

By the way, I feel obliged to respond here to critics who have suggested that the winners of the 2000 and the 2016 Presidential elections are somehow illegitimate because they did not win the popular vote. This is nonsense. George W Bush and Donald Trump won their elections based on the rules of the game at the time the game was played. Any criticism about their legitimacy is like claiming that the losing football team should be awarded the victory because they gained more yards than their opponent. I would say, if we do not like the rules of the game, then we must change the rules, but amendments only affect future contests. What might have happened if the rules had been different in 2000 or in 2016? Maybe the winners – Bush and Trump – would have employed different strategies, maybe they would have campaigned in California, and maybe they would have won the popular vote too. Let us be clear: The challenge is to fix the rules going forward, not to re-litigate the elections of the past.

---

[4] Daniller, A. (2020). "A majority of Americans continue to favor replacing the Electoral College with a nationwide popular vote". Pew Research Center (March 13). [Available online at https://www.pewresearch.org/fact-tank/2020/03/13/a-majority-of-americans-continue-to-favor-replacing-electoral-college-with-a-nationwide-popular-vote/, accessed on 2/5/2022.]

Challenge 2. Senate Structure

Consider this scenario. You are attending a high school reunion at a state park, and 66 of your classmates show up. You all agree to go on a nature walk but must choose between Trail A, an easy 2-mile stroll through the forest, and Trail B, 1.5 miles of steep, rocky terrain with little protection from the sun.

Jokingly, you all agree that, since we live in a democracy, this decision too should be made democratically. And so it is. The vote is 65 in favor of Trail A and one in favor of Trail B. Based on our time-honored democratic tradition, you all march off together – on TRAIL B!

The one lonely vote for Trail B outweighed 65 votes for Trail A!

Does that sound very democratic to you? Yet that is precisely how American "democracy" works in the makeup of the US Senate.

Let me explain.

Proportional Representation

The United States Senate is not a representative body. It does not represent the people of the United States and was never intended to. Rather, the framers of the Constitution designed the House of Representatives (the so-called "People's House") to represent the people and the Senate to represent the states. In this scheme, every state is equal: each state has two Senators, as provided by Article I Section 3 of the Constitution.

The original Constitution provided that the Senators from each state would be chosen by their respective state legislatures. Only later did states and citizens begin to recognize the value of adopting the more democratic and more representative practice of direct election of Senators by the people. Finally, direct election was mandated by the 17th Amendment to the Constitution, adopted in 1913. (By the way, the fact that we changed the method of Senate elections and removed the power of state legislatures to select Senators proves that we do have the ability to modify the Constitution and to move slowly toward a more representative democracy.) (Also, by the way, I am rather surprised that no one has successfully argued before the Supreme Court that, following adoption of the 17th amendment, the principle of "one man, one vote" should mandate proportional representation in the Senate.)

Perhaps it is time to make another move toward representative democracy in the makeup of the upper chamber of our national legislature.

Did you know that a citizen of Wyoming has 66 times more power in selecting his Senator than a citizen of California has in selecting his Senator? (That is, in the class reunion scenario at the top of this essay, if the 65 folks who voted for Trail A came from California, and the one classmate who voted for Trail B came from Wyoming, then Trail B gets selected fair and square – those are just the rules of our democracy.) Did you know that a citizen of Vermont has 40 times more power in choosing a Senator than a citizen of Texas? The populations of these states are as follows:

State	Census in 2010	Senators	Population per Senator
California	37,253,956	2	18,626,978
Wyoming	563,626	2	281,813

Texas	25,145,561	2	12,572,781
Vermont	625,741	2	312,871

Now, if Senator A represents 20 million people, while Senator B represents only a half million people, then each voter in Senator B's state has 40 times as much power to influence the Senate as each voter in Senator A's state. When it comes to the next Senatorial election, voters in Senator A's state who oppose his reelection must convince 40 times as many voters as compared to the voters in Senator B's state. This is inherently unfair. Here is a table of all 50 states, showing the Relative Power Per Person (RP/PP) in each state relative to the power of a person in California, which, with the largest population, has by definition the least power per citizen in choosing his state's Senators:

State	RP/PP	State	RP/PP	State	RP/PP
California	1.0	Missouri	6.2	Nevada	13.8
Texas	1.5	Maryland	6.5	New Mexico	18.1
New York	1.9	Wisconsin	6.6	West Virginia	20.1
Florida	2.0	Minnesota	7.0	Nebraska	20.4
Illinois	2.9	Colorado	7.4	Idaho	23.8
Pennsylvania	2.9	Alabama	7.8	Hawaii	27.4
Ohio	3.2	South Carolina	8.1	Maine	28.0
Michigan	3.8	Louisiana	8.2	New Hampshire	28.3
Georgia	3.8	Kentucky	8.6	Rhode Island	35.4
North Carolina	3.9	Oregon	9.7	Montana	37.7
New Jersey	4.2	Oklahoma	9.9	Delaware	41.5

Virginia	4.7	Connecticut	10.4	South Dakota	45.8
Washington	5.5	Iowa	12.2	Alaska	52.5
Massachusetts	5.7	Mississippi	12.6	North Dakota	55.4
Indiana	5.7	Arkansas	12.8	Vermont	59.5
Arizona	5.8	Kansas	13.1	Wyoming	66.1
Tennessee	5.9	Utah	13.5		

Of course, the relative power of each citizen in the Senate has always been unfair, but two huge facts made it less unfair when the Constitution was written than it is now. First, as pointed out above, the framers of the Constitution were not trying to make a democratic Senate in terms of representing people; rather, they were trying to create a body that would represent states, and in fact they assigned to state legislatures the power to choose that state's Senators. But as time passed, Americans came to value the notions that Senators should represent people and that people should directly elect them. Second, the populations of the thirteen original states were not as dramatically lopsided as the populations of the 50 states are today. Here are the populations of the thirteen original states in the first census after the Constitution was adopted (1790) along with the RP/PP of each citizen relative to the voting power of a citizen of Virginia (since Virginia had the most people):

State	Population in the 1790 census	RP/PP
Virginia	747,610	1.0
Pennsylvania	434,373	1.7
North Carolina	393,751	1.9
Massachusetts	378,787	2.0
New York	340,120	2.2

Maryland	319,728	2.3
South Carolina	249, 073	3.0
Connecticut	237,946	3.1
New Jersey	184,139	4.1
New Hampshire	141,885	5.3
Georgia	82,548	9.1
Rhode Island	69,825	10.7
Delaware	59,094	12.7

As you can see, the difference in Senatorial power per person between the least populous state (Delaware) and the most populous (Virginia) was 12.7 to 1 – as compared to today when the largest difference is 66 (Wyoming) to 1 (California), and 19 states have a difference greater than the most lopsided difference in the first Senate under the 1787 Constitution.

Iterative and Perpetual Characteristics of the Senate's Undemocratic Imbalance

Due to the undemocratic imbalance in the Senate, all legislation is held hostage. Because of the Senate's traditional filibuster rules (where 41 Senators can block any legislation by talking it to death), it is possible today for Senators from the 21 least populous states, representing only 10% of the population, to prevent Senate action on any bill. Again, this is hardly a democratic state of affairs.

This imbalance stretches two steps further:

a) The Constitution incorporates the Senate's unfairness into the formula for allocating the number of electors from each state to the electoral college: the number of electors in each state equals the total number of Senators and Representatives, giving a disproportionate number of electors to the states with less population.

35

b) Article V of the Constitution precludes any constitutional amendment that reduces any state's equal representation in the Senate without its consent. Hence, we may not be able to fix this problem with a normal constitutional amendment unless the legislatures of all 50 states agree.

Provenance of Structural Unfairness in our Constitutional System

---

"In America, everything is about race."

An old adage, oft-quoted by African-American authors

This oft-quoted adage certainly applies to the deliberations of the Constitutional Convention in 1787. James Madison, among others, argued for direct election of the President by nationwide popular vote. However, other delegates from slave-holding states argued against universal suffrage: if the Convention adopted universal suffrage for President and for both Houses of Congress, the Southern states would always lose out. Northern states would let almost everybody vote while the Southern states would refuse to enfranchise slaves, indentured servants, or people without money or property. Hence, given the numbers, Northerners would probably win every Presidential election.

Therefore, the Southern delegates developed a strategy to maintain their political hegemony (note: five of the first six Presidents came from Virginia). This strategy was to apportion seats in the House based on total population including slaves and to count states rather than population for the upper chamber of the legislature. The second half of this proposition was meant to entice convention delegates from states with smaller populations to come on board since this plan gives disproportionate power to small states. The "compromise", such as it was, was to count only 3/5 of the slaves as people for the purpose of allocating seats in the House yet overlook population entirely when allocating seats for the Senate. Furthermore, while voters (white, male, over 21, and with property) would elect members of the House, state legislatures would choose each state's senators. As part of this same compromise, another body, the electoral college, again skewed in favor of states with less population, would choose the President.

In addition to considerations of race, our forebears also had an innate fear of mob rule – entrusting our government to the passing whims of a radical majority. Their fears were not entirely unreasonable. The men who made up the Constitutional Convention of 1787 were products of monarchy and aristocracy, which represented stability if nothing else. They were already taking a huge leap into the unknown, resting the reins of power in the hands of a much wider electorate.

Previous Fixes

Before proposing a solution to the inherent unfairness in the current makeup of the Senate, we will consider what has happened historically when the people decide to change an undemocratic institution. We have instructive examples in the United States and in Great Britain:

- In the US:
    - When the US Constitution was being drafted, the British House of Commons had numerous parliamentary districts based on geography and tradition rather than population. Some districts had close to zero residents. These were derisively referred to as "rotten boroughs". This was such a problem that the American Framers included a constitutional provision for redistributing seats in the House of Representatives every ten years based on a decennial census.
    - When the size of the House threatened to become too large and unwieldy, in 1911 we fixed the size of the House at 435 seats with the number of seats awarded to each state based on the most recent census.
    - As mentioned earlier, we also amended the Constitution to require direct election of the Senate by the people (Amendment 17, ratified 1913)
- In the UK:

- An 1832 reform fixed the "rotten boroughs" problem by changing the makeup of the House of Commons, with districts based on population, revised regularly based on the census.
- The Chartists Movement (1836-1848) campaigned for many democratic reforms including One man, One vote.
- The House of Lords was originally comprised of church leaders (Spiritual Lords) and hereditary members of the nobility or "peers" (Temporal Lords). The king and prime minister could appoint additional members to Lords. This system was so unrepresentative of the people that the country demanded institutional changes in both the makeup and the power of the House of Lords. Over time, the House of Lords has become both more representative and less powerful.
- Citizens of the constituent nations that comprise the United Kingdom have even come to view the House of Commons as somewhat unrepresentative. For this reason, Northern Ireland and Scotland now have their own parliaments, with plans afoot for the continuing "devolution" of power from the central government to Scotland, Northern Ireland, England, and Wales.

Conclusion: Institutions do change, and representative democracies do have the power and ability to institute changes intended to make themselves more representative.

It is high time that Americans make their Senate proportionally representative of the people who elect them. Every American should have an equal chance to choose their Senator.

Challenge 3. Gerrymanders

Decennial Reapportionment

In the beginning our Founding Fathers knew that England had a significant problem concerning the boundaries of election districts for the House of Commons. The district boundaries had evolved historically, but by the 18th century, those boundaries no longer reflected (if indeed they ever had reflected) the number of people living within each election district. It became so distorted that some election districts, known derisively as "rotten boroughs", had fewer than 100 electors, and so those few citizens could elect (almost appoint) a Member of Parliament. The Founding Fathers sought a permanent fix.

As a reaction to England's history, our Framers decreed that the election districts for the House of Representatives would be redrawn every 10 years based on a decennial census. Hence each state has a process for redrawing Congressional Districts every 10 years. In most states, the governor and state legislature control this process. If the same political party controls both the governorship and the legislature, then that party controls the redistricting process. Therein lies the problem.

The Practice of Gerrymandering

"Gerrymandering" is the practice of drawing the boundaries of an election district to favor or punish particular candidates or a particular political party. In 1812, Massachusetts Gov. Elbridge Gerry engineered adoption of an obtusely shaped election district to favor his own political party. Cartoonists thought the shape looked like a salamander, and so the term "Gerry-mander" was born – a conflation of the governor's name plus "salamander".[5] Through much litigation over the next two centuries, courts have generally permitted strangely shaped election districts, as long as

- populations of each district are roughly equal,

- every district consists entirely of contiguous land areas, and

- no protected class of citizens (such as a racial minority) is unfairly marginalized as a result.

---

[5] "Gerry-mander": Cartoonist Elkanah Tisdale, Boston Sentinel, 1812 (Public Domain)

However, generally those districts that clearly favor one political party over another have been allowed.

In modern times gerrymandering has become a science in which incumbents draw boundaries that perpetuate the party in power. This is certainly one of the reasons that our current House of Representatives cannot get anything done, why incumbents are almost always re-elected, and why Congressional leaders cannot get Members of Congress to go along with any consistent program – no matter what the people want. It is also a significant factor in explaining why state legislatures are so resistant to change. The fact is that nearly every incumbent

41

resides in a "safe" district, one in which the current Member of Congress has little need to worry about the opposition party. In fact, the only threat that many incumbents fear is a primary challenge from their own party. Gerrymandering is effective for both major parties in almost all districts in almost all states. For example, in the 2014 elections, 416 of the 435 members of the House of Representatives sought reelection, and 393 (or 94%) of them were reelected.

Disenfranchised Voters

Partisan gerrymandering generally comes in two forms, called "cracking" and "packing", both designed to disenfranchise voters in the minority party.

Cracking occurs when the dominant party in a state targets a community with a high concentration of voters from the minority party. To prevent that party from winning the election that that community might normally be expected to win, the dominant party draws congressional district boundaries that break up (or "crack") that community into two or more partitions assigned to different CDs in which the state's dominant party still has a majority.

Packing occurs when the minority party might have a competitive advantage in several adjoining districts. To prevent the minority party from winning multiple elections, the dominant party artificially skews the district boundaries so that the minority party's voters are packed into one district, where the minority party candidate will win by an overwhelming margin, but the dominant party's candidates will win all the other adjoining CDs.

In both cracking and packing, the result of partisan gerrymandering is that the power of the minority party's voters is weakened or extinguished.

CD boundaries are also sometimes artificially rigged to reward a favored candidate or incumbent politician or to punish an unfavored one. The politicians in charge of drawing the boundaries have created unnatural districts so as to include or exclude the residence of a particular person, or to force two incumbents into the same district. Since voters often insist that their Congressperson live within the CD (while the Constitution only requires a Member of Congress to live within the state), a re-districting scheme that places two incumbents in the same district obviously disadvantages one or both of them.

In addition to disenfranchising large groups of voters, we can also point to the negative effect on individual voters. Ongoing research at the University of North Carolina demonstrates that citizen engagement of individual voters lessens significantly when a community is split into two or more congressional districts. Citizens in such split communities are less likely to 1) know who their

Congressperson is, 2) contact or meet their Congressperson, or 3) believe that their Congressperson represents their own views or the views of their community.[6]

Worst Cases in Practice

Americans sometimes kid themselves into thinking that this is only a peripheral issue and that most Congressional Districts are drawn pretty fairly with only a few disputable boundaries. So let me give you a few examples of egregious gerrymanders from the 21st century.

Following the 2010 Census, many state legislatures that have a single party controlling both houses of the state legislature as well as the governorship opted for extreme partisan gerrymandering in order to solidify the dominant party's control of seats in the U.S. Congress. Here are three examples from North Carolina (Republican), Maryland (Democratic), and Pennsylvania (Republican). All three of these CD boundaries were used in the Congressional elections of 2012 and 2014.

North Carolina 12th CD boundaries (2014 election)

Approximate extent of North Carolina CD 12, splitting Forsyth, Guilford, Davidson, Rowan, Cabarrus, and Mecklenburg counties, and maintaining no community intact.

The U.S. Supreme Court threw out North Carolina's 12th CD before the 2016 elections, stating that this was an unconstitutional racial gerrymander. North Carolina had "packed" black populations across the North Carolina Piedmont into this one district, so that the black community could elect one Congressman, but would not affect elections anywhere else.

---

[6] Curiel, J. and T. Steelman, "How to measure the impact of partisan gerrymandering". Presentation at Reason, Reform & Redistricting Conference, Duke University, January 2019.

Ripley's Believe It Or Not -- the actual boundaries of Maryland's 3rd CD

Approximate extent of Maryland CD 3, with pieces of Montgomery, Baltimore, Howard, and Anne Arundel counties and a piece of Baltimore City

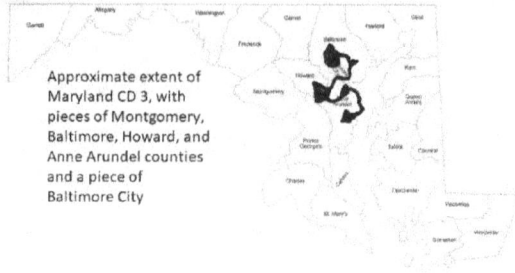

Maryland's 3rd CD, a truly contorted figure, was still in use in 2020. Democrats in the state legislature drew this district to protect John Sarbanes, the incumbent since 2007. One commentator dubbed it a "Marymander".[7]

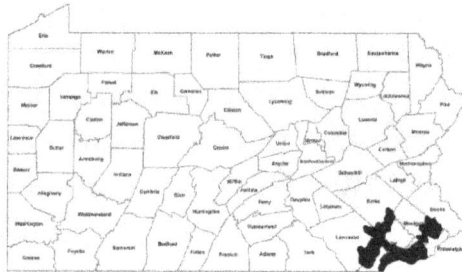

The actual boundaries of Pennsylvania CD 7 from 2012 through 2016

Approximate extent of Pennsylvania's CD 7 (before 2018). Another Rorschach inkblot?

Pennsylvania's 7th CD (like all Pennsylvania CDs) was redrawn by order of the Pennsylvania Supreme Court for the 2018 elections.

Compare these three modern examples with Gov. Gerry's original "salamander-gerrymander". We have obviously gotten much more sophisticated at drawing crazy boundaries to suit a particular political purpose.

---

[7] "Welcome to America's Most Gerrymandered District", The New Republic (Nov. 8, 2012). Accessed on May 9, 2019, at https://newrepublic.com/article/109938/marylands-3rd-district-americas-most-gerrymandered-congressional-district

Worst Case in Theory

Here is a rather dense mathematical analysis of gerrymandering, presenting one simple but extreme hypothetical example of how gerrymandering works and how bad it can get.

- In this fictitious example, a state's 10,000 voters elect a legislative assembly with 100 members from 100 election districts with 100 voters per district. In an election held yesterday, 5500 voters (that is, 55%) voted for Party A, and 4500 voters (45%) voted for Party B. So Party A won the popular vote across the whole state by 10 points. What might the legislative assembly look like after this election?

- Without gerrymandering, Party A can be expected to win 70 seats, give or take. With a 10 point advantage in the popular vote, you might expect it to win every district by 10 points and thus win all 100 seats. Or, since Party A won 55% of the vote, you might expect it to win exactly 55% of the seats. But neither of these scenarios is at all likely for these reasons:

  - In the first scenario Party A wins every seat, which can only happen if Party A's majority is consistent across every district in the state. But such an even distribution rarely occurs because voters in both parties probably reside throughout the state with pockets of strength in certain areas. Further a party that loses every election will not remain a party for long, while a party that wins every election will soon split into factions and become two or more parties.

  - In the second scenario Party A wins exactly 55 seats and wins 55% of the total vote. Party A would need to win those 55 seats by much more than an average of 10 points so that it could lose 45 seats by a small margin. If one party wins 55 seats, it's much more likely that it will have ~51% of the popular vote.

  - So the most likely outcome, without gerrymandering, is that Party A will win ~70 seats, give or take. It will win many seats by about 10 points, will win fewer seats by more than 10 or by less than 10 points, and will narrowly lose some number of seats. How many it wins depends on how evenly distributed Party A's voters are across all the districts.

- With gerrymandering, consider what happens. Note that a political party wants to win not only a majority (in this case, at least 51 seats) but also, if possible, a veto-proof majority (in this case, 67 seats). Remember that Party A has a 55% to 45% popular majority, so Party A's objective in drawing district boundaries is to maintain that 10 point spread in its favor in every district. That's probably impossible, but it's not improbable that Party A could concentrate Party B's 4500 voters in 10 districts. Let's say Party B wins those 10 districts 63% to 37%, thereby accounting for 630 of Party B's voters. Then Party B's remaining 3870 voters are distributed across the remaining 90 districts, giving it 43 votes in each of those districts on average. As a result, Party A wins a solidly veto-proof 90 seats in the legislature.

- But let's say that the minority party, Party B, controls the election districts for whatever reason (perhaps Party B was the majority party the last time the election districts were drawn up). Party B has arranged these districts so that Party B's 4500 voters are concentrated in 80 election districts, and Party B wins each of those contests by a small majority (52 votes to 48). In the other 20 districts, Party A receives 83 votes while Party B gets 17, so Party A elects just 20 representatives. As a result, Party B wins a solidly veto-proof 80 seats in the legislature. What a surprising result!

- The table below shows these results side by side.

	Gerrymandering		
	None	by Party A	by Party B
Districts won by Party A	70	90	20
Party A votes per district	65	57	83
Subtotal Party A votes	4550	5130	1660

Party B votes per district	35	43	17
Subtotal Party B votes	2450	3870	340
Districts won by Party B	30	10	80
Party A votes per district	32	37	48
Subtotal Party A votes	950	370	3840
Party B votes per district	68	63	52
Subtotal Party B votes	2050	630	4160
Total Party A votes	5500	5500	5500
Total Party B votes	4500	4500	4500
Total votes	10000	10000	10000

This might be even more dramatic as a graph. Even though Party A wins 55% of the vote, if Party B controls the district boundaries, Party B could end up with 80% of the seats:

Worst Case in Theory: State legislature has 100 seats & 100 elections.
Party A gets 55% of the vote, Party B gets 45%.
How many seats does each party get?

No Gerrymander   Gerrymander by Party A   Gerrymander by Party B

▨ Party A Seats ▥ Party B Seats

Why and How We Need a Fix, and What Clearly Will Not Work

Unfortunately, gerrymandering has become the common practice whenever either party controls the redistricting process in any state. By the way, we should not blame politicians for this state of affairs. For any species, the two most important biological imperatives are reproduction (that is, preservation of the species) and survival (that is, preservation of the individual). Politicians behave like any other species. We may hire them to do the public's business; but, left to their own devices, they will focus first on their party's and their own political survival. We the people are unlikely to change the nature of politicians, nor can we expect them to instigate change themselves, nor can we solve the problem by exchanging current politicians for new ones. To get back to the original issue: The systemic problem is that the process of redrawing Congressional Districts after each census is largely in the hands of politicians, who stand the most to gain from gerrymandered districts.

A very good summary of the state of redistricting reform in 2015 was published by US News & World Report (https://www.usnews.com/news/articles/2015/12/01/redistricting-reform-gains-steam).

An added thought indirectly related to gerrymandering:
While politicians gerrymander districts to favor
themselves or their own party, race, or ideology, they also
attempt to inhibit voting among the groups they do not
like. Voter suppression efforts include Voter ID laws,
fewer polling places, limited voting hours, and similar
restrictions – just like the poll tax of yesteryear, which we
eliminated by the 24th Amendment to the Constitution. But
what if we used the number of votes cast in each state in
previous elections rather than population figures as a basis
for apportioning House seats? Then states which inhibit
voting would end up with fewer seats in Congress –
probably a reasonable penalty for states that disenfranchise
their own citizens.

Finally, we can no longer look to the Supreme Court for relief in this matter. In
June 2019 in the landmark Ruch v. Common Cause case[8], the Supreme Court
concluded that the U.S. Constitution is silent on partisan gerrymandering, that
federal courts cannot intervene in Congressional redistricting cases based on
constitutional arguments, and that plaintiffs in such cases must look elsewhere for
relief – which leaves state law and constitutions and courts as well as federal laws.

State Legislative Districts

Gerrymandering may be even more significant when drawing district boundaries
for state legislatures. This is true for three reasons: 1) State laws often affect
citizens more directly than federal laws. Hence the fair representation of citizens in
state legislatures is doubly important. 2) State legislatures usually control the
process for drawing the boundaries of federal Congressional Districts. 3) Most
members of Congress served first in their state legislature, so the state legislatures

---

[8] Supreme Court of the United States (June 2019). "Rucho et al. v. Common Cause et al."
Accessed from https://www.supremecourt.gov/opinions/18pdf/18-422_9ol1.pdf.

serve to a considerable extent as Congress' J.V. Your local state delegate has a reasonable chance of becoming your future Congressman.

Because state legislative districts are so carefully drawn to favor the incumbent politician/party, many would-be candidates choose not to run for elected office at all. They can see that "the fix is in", so there is little point in competing against a rigged system.

Fixing the gerrymander challenge with respect to state legislative district boundaries would go a long way toward repairing our damaged politics.

Challenge 4. Other Election System Deficiencies

First-Past-The-Post (FPTP) Voting

All Congressional elections (both Senate and House) have a single winner. Each voter votes for a single candidate, and the candidate who gets the most votes wins the election even when that candidate earns only a plurality (not a majority) of votes cast. Among political scientists and voting system experts, our system of voting is known as "First Past the Post (FPTP)". (A few states require a runoff election between the top two vote-getters if no one has a majority, or in some cases if no one has more than 40%; and as of 2016, Maine has adopted Ranked Choice Voting – but these are the exceptions.) When the winner has earned a plurality but not a majority, at least four negative consequences ensue:

a) A winner by plurality has less authority, less of a mandate to lead or govern, than a winner by majority.

b) In a three- or four-person contest, candidates tend to focus only on their own base voters, paying little attention to the voters of the other candidates. Rather than appealing to voters with disparate views, each candidate works to split the opposition, get 100% support from their own base, and thus win by a plurality. When elected, winners by plurality often continue to appeal to their base supporters and make only a token effort to represent the majority who voted for their opponents.

c) In a three-candidate race, two candidates with similar majority views may split their combined 60% majority into equal shares of 30%, while a third candidate with minority views earns 40% and is declared the winner.

d) A spoiler candidate, who cannot possibly win, may yet draw enough support away from an "acceptable" candidate so that another candidate, whom most voters do not want, ends up winning with a plurality.

Conclusion: We should adopt a system of voting which ensures that the winner has support from a majority of the electorate.

The Two-Party System

Many of our challenges stem from the dominance of the Republican and Democratic parties. The two-party system has become so entrenched that we cannot envision politics without Republicans and Democrats. We need to remind ourselves of the strong feeling of the Founding Fathers on this subject: George Washington was not alone in warning us about the evils of "factions" (the 18th century word for political parties). Today numerous state and federal laws provide legal status to the two major parties and make it very difficult to implement reforms. Yet we need to confront the dominance of the two-party system if we are ever to return real power to the people of this country.

While decrying the dominance of our two-party system, we must also acknowledge the benefits of political parties. A political party allows people to come together around shared ideas, policies, programs, and priorities. They allow like-minded candidates to support each other. They allow all party members to work together on political campaigns whether those campaigns are geared to electing particular candidates or supporting particular agendas. On the other hand, we must also recognize that powerful political parties can squash reforms within a party, block grassroots political movements, and perpetuate the status quo.

One of the biggest problems of the two-party system is its tendency to produce extremism in both parties. The ideologues of the right and of the left find it much easier to take over the machinery of one political party than to convince a majority of their fellow citizens of the correctness of their views. But with the two major parties dominating the process, often with the support of state and federal laws, a third party, a new movement, or a middle-of-the-road independent usually cannot gain a nomination. A Republican Presidential candidate with moderate views, especially one willing to compromise with Democrats, may be unacceptable to the conservative ideologues who dominate the party apparatus; and so that candidate cannot win the Republican nomination. Similarly, on the Democratic side, a Presidential candidate with moderate views who is willing to work with Republicans may be completely unacceptable to the liberal ideologues who dominate the Democratic party; and so that candidate likewise cannot win his party's nomination. The result is a system that tends to nominate a Republican candidate too conservative for a majority of Americans along with a Democratic candidate too liberal for a majority of Americans. That's why we often end up with candidates with huge unfavourability ratings among all Americans.

Meanwhile, fewer and fewer voters identify with either major party. In the 16 Gallup polls concerning party affiliation taken from November 2020 through January 2022, an average of 26% of voters self-identified as Republican, 29% as Democrat, and 42% as Independent.[9] As a result, few of those unaffiliated voters (42% of the electorate) ever get a chance to be heard in selecting either major party candidate for any office.

Let me rephrase this conclusion in a slightly different way. Over a third of the electorate align themselves with neither major political party, so they do not get to participate in choosing the major party candidate for any office. Among those who do register as Republican or Democrat, the overwhelming majority either live in states without primary elections or they fail to show up for the primary. Hence the percentage of eligible voters who select our general election candidates is quite small. In the race for President in 2016, only 9% of America chose either Trump or Clinton as their candidate![10] Let that sink in: only 9% of us voted for either of the winning candidates in the Presidential primaries!

---

[9] https://news.gallup.com/poll/15370/party-affiliation.aspx (accessed on Feb 5, 2022).

[10] "Only 9% of America Chose Trump and Clinton as the Nominees". https://www.nytimes.com/interactive/2016/08/01/us/elections/nine-percent-of-america-selected-trump-and-clinton.html?_r=0. Accessed on June 15, 2017.

For two centuries (1789-1976) the Tammany Hall political organization in New York City controlled the city's Democratic Party machinery. Tammany Hall's most notorious and "entrenched" leader was William "Boss" Tweed, who once famously remarked that voters could elect anybody they want as long as he got to pick the candidates.[11] When people today complain about a "rigged" system and a lack of choice, Boss Tweed comes immediately to mind.

"I don't care who does the electing, as long as I get to do the nominating" – William "Boss" Tweed

---

As to the "legal entrenchment" of our two-party system, consider how the Presidential primary system works: each of the two major parties nominates a Presidential candidate, and for all practical purposes, those two candidates are our only choices for President. Republicans and Democrats may agree on little else, but they do agree on this one feature of our politics: They all love the two-party system.

---

[11] Top 6 Quotes from Boss Tweed, *AZ Quotes,* http://www.azquotes.com/author/14885-Boss_Tweed [accessed on June 15, 2017].

Caucuses, Conventions, and Closed Primaries

*Independents Need Not Apply

We have evolved a two-stage election system in this country: Stage 1 winnows the field of candidates, ultimately nominating one person from each political party (plus the occasional independent nominee), while Stage 2 (the general election) allows voters to determine the winner of each contest from those nominees who have survived Stage 1. The focus of this discussion is on Stage 1.

Stage 1 consists of primary elections, most of which occur within a political party, as well as caucuses and conventions, all of which occur within a political party. Primaries are either open or closed or mixed: Open primaries are open to all voters; closed primaries are restricted to voters who belong to a particular political party. Caucuses and conventions are gatherings of party activists. In states with caucus systems, caucuses occur simultaneously in districts throughout the state. Each local caucus selects delegates to a state convention, where the party's nominee is selected. The winners of Stage 1 are the party nominees who appear on the general election ballot.[12]

---

[12] Only a handful of jurisdictions have an alternative Stage 1 system. Of these, the most popular is a single primary open to candidates of all parties. The two candidates with the most votes survive the

The challenges of the prevailing Stage 1 models are these:

a) Caucuses and state nominating conventions are inherently unrepresentative. These processes attract party activists, a far smaller population than the general public. We need to take some of the parties' power back to the people. There is no good reason that, when it comes to a general election, our only choices are nominees that have been chosen by a relatively small group of activists.

b) The current system produces general election nominees who reflect the views of the party faithful rather than nominees with broad public support. At the end of the nominating process (whether by primary or caucus or party convention or some combination of these), our nominees often reflect the most extreme views of one wing of each political party. As often as not, the public is disenchanted with all the nominees.

c) In many instances, two or three of the most popular candidates all belong to the same party. Nevertheless, with only a few exceptions, our state election systems produce only one general election nominee from each party.

d) A majority of Americans reside in a state dominated by one political party. If a voter belongs to the other party or to no party at all, that voter has no opportunity to participate in a meaningful way in the selection of general election candidates for any office.

e) A separate primary ballot exists for each party, and that ballot lists one party's candidates for every office. Except for primaries in a very few states, a voter can vote in only one party's primary. On primary election day, on my party's ballot, I can select my preferred candidate for President, Governor, or senator from among those running for each office from my party. I do not get to participate at all in the primary for local offices, such as county commissioners, county sheriff, mayor, or school board, because my party usually fields zero candidates for those

---

primary and compete head-to-head in the general election. Variations on this system exist, but suffice it to say that such systems are the exception.

offices. Then in the general election, the person who won the primary from the other party for those local offices runs unopposed. No wonder voters are discouraged!

f) Again, except for primaries in a very few states, if my preferred candidate for President is in one party, and my preferred candidate for senator is in the other party, and my preferred candidate for congressman is in a third party, I cannot vote all three of my preferences in the primary election. That is because the two major parties have rigged the system, forcing me to make all my primary election selections from the same political party.

Electioneering Forever

Imagine you are the owner of an automobile dealership. Just after you hire John as a master mechanic, your Service Manager announces that he plans on retiring in three years. Your new master mechanic John starts out okay, but after only six months fixing cars and satisfying customers, he begins campaigning for the Service Manager position, which is going to become available 2 ½ years from now.

John starts spending more and more of his time cozying up to you, partying with big shots, and getting community leaders to write to you or speak to you on his behalf, recommending John as the next Service Manager. It seems that after only six months on the job, John is no longer functioning as a master mechanic; rather, he is functioning as heir apparent and campaigner-in-chief for his next gig. While you were very keen on John for the first six months, now you are no longer so sure – in fact, his constant pandering has become boring, and meanwhile his real job is not getting done.

If that scenario sounds familiar, it's because it is: That is the behavior of many of our elected representatives. We hired them to govern – as President, Vice President, senator, congressman, or governor. Yet, after doing that job for only a short while, they start spending most of their time glad-handing, pandering, soliciting contributions from the donor class, and campaigning for the next election – be it re-election to their current position or a higher office. American politicians fail to govern and fail to tend to our real and myriad national and state problems at least partly because they are too busy campaigning and raising money.

Don't you wish they'd spend a bit more time doing the job we (the public) hired them to do, before auditioning for their next appointment?

We also have the problem that the incessant campaigning is boring. How many different ways can a politician repeat the same talking points without ever actually doing anything? Congress' job approval rating hovers around 10%, and the public is totally apathetic. It's rare for us to get excited about politics, partly because the politicians are all about scoring political points and very little about accomplishing something on behalf of the people they nominally serve.

We really should consider establishing an abbreviated and fixed election timetable, which might help us become less apathetic and more involved the first couple times we did it.

Voting Rights Restrictions

Just being able to vote is still a challenge in many jurisdictions around the country. This is surely something we should have solved by now – and we can easily solve it if people truly believe in democracy. (Go back to the Preface of this work if you need a primer on this topic ☺.)

Unfortunately, there still seem to be some among us who do not believe in democracy for all, and some of those folks hold positions of power or influence, and they sometimes exercise that power to place roadblocks targeted at people that they would rather not see casting a ballot. Of course, persuading someone to come around to your point of view, while perhaps difficult in the short run, is far more effective in the long run than trying to prevent that person from expressing a point of view different from your own at the ballot box. But I digress.

The challenges include:

   a) Making it difficult or inconvenient to register to vote;
   b) Limiting vote-by-mail (absentee voting, for any reason);
   c) Limiting in-person early voting dates, hours, and locations;

d) Providing inadequate polling locations, inadequate staffing at polling locations, inadequate numbers of voting machines, and too few hours in which to vote;

e) Requiring unreasonable voter identification; requiring cumbersome paperwork for provisional voting when a voter's right to vote is questioned.

Protests against these restrictions have been met consistently with arguments about the need to prevent voter fraud. However, every responsible study of this subject has proven that the incidence of voter fraud in this country is negligible.

If we are true to our democratic ideals, then we need to do everything we can to ensure that all eligible citizens are registered to vote, that we make voting as convenient and accessible for all citizens as we can, and that we then actively encourage them to get out and vote. We might also incentivize states to encourage voter turnout – for example, by apportioning House seats based on the number of people who vote in each state rather than on the number of people who live there.

Congress for Sale

The underlying principle concerning campaign financing reform was stated in the Preface: Every voice deserves to be heard, and no voice should be allowed to drown out all other voices solely because the speaker has more money than most everyone else.

The fight against the undue influence of money in American politics has a long and colorful history. Many Americans may not realize that overt payment for your vote was a common practice until we adopted the secret ballot after the acrimonious Presidential election of 1884. Government jobs were also for sale. Until the Pendleton Act of 1883, which established the federal civil service, many people with government jobs had to contribute a portion of their pay to the political party that had appointed them and whose continuing protection was needed in order to remain employed. Meanwhile, vendors who wanted government contracts contributed Big Money to the party in power. In sum, politicians paid for your vote, government employees paid the politicians for their jobs, and contractors paid politicians for their government contracts. The whole system was essentially for sale.

Though we've come a long way, most observers think we still have a long way to go.

In 2006, the Supreme Court decided the *Citizens United* case, holding that businesses and organizations have a First Amendment right to express their opinion through paid political campaigns essentially without restriction. This decision invalidated limits on campaign expenditures that had been incorporated in several earlier laws.

Financial Disclosures, Transparency, and Nepotism

I was traveling through Southeast Asia while drafting this essay, and I was amazed at the number of countries that give lip-service to democracy while suffering from blatant corruption and venality of public officials. The problems are obvious, systemic, and intractable:

- High public officials have direct financial interests which conflict with their official duties.

- High public officials use close family members to control various government departments and to simultaneously control major corporations and sectors of the economy.

- The public is generally uninformed about these matters. Those few who do know about them are not in any position to do anything about them.

In the USA, we have had our own share of similar scandals. Congress has nibbled at the edges of these problems, but existing legal strictures are rather weak and only marginally effective. We deserve better. We deserve public officials who are completely open and transparent with respect to their personal wealth, who disclose their continuing financial interests, and who avoid using family members to expand their political control or power or to further their own financial interests.

We can try to operationalize these principles through federal laws, but it's unclear whether such rules would withstand challenges on constitutional grounds, especially given the Supreme Court's decision in *Citizens United*. Therefore, it may be necessary to address these matters through one or more constitutional amendments.

Part II. Fixes

Ship of State

Introduction to Part II

Americans can ameliorate or resolve each of the challenges outlined in Part I through new legislation at the state or federal level, through state or federal constitutional amendments, and through social change. The reforms will enhance the power of citizens to control their own lives (that is, freedom) and to control their government (that is, democracy). (A new Constitution II could fix most of these problems all at once; that is the subject of Part III.)

Three of these fixes, "Ranked Choice Voting", "Fix the Two-Party System", and "Empower Voters to Amend the Constitution", relate to more than one challenge. To avoid repetition as we present the fixes to each specific challenge, we start with these three Big Fixes.

All the Part I challenges relate directly or indirectly to federal elections, and so we address these under "Election System Fixes", namely, "Presidential Selection

Fixes", "U.S. Senate Fix", "Gerrymander Fix", and "Other Election System Fixes". For each of the elections-related fixes, we then examine the methods of realization – state or federal laws, constitutional amendments, or cultural shifts. We then present "The Amendment on Federal Elections", a comprehensive constitutional amendment which could fix all of our electoral shortcomings at once.

Three Big Fixes

Big Fix 1. Ranked Choice Voting

Relevance

This fix relates directly to Challenge 4. "Other election system challenges", especially the dearth of runoff elections. However, this fix also relates to Challenge 1 (regarding how we choose the President and Vice President) and Challenge 3 (the problem of gerrymandering). Therefore, because it has such general applicability to all elections, it deserves to be argued first.

The problem is that the traditional First-Past-The-Post (FPTP) voting scheme leads to undemocratic outcomes, elected officials who often fail to represent the majority of their constituents, and literally millions of voters with no effective representation at all.

Restating the Problem

We have far too many election winners who win with a plurality, that is, with less than majority support from the voters, both in our primary and in our general elections. A person might become Mayor or Congressman or Governor, and only have achieved 40% of the vote, while two or more competitors split the other 60%. It's difficult to claim to have a mandate when you have earned the trust of only 40% of the voters. Governing after such an election, a public official might only look to that 40% base of voters for support.

Ranked Choice Voting solves this problem by ensuring that the winning candidate has at least some level of support from a majority of the voters.

What is Ranked Choice Voting (RCV)?

RCV is an improvement over runoffs between the top two finishers in a traditional, First-Past-The-Post voting scheme. In the traditional runoff, if no candidate wins a majority of the vote (or, in some jurisdictions, if no candidate wins at least 40%), then a subsequent runoff election between the top two finishers decides the contest. Note that, in the runoff election, every voter casts a complete ballot. That is, a voter is not penalized for having chosen a candidate who was eliminated in round 1. Rather, the question voters face in the runoff is, "Which of these two remaining candidates do you prefer?"

An RCV "instant runoff" is a more efficient method of conducting a traditional runoff.

Ranked Choice Voting Procedures

RCV from the voter's perspective

General Election Ballot			
Vote for up to 3 : Mark your 1ST, 2ND, and 3RD choices			
CANDIDATE	1ST CHOICE	2ND CHOICE	3RD CHOICE
ADAMS		X	
IVY	X		
BROWN			
ALSORAN			X

From the standpoint of the voter, Ranked Choice Voting is easy and straightforward. After selecting their 1st choice for any office, voters are allowed (but not required) to also select a 2nd choice, 3rd choice, and so on, limited only by the number of names on the ballot.

Since this can become unwieldy – imagine voters trying to rate 36 candidates on a ballot while hundreds of other voters wait in line to vote – I propose limiting the number of selections to three in primary elections (which could have any number of candidates) and to two in general elections (which will have only three names on the ballot).

Counting of ballots in primary elections

The number of successful candidates in a primary election is three, and these three primary winners are the only names that will appear on the general election ballot. This is the procedure for counting votes:

1. Count the 1st choice votes for each candidate, and rank order the results. Repeat steps 2 through 4 until only three candidates remain, or until three candidates each exceed 25% of the total vote. (Note: it is mathematically impossible for four candidates to exceed 25%.)

2. Eliminate the candidate with the fewest votes.

3. Reassign each vote for the eliminated candidate to each voter's next highest choice for a candidate not yet eliminated.

4. If a ballot for the eliminated candidate contains no choice for a candidate not yet eliminated, then that ballot is exhausted and is no longer counted as part of the total vote.

Counting of ballots in general elections

1. Count the 1st choice votes for each candidate, and rank order the results. Repeat steps 2 through 4 until one candidate has a majority of the total vote.

2. Eliminate the candidate with the fewest votes.

3. Reassign each vote for the eliminated candidate to each voter's second choice.

4. If a ballot for the eliminated candidate contains no second choice, then that ballot is exhausted and is no longer counted as part of the total vote.

Logistics note on counting ballots

The centralized vote tabulation authority in any election need not collect the entire ballot information from each voter. Rather, each polling place needs to report only its first choice results. The centralized vote tabulation authority (whether for a Congressional District, a state, or the nation as a whole) then ranks all the fist choice results. As needed, the centralized authority eliminates the candidate with the fewest votes and then requests new vote totals from the feeder locations after the feeder location has replaced votes for the eliminated candidate with each voter's second (or third) choice.

Expected RCV Results

RCV produces winners with wider support than a system that declares the person with a plurality as the winner.

Here is a typical general election example: In a village with 100 voters, 60 voters belong to Party A and 40 voters give their allegiance to Party B. One year, in the election for mayor, Party A and Party B each field one candidate, ADAMS and BROWN, respectively. Then a former Party A mayor, IVY, who does not like ADAMS, decides to run as an Independent, and another local candidate named AlsoRan also runs. Perhaps Party A's 60 voters give 35 votes to the official Party A candidate ADAMS, 23 votes to the Independent former mayor IVY, and 2 votes to AlsoRan. Meanwhile all 40 of Party B's voters support the one Party B candidate BROWN. Here is a table of the results:

Election Results in FPTP Voting Stystem	
Candidate	Votes
Adams	35
Ivy	23
Brown	40 – WINNER
AlsoRan	2

In our current First-Past-the-Post voting scheme, BROWN is elected as the next mayor with only 40 votes.

With RCV, a different outcome is plausible. Let's say that the 23 Party A voters who defected to the Independent IVY as their 1st choice choose the regular Party A candidate ADAMS as their 2nd choice. That is to say, while they may prefer IVY to ADAMS, they clearly prefer their own Party A's candidate ADAMS to Party B's BROWN. The two voters who selected AlsoRan as their first choice also select ADAMS as their second choice.

When no mayoral candidate has 51 1st choice votes after Round 1, the candidate with the fewest 1st choice votes, AlsoRan, is eliminated, (and his 2 votes are reassigned to Adams); and when still no one has 51, the Independent IVY is also eliminated, causing the reassignment of IVY's 23 1st choice votes to each voter's 2nd choice, namely, the official Party A candidate ADAMS, giving ADAMS a revised 60 votes and the win. In terms of governing, the new mayor can claim to have some measure of support from most of the voters and is also more likely to hear the voices of those who originally had supported the Independent.

1st and 2nd Choice Vote Totals in RCV Voting System		
Candidate	1st Choice	2nd Choice
Adams	35	(35 for Ivy)
Ivy	23	(23 for Adams)
Brown	40	(40 for AlsoRan)
AlsoRan	2	(2 for Adams)

RCV Election Results			
Candidate	Round 1	Round 2	Round 3
Adams	35	37	60-WINNER
Ivy	23	23	(eliminated; votes reassigned to Adams)
Brown	40	40	40
AlsoRan	2	(eliminated; votes reassigned to Adams)	

(These results are less complex than a real election in two ways: In a real election, more variability in the 2nd choices could be expected, and in this simplified example, 3rd choices never come into play.) Here is a table showing the 1st and the simplified 2nd choice vote totals:

Because everyone recognized the possibility of this scenario coming true, with RCV the candidates are more likely to try to appeal to the voters who support their opponents. Candidates will use an argument along the lines of, "I understand your support for one of my opponents as your 1st choice, but I would certainly like to earn your vote as your 2nd choice." Then, in a close three-way election, the candidate best able to appeal to his opponents' voters is most likely to win. That outcome is good for democracy.

Additional Rationale

Basically, the credibility of a democratic electoral process derives from the winner's ability to claim the support of a majority or near majority of the voters.

Credibility also depends on the public's perception that the process is inclusive, fair, and reflects the views of most of the constituents. In many three-candidate races, the winner cannot claim support from a majority or near majority of voters, nor does the public perceive the process as fair.

First-Past-The-Post (FPTP) vote-counting is a major impediment to new grassroots movements, new political parties, and lesser-known candidates. Voters shy away from voting for a third party or for an attractive but upstart candidate because they are afraid to "throw away their vote" on a candidate or a cause that cannot possibly win. RCV eliminates that barrier.

We have long had exactly two major political parties, and so most of our general elections come down to a choice between the Republican and the Democrat. Occasionally, we have three candidates with significant public support, and these general elections present situations in which RCV works really well.

We also often have primary elections with three or more candidates, and again the RCV system improves the process. All the candidates who survive the primary will have demonstrated significant support among the electorate, and nobody makes it to the general election just because several other candidates split the vote.

Critics and Costs

Critics: The major criticism of RCV is that voters find it confusing; and, say some, many voters simply refuse to vote for any candidate beyond their 1ˢᵗ choice. But experience with RCV does not support this contention.

Costs: The jury is out as to whether RCV would save or cost money. It certainly saves the cost of holding a traditional runoff election, where such a runoff would otherwise be required. But voting machinery may need to be replaced to support RCV, and funding for voter education would also be needed. These are all one-time costs, while RCV's benefits continue indefinitely.

RCV in the US and Around the World

32 of the 50 US states have adopted or have pending legislation to require or to permit Ranked Choice Voting in municipal, state, or federal elections or party caucuses and conventions. Of these 32, Maine has adopted RCV statewide; 9 states (MD, MA, TN, FL, MN, CO, NM, CA, and OR) mandate or allow RCV for municipal elections; 5 states (LA, AR, MS, AL, and SC) use RCV for military and

overseas voters (where mailing delays would make it difficult for those voters to participate in runoff elections); 4 states (UT, TX, IA, and VA) use RCV in party elections; and the other 13 states have legislation pending in 2017 to implement or permit RCV in some of their elections.

Australia uses RCV for its national parliamentary elections. In their system, every Australian citizen is required to vote, and every voter must rank order all the candidates on the ballot in order of their preference. In the most recent elections for the Australian Parliament, the candidate receiving the most first place votes won 90% of the seats in parliament; but 10% of the seats were won by a candidate who received fewer first place votes in the initial count, but who captured a majority of the votes only as candidates at the bottom of the tally sheet were successively eliminated.

There are many variations on the Ranked Choice Voting basic scheme, sometimes called Instant Runoff Voting (IRV): see this article on Instant Runoff Voting (IRV) in Wikipedia for the details (https://en.wikipedia.org/wiki/Instant-runoff_voting).[13] The article lists the historical and current uses of IRV around the world. For details on American use of RCV and prospects for wider adoption, see the articles at http://www.FairVote.org.

Congress's Power to Act

RCV can probably be implemented by a federal statute, safe from a constitutional challenge, at least with respect to Congressional elections. The Constitution clearly states that Congress has the power to fix the "Times, Places, and Manner of elections for Senators and Representatives", and Ranked Choice Voting deals with the manner of elections.

One can argue that this power extends to the election of the electors for President and Vice President (the members of the electoral college) since the Constitution clearly wanted to give Congress the power to control elections for federal offices by the people. At the time of the writing of the Constitution, the people were not constitutionally empowered to vote for Presidential electors. Now that we are everywhere so empowered, Congress probably has the right to fix the manner of elections for President as well. Constitutional scholars can argue whether Congress has this power.

---

[13] Admittedly, Wikipedia is not the world's most reliable source of information, but this long and well-referenced article seems to be an excellent primer on this topic.

Big Fix 2. Restrain the Two-Party System

Open Primaries

When the United States began, the Founding Fathers were very concerned about the formation of "factions" (that is, political parties), which could do great damage to the functioning of the Republic. Obviously, we have become wedded to the dominance of political parties in every phase and at every level of our politics. We need to rediscover our Founders' fear of "factions". One such improvement would be the adoption of open primaries, in which all candidates compete (regardless of party affiliation) and in which all voters can vote.

We need to mandate open primaries for all federal offices (President and both chambers of Congress). These are the rules for primaries that we should adopt:

- Any eligible candidate may compete in any primary, subject to state rules for qualifying for the ballot.

- One primary will take place for each elected office. Candidates from every political party and from no party (independents) may participate. A candidate may choose to indicate affiliation with a political party on the ballot.

- All registered voters are eligible to vote in every primary for every office within the jurisdiction where they legally reside.

These are the rules for all primaries:

- The number of successful primary candidates is three.

- The only way to appear on the general election ballot is to earn sufficient support in the primary to qualify for the general election. Therefore, the general election ballot will have at most three names.

- The RCV procedure for counting ballots in a primary election provides for three winners. Naturally, each voter wants the list of successful primary candidates to include the voter's preferred candidate, but, if the voter's preferred candidate does not make the cut, the voter might very well want the list to include the voter's 2nd or 3rd choice.

The proposed rules on open primaries will allow all registered voters (Democratic, Republican, any 3rd party, or Independent) to participate in all primaries and will allow voters registered as Republican or Democratic to select a primary candidate from the opposite party. These changes can only be an improvement for our democracy.

Party Caucuses and Conventions

A caucus or a convention of Democrats or Republicans is much less likely to select a candidate acceptable to the entire electorate than a primary election open to all voters. Voters should select all general election candidates through primaries rather than caucuses and party conventions. Party activists will not like this change, of course; nonetheless, it would be good for our democracy.

Political parties may continue to hold elections for party offices, and they may hold caucuses and conventions at any level at their own expense. Such activities are completely independent from the public primary elections. Endorsement by a political party helps a candidate raise money and enlist volunteers for a campaign, but that endorsement gains nothing from a legal standpoint. That is, candidates must still qualify to appear on the primary ballot according to the rules of each state, and they must survive the primary to compete in the general election.

All Other Laws, Regulations, and Practices

Statutes and regulations should not favor political parties. Period.

The objective here is not to end political parties. As mentioned earlier, political parties can be quite useful in a democracy. Rather, the objective is to improve ballot access for all candidates, equitable treatment of all candidates, and inclusion of all voters.

Big Fix 3. Empower Voters to Amend the Constitution

The Founding Fathers trusted neither the King nor the people *en masse* – in their view the tyranny of the mob was no better than the tyranny of an autocrat. That is at least a partial explanation for the very limited power of everyday-joe-citizens in the Constitution. This is pointedly true with respect to amending the Constitution.

Article V of the Constitution specifies the two procedures that can be followed to propose amendments to the Constitution: 1) an amendment can be proposed by two-thirds of both Houses of Congress, or 2) two-thirds of the state legislatures can require Congress to call for a convention that will propose constitutional amendments. In either case, Congress then submits the proposed amendments to the states, specifying whether these amendments will be considered by state legislatures or by state conventions. Proposed amendments that are ratified by three-fourths of the states (either legislatures or conventions, as specified by Congress) become part of the Constitution.

Note that regular citizens have little say in any of this. That is most certainly a challenge.

I believe in democracy. When most of the people want to change our constitution, then their collective opinion should carry the day. At the same time, popular opinion should not be just a temporary infatuation with an idea or politician; rather, the collective, considered opinion of the citizenry, taken over time, should determine our collective course.

The reason I have included this fix as one of the three Big Fixes is that a significant number of the fixes proposed in this book either require a constitutional amendment or would work better with a constitutional amendment (including, for example, replacement of the electoral college or re-making the US Senate into a representative body). Since the existing procedure for amending the Constitution cuts out all but a few thousand federal and state legislators, it behooves us to come up with a new procedure in which Joe and Jane Citizen cast the deciding vote.

In addition to casting the deciding vote on proposed constitutional amendments, Joe and Jane Citizen should also have a way of introducing or proposing a constitutional amendment without waiting for the political class to act. My proposal here is that we use the existing procedures in every state for amending their state constitutions. In about half the states, the citizens can use a petition system to put a state constitutional amendment on the ballot, and in almost all the states, voters must ratify a state constitutional amendment whether proposed by citizen petition or by the legislature. If half of the states, following their own states' procedures for amending their state constitutions, comprising at least half of the US population, propose an amendment to the US Constitution, then that proposed amendment will be submitted to the people. Ratification by the people requires two positive votes in two general elections separated by a new Congress and a new President – preventing adoption of an amendment on the basis of a temporary frenzy or infatuation with a particular personality.

In the revised amendment procedure, I am recommending that Congress may propose a constitutional amendment by majority vote in both chambers, as opposed to the two-thirds majority currently required. The rationale for this change is that we are consciously shifting power from the professional politicians to the people. We are not making it easier to amend the Constitution, as you will see in the suggested wording of this Article V replacement; rather, we are making it more difficult for a small clique of elected officials to obstruct the will of the people.

Here is suggested wording for the proposed constitutional amendment. This amendment will be referenced as the Amendment on Amendments throughout this document.

Amendment on Amendments

This amendment replaces Article V of the Constitution.

Section 1. Proposing an Amendment

This section prescribes two methods for proposing an amendment to the Constitution.

- **Method 1.** The Congress, whenever a majority of both chambers shall deem it necessary, shall propose an amendment to this Constitution.

- **Method 2.** Each of the several states may propose a constitutional amendment by approving the amendment according to the procedures of each state for amending their own state constitutions. When at least half of the states comprising at least half of the US population propose such an amendment, then this amendment becomes a proposed amendment.

When an amendment to this Constitution has been proposed according to either method specified in this Section, that amendment shall be valid to all intents and purposes as part of this Constitution, when ratified by the people as specified in Section 3.

Section 2. Constitutional Convention

This section prescribes two methods for proposing a Constitutional Convention charged with the task of drafting a new Constitution.

- **Method 1.** On the application of the legislatures of two thirds of the several states, Congress shall call a Constitutional Convention for the purpose of drafting a new Constitution.

- **Method 2.** Each of the several states may propose a Constitutional Convention charged with drafting a new Constitution by approving the call for a Constitutional Convention according to the procedures of each state for amending their own state constitutions. When at least half of the states comprising at least half of the US population propose a Constitutional Convention, Congress shall call a Constitutional Convention for the purpose of drafting a new Constitution.

When states have called for a Constitutional Convention according to either method specified in this Section, Congress shall convene said convention. The product of said convention shall be the Proposed New Constitution, which shall be valid and will replace this Constitution when ratified by the people as specified in Section 3.

Section 3. Ratification

Two General Elections. Ratification requires the approval of voters in two general elections. Between these two general elections, at least one new Congress must have convened and a new person must hold the office of President.

Ratification Threshold. In both of these two general elections, ratification requires the approval of 1) a majority of all votes cast, and 2) a majority of votes cast in 60% of the states containing 60% of the population.

Election System Fixes (Challenges 1-4)

If we are able to adopt Ranked Choice Voting, eliminate preferences for the two-party system, and empower citizens to amend the constitution, then wholesale improvements to our election system become possible.

The reforms argued here include fixes to the Presidential selection process, the unrepresentative U.S. Senate, Congressional redistricting, and other election reforms.

Challenge 1. Presidential Selection Fixes

We need to improve the process in three ways: 1) shorten, simplify, and democratize the process of choosing Presidential candidates; 2) replace the position of Vice President with a Chancellor of the Senate; and 3) provide for direct election of the President by the people, that is, do away with the electoral college.

Bob Spear

Shorten, Simplify, and Democratize the Process of Choosing Presidential Candidates

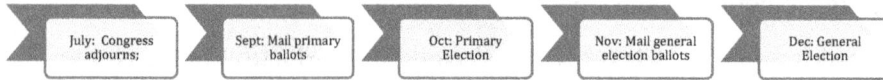

| July: Congress adjourns; | Sept: Mail primary ballots | Oct: Primary Election | Nov: Mail general election ballots | Dec: General Election |

Our election season is way too long. The presidential primaries drag on forever. How many different ways can candidates repeat the same talking points? Since many candidates for federal offices currently hold elected office, the interminable campaign process also detracts from these candidates' ability to do their day jobs. And finally, the lame-duck session of Congress following the general election is an affront to democracy, as Congresspersons already rejected by their constituents still fashion policies and laws going forward.

The existing primary/caucus/convention mish-mash disenfranchises the 40% of registered voters who do not identify with either major political party.

The 20th Amendment to the Constitution moved the Presidential inauguration from March to January 20. If we want to shorten and streamline the entire Presidential election season while retaining the current constitutionally-mandated inauguration day, then the Presidential primary must occur later in the election year. Further, to minimize the delay between the general election and the beginning of the newly-elected Government, the general election should be held much later in the calendar year.

Not only are Presidential campaigns too long, so are the 538 contests for the Senate and the House.

So let's do something about this. Let's force politicians to restrict their campaigning to a limited and designated time period before each election, which might accomplish two things: 1) We will not need to endure incessant TV ads (with the same repetitive sound bites and talking points *ad nauseam*) and campaign signs and literature and robocalls and solicitations for money 24/7 as we suffer through today, leaving us perchance the opportunity to become excited about politics and a particular campaign when the designated time for campaigning rolls around; and 2) Maybe, just maybe, if politicians do not need to spend all of their time raising money and campaigning, perhaps they will find time to actually tend to the people's business, and if they did that, then maybe, just maybe, their collective job approval rating would move somewhere north of abysmal.

But how, I hear you ask, can we make this happen?

First, consider how our British cousins do it. They do not tolerate incessant political campaigns. In 2015, the election season began with the dissolution of Parliament on March 30, and elections took place six weeks later, on May 7. Our British cousins crammed all of the campaigning into those six weeks. Every day, a spokesperson for each major party held a press conference to discuss their party's platform, while all the Members of Parliament and candidates were out on the hustings, and every party and political organization ran a zillion ads. Meanwhile, no one was failing to do their day job, because Parliament had been dissolved and was not in session. When the election was over, the leader of the winning party asked Her Majesty for leave to form a new Government. The Queen accepted the new Prime Minister, who moved into #10 Downing Street the same day, and the new Parliament convened before the end of May. I probably got a few of the details wrong here, but you pretty much get the picture. The campaign was brief but intense, and when it was over, it was over.

So how can we accomplish a similar result, but based on our American political system?

The solution is a national election schedule, encompassing a single date for all primary elections (Presidential as well as Congressional), a much shorter campaign season, and elimination of the lame-duck session of Congress. The balloting procedure will also be greatly simplified by making ours an entirely vote-by-mail, paper-ballot system. Voters can mail their completed ballots or drop them off at designated collection boxes throughout the voting window. Here is the proposed schedule:

- July: Congress adjourns *sine die,* and the election campaign season begins on or before July 4 in even-numbered years. Congress does not meet again until the new Congress convenes in January following the election. As soon as Congress adjourns on or about Independence Day, candidates may declare their candidacies and begin campaigning. No candidate for Federal office, whether currently a member of Congress or not, may engage in fundraising while Congress is in session.

- States conduct all elections, as at present. On September 15, voting authorities in each state mail primary ballots to all registered voters. As this will be an open primary, the ballot in each state and for each Federal office will contain the names of all candidates who have qualified for the primary in that state.

- October 1 – 15: Voting authorities receive, process, and count all primary ballots received. Voting authorities must accept all ballots received by October 15. Each day from October 11 to 15, voting authorities must announce the 1st choice results. Voting authorities announce the final tallies, including the results of RCV procedures, as soon as possible after polls close on October 15. Every primary election for a federal office (president, senator, or House member) has three winners, and these primary winners are the only contestants in the general election.

- For the presidential primary and general elections, the Federal Election Commission shall appoint a National Vote Tabulation Authority, whose function is to collect election results from every jurisdiction and announce the overall results to the country.

- October 22: Each of the three successful presidential candidates must announce his/her vice presidential running mate.

- November 15: States mail general election ballots to all registered voters.

- December 1 – 15: Voting authorities receive, process, and count all ballots received. Voting authorities must accept all ballots received by December 15. Each day from December 11 to 15, voting authorities must announce the 1st choice results. Voting authorities announce the final tallies, including the results of RCV procedures, as soon as possible after polls close on December 15.

- January 2: The newly-elected Congress convenes.

- January 20: Inauguration of the newly-elected president.

This scheme includes the following features:

- Each presidential candidate must qualify to appear on the primary ballot in each state by following the rules of that state. This procedure actually benefits new parties and upstart candidates, who may have zero chance of winning the presidency in this election cycle, but who can establish themselves in targeted states, perhaps positioning themselves for a serious run the next time around. We do not want to enshrine a new system that precludes new parties or new coalitions – which would have us jumping out of the pot and into the fire.

- To appear on any Presidential or Congressional primary ballot, a candidate must sign an affidavit authorizing the IRS, on November 1, to release the tax returns of the candidate and his/her spouse for the preceding five years, if that candidate should qualify for the general election. (Knowing this requirement and the public's expectation of transparency, most candidates are likely to release their tax returns early in the primary season.)
- One primary ballot will contain the names of all candidates regardless of party. A candidate may choose to indicate a party affiliation on the ballot.
- State primary rules in most states will need to be modified so that only one primary is held (rather than a primary for each party and rather than caucuses and state-level party conventions).
- If Ranked Choice Voting (RCV) in Presidential Primary elections is adopted, in successive rounds of ballot counting, the National Vote Tabulation Authority (NVTA) will notify state election officials of the names of candidates who have been eliminated, and the states will thereupon report new 1st choice vote totals absent the eliminated candidates. This will continue until only three candidates remain.
- Whether or not RCV in Presidential primaries is adopted, NVTA will announce the three primary winners of the national primary, who will face off in the general election. These are the only candidates who will appear on the ballot for the general election.
- In the general election, the NVTA will announce the nationwide results. If RCV is adopted for the Presidential general election, and if none of the three finalists has a majority of 1st choice votes, then the NVTA will announce the candidate who is eliminated and will ask the states to recount and resubmit their 1st choice totals after applying the RCV procedure.
- After the General Election, the nation will take a short break from politics, celebrate the Holiday Season, and forgo the lame-duck session of Congress.

Thoughts concerning the length of our Presidential campaigns:

- July 4 to December 15 should be enough time for both the primary and general elections. If the campaigns are thus limited, voters can avoid watching the same ads, hearing the same talking points, and listening to the same stump speeches for 18 seemingly interminable months as at present.

Candidates can rest and reflect a bit more. Voters can avoid boredom and exhaustion.

- Of course a shortened campaign season should be paired with a shortened fundraising season. One useful suggestion in this regard is to prohibit any fundraising by any candidate or his/her campaign while Congress is in session. This rule would have to apply to all candidates, not just those currently serving in Congress. We'd all welcome relief from incessant fundraising appeals.

- Meanwhile, if we curtail the campaign season as suggested here, the candidates (most of whom are currently serving elected officials) can continue doing their day jobs, that is, serving us, rather than pontificating on the stump and begging for money.

Thoughts on the timing of the elections:

- An 1845 federal law established election day as the first Tuesday after the first Monday in November. This schedule accommodated farmers (that is, most of the voters in 1845). Those rural voters could attend religious services on Sunday, travel to the county seat on Monday (often the sole polling location in a county), vote on Tuesday morning and return home, and then participate in market day (Wednesday). November was chosen, of course, to follow the fall harvest.

- This reasoning was great in 1845 but not so much today, when 3% of the voters are farmers. For the convenience of most voters and workers and to encourage greater voter participation in elections, all our elections should include a two-week voting window and require no travel, since all voters will cast their ballots by mail.

- Five states (Colorado, Hawaii, Oregon, Utah, and Washington) have now demonstrated the efficacy, fairness, and integrity of mail-in ballots as the only or the preferred method of casting your ballot. Critics of all-mail systems have claimed that such systems are subject to widespread voter fraud and/or that such systems favor Republicans or favor Democrats. Serious studies of the existing all-mail systems have debunked all these claims.

- This schedule of primaries and general election can be adopted by an Act of Congress. The Constitution specifies only that the new Congress will convene on January 3 and the new President will take office on January 20. Therefore, modifying the schedule of primaries and the general election does not require a constitutional amendment.

Four huge benefits to the public accrue from this proposal: 1) Congress can keep working until July 4 of every election year. 2) Congress does not need to pretend to keep working during the fall campaign season when every day spent in Washington takes the candidates away from the task they are really invested in – campaigning. 3) The public only needs to tolerate repetitive campaign ads and stump speeches from July 4 until the general election, in contrast to the 18-month marathon we all must endure at present. 4) We can do away entirely with the lame-duck session of Congress, and we will have a much shorter period between the general election and the start of a new Congress and inauguration of a new President in January.

Implementing this abbreviated election season requires some national legislation, but even more importantly, it requires a cultural shift. People must recognize the value in overhauling our current perpetual campaigning practices, and citizens will have to demand a shortened campaign season.

Some currently elected officials will oppose this change because change is always fraught with uncertainty. The current officials know how the current system works, and even if they do not like perpetual campaigning and fundraising, they have mastered the art and they know that it keeps them in office. However, one can hope that enough of them will see the advantage to the public in adopting these changes and perhaps also political advantage to themselves in becoming reform advocates.

Because of the free speech clause of the First Amendment, we cannot stop politicians from campaigning outside the "official" campaign season, which will begin on Independence Day. However, news media can refuse to cover campaign events and can also point out that those conducting such events are violating the spirit of the rule that the public insisted on. Finally, the voters can punish such violators at the polls. The shortened campaign season may take some time to really sink in, but voters are bound to prefer it over the existing interminable cacophony.

We really should consider giving an abbreviated and fixed election timetable a chance. If nothing else, it would at least help all of us become less apathetic and more involved the first couple times we did it.

Replace the Vice President with an Elected Chancellor of the Senate

Some have argued that the Presidential candidate should be able to choose his running mate because after the election this pair is more likely to function as a team if they are united throughout the campaign.

Here are my responses to that argument:

- As to the Vice President's role as a member of the President's team, the President can appoint as many advisors as he likes and does not need a Vice President for that role. In fact, through most of our history, the President has largely ignored his Vice President. For example, FDR chose Missouri Senator Harry Truman as his new Vice-Presidential candidate in 1944 without knowing him at all, and when Roosevelt died in April 1945, Roosevelt and Truman had met each other no more than eight times, usually with a group of legislators. When Truman became President, he had not yet been briefed on the Manhattan Project (the development of the atomic bomb).

- We also have the inarguable truth that many modern Vice-Presidential candidates were far from the cream of the crop: Truman selected the quite

92

elderly Kentucky Senator Alben Barkley in 1948 (ever hear of him?); Nixon chose the inexperienced and rather sketchy Maryland Governor Spiro Agnew in 1968, who resigned in disgrace the year before Nixon himself did the same; George H.W. Bush selected the intellectual lightweight and disinterested Indiana Senator Dan Quayle in 1988; and, in the most unqualified selection of all, Senator John McCain in 2008 picked first-term Alaska Governor Sarah Palin. Even as long ago as 1812, President James Madison teamed up with Massachusetts Governor Elbridge Gerry as his running mate, heretofore famous mainly for the "Gerry-mander". Certainly the voters could find better candidates.

What are the duties of the Vice President? Essentially, there are two duties: 1) succeed the President if that position becomes vacant and 2) preside over the Senate. We could solve the issue most directly through a constitutional amendment to

- Replace the position of Vice President of the United States with the position of Chancellor of the Senate (the presiding officer of the Senate);

- Hold a direct national election for Chancellor. Like the presidency, this position could have a four-year term of office; but to keep it distinct from the Presidential election, the Chancellor election could be held at the time of the general election in non-Presidential election years, that is, even-numbered years not evenly divisible by 4. In this way, the Chancellor could very well develop a national following and gain meaningful experience in preparation for a run for the presidency two years later;

- Make the Chancellor first in the line of succession to the presidency; and

- Give the Chancellor meaningful responsibilities. The Chancellor should take over the responsibility for making all judicial appointments. The Chancellor should also truly preside over the Senate, controlling the agenda and the debate, and appointing the other Senate officers, such as the Chancellor Pro-Tempore and committee assignments – in the same fashion that the Speaker runs the House of Representatives.

14 Vice Presidents have become President in our history, either through the death or resignation of the President or through a subsequent election in which a sitting or former Vice President is seen as having a considerable built-in advantage over any other Presidential aspirant. Therefore, in a democracy, it is reasonable that the people should choose the second-most important job under our Constitution, rather than leaving that selection to a single person, who, at the time the decision is made,

has not yet been elected as President. This is the main argument for making the election of Chancellor distinct from the election of the President.

Reassigning the responsibility for judicial appointments to someone other than the President could be part of the constitutional effort to regain balance among the three branches of government and strip away some of the inordinate power of the presidency. Although we have three distinct branches of government, there are points at which one branch is intimately involved in another branch. While the President obviously should make all executive branch appointments, the appointment of judges is a point at which he is involved in the judiciary. It might make more sense to let the Chancellor of the Senate perform that function. And if we made that change, then one of the major issues in the national election for Chancellor would be the candidates' potential selections for the federal judiciary.

The comprehensive amendment on Federal elections at the end of Part II of this book as well as the revised Constitution in Part III include the replacement of the Vice President with the new position of Chancellor. This change makes much more sense were it adopted in conjunction with a series of other related changes.

Until this constitutional amendment is adopted, I suggest that each successful Presidential primary candidate announce his/her choice of a Vice Presidential running mate by October 22.

Provide for Direct Election of the President and Vice President

In 1823 the former President James Madison returned to his earlier view in favor of universal suffrage and against the electoral college as it had evolved. By that time, almost all states had adopted the winner-take-all practice still used by 48 of the 50 states today: the winner of the statewide popular vote receives all of that state's electoral votes. Madison also opposed the provision that gives the election to the House of Representatives with one vote per state when no candidate has a majority of the electoral votes. Madison proposed a constitutional amendment[14] (which obviously never passed) (see sidebar).

Interesting sidebar: James Madison's Constitutional Amendment

Proposed in 1823. Never passed. Key elements:

[14] http://www.fairvote.org/why-james-madison-wanted-to-change-the-way-we-vote-for-President. [Accessed on June 16, 2017.]

a) Voters in Presidential election districts in each state choose Presidential electors, with no more than two electors per district.

b) Each elector chooses two persons for President, a 1st choice and a 2nd choice.

c) If one person receives a majority of the 1st choice votes, then that person becomes President.

d) If no one receives a majority of 1st choice votes, then the 2nd choice votes are added, and if one person receives a majority, he becomes President.

e) If still no one has a majority, then Congress in a joint session of both chambers selects the President from the two names with the most 1st plus 2nd choice votes.

When we consider improvements to the manner of choosing the President, James Madison's proposed constitutional amendment might be a good place to open the discussion.

As Madison's proposal demonstrates, Americans have long debated the elimination of the electoral college. I believe strongly that Madison was right, and that direct election is by far the best and only truly fair solution. The arguments are thoroughly spelled out in *Every Vote Equal*[15], a monograph which argues in favor of the National Popular Vote Interstate Compact (explained below), but which also provides a detailed analysis of the reasons why direct election is preferred. Later in Part II, the Amendment on Federal Elections specifies direct election of the President using Ranked Choice Voting, and in Part III, the revised U.S Constitution does the same – That is to say, if we are going to change the Constitution, we should go all the way to direct election of the President and do away with both the Electoral College and the untenable procedure for throwing the election to the House of Representatives.

However, if we wish to move in the direction of direct election but without amending the Constitution – a less daunting task – then here are three alternatives along with the pros and cons of each.

Each alternative still works within the framework of the electoral college as provided in the Constitution. We currently have 538 electoral votes, made up of 435 electoral votes equal to the number of seats in the House of Representatives,

---

[15] J.R. Koza et al. (2013). *Every Vote Equal.*

100 electoral votes equal to the number of seats in the Senate, and 3 electoral votes for Washington, DC. (The 3 votes for DC are based on the electoral votes that DC would have if it were a state – one seat in the House and 2 in the Senate.) If one candidate receives a majority of the electoral votes (270), that candidate is elected President. If no candidate receives a majority, the House of Representatives determines the winner, and each state delegation has one vote.

Because the Constitution specifically empowers states to choose their electors however they see fit, any scheme that garners 270 electoral votes will work. As an extreme example, we could adopt simple random selection: People who want to be President throw their names into a hat, and one name is randomly drawn as the winner. If states with 270 electoral votes agree to give all their electoral votes to that randomly-selected candidate, then that person becomes President.

The following three alternatives are feasible.

Alternative 1: The National Popular Vote Interstate Compact (NPVIC)

NPVIC could bring about the direct election of the President by popular vote without needing to amend the Constitution. Under this initiative, identical laws have been introduced in 47 states, which provide that that state will cast all its electoral votes for the candidate who wins the national popular vote. These state laws only become effective when states having at least 270 electoral votes in aggregate have adopted NPVIC.

Pros and cons of Alternative 1

The pros of the NPVIC proposal are easy to see. Every vote counts equally. This feature eliminates the preference given to voters in less-populous states. NPVIC also eliminates the state-by-state winner-take-all system, which currently causes most states and most voters to be ignored. As a result, the notion of "swing states" would disappear. It would no longer matter whether a candidate "won" a particular state or not. 70% of American voters believe that the candidate with the most votes should become President. NPVIC gives us that result without amending the Constitution.

The Con of this proposal is that the need for candidates to appeal to every geographic region of the nation would be reduced. (Of course, one can argue rather persuasively that the current system also does not require candidates to appeal across many regions since the entire Presidential election campaign focuses only on eight or nine "swing" states.) Another Con is that, by not amending the

Constitution, NPVIC could be undone by states that change their mind and drop out or fail to follow the compact. Hence, the failure to amend the Constitution is a two-edged sword: what a state legislature can do, that state legislature can undo a week later.

Can NPVIC succeed?

As of this writing, 15 states plus Washington, DC have passed the National Popular Vote Interstate Compact. These states control 196 electoral votes, 72% of the number needed to reach 270. However, the states that have adopted NPVIC (MD, NJ, IL, HI, WA, MA, VT, CA, RI, NY, CT, CO, DE, NM, OR, and DC) are primarily the more progressive states; gaining the requisite 74 additional electoral votes will be difficult. NPVIC may well be the current effort closest to a successful conclusion, but success is still very far away. Some folks prefer to retain the current electoral college with its built-in protections for less populous states and its requirement that a successful candidate demonstrate support across all regions of the country.

Alternative 2: Voting by Congressional District, as in Maine and Nebraska

In Maine and Nebraska, the winner of the Presidential election in each congressional district (CD) is awarded one electoral vote (representing the electoral votes allocated to that state based on its seats in the House), and the winner statewide is awarded two electoral votes (representing the electoral votes allocated to that state based on its seats in the Senate).

Pros and cons of Alternative 2

This system is much fairer than the winner-take-all approach followed in the other 48 states although it does not eliminate the built-in preference for states with small populations. Another Pro is that it does not require a constitutional amendment; but a Con is that it would not be really effective unless it were implemented in all 50 states, a tough nut to crack. Probably the biggest Con is that it gives no credit at all to the candidate who wins the national popular vote, which makes Alternative 2 much less popular among reformers than NPVIC.

Can Alternative 2 succeed?

Maine and Nebraska adopted this system for reasons unique to the internal politics of those states. Its chances of wider adoption in its present form are slim. Most states perceive only a loss of power and influence by dividing their electoral votes among multiple candidates.

Alternative 2 might have greater appeal if its implementation followed the NPVIC model. Specifically, states would agree to cast all their electoral votes for the candidate who wins according to this system, but implementation would only take place after states with at least 270 electoral votes adopted it.

Alternative 3: Local-State-National (LSN) Voting – A Hybrid Solution

This system represents a hybrid, giving weight to each vote at the local, state, and national levels. Basically, each vote contributes to the preferred candidate winning within a congressional district (CD), within a state, and across the whole nation. Like the NPVIC, this solution can be implemented as soon as states with at least 270 electoral votes adopt it.

Here is how LSN Voting works:

Under the LSN voting scheme, the number of LSN votes equals the number of electoral votes (538). LSN votes are tabulated as follows:

- One LSN vote is awarded to the winner of each CD. This is the "Local" component of LSN voting. This accounts for 436 LSN votes.

- One LSN vote is awarded to the winner of each state. This is the "State" component of LSN voting. This accounts for 51 LSN votes.

- One LSN vote is awarded to the winner of the national popular vote for each state in the Union. This is the "National" component of LSN voting. This accounts for 51 LSN votes.

- If one candidate has at least 270 LSN votes, that candidate is the winner. If no candidate has at least 270 LSN votes, then the winner of the national popular vote is the winner of the election.

The Local-State-National Interstate Compact (LSNIC): States adopting the LSN voting scheme agree to cast all their electoral votes for the candidate who wins the election according to the LSN voting scheme. These state laws only become effective when states with 270 electoral votes have adopted it.

Pros and cons of Alternative 3

LSN Voting accomplishes all the major objectives of reform:

1. Values every voter in every congressional district, every state, and the nation as a whole;

2. Retains a role for the states, while also recognizing both a smaller (local CD) and larger (national) component of each voter's choice;
3. Requires the winning candidate to have broad appeal at all three levels (local, state, and national) and across all regions of the country;
4. Bypasses the electoral college, removing any possibility that "faithless electors" could alter the outcome of the contest; and
5. Eliminates the possibility that the Presidential election will ever be thrown into the House of Representatives.

Can the LSN solution succeed?

In terms of effectiveness and possibility of adoption, this compromise proposal might satisfy sufficiently those who want every vote to count and want the winner of the popular vote to win the election. It might also satisfy those who want the winner to have broad appeal across the nation and want the states to still matter.

The major parties will likely rail against this proposal (since it reduces their clout), and they are very likely to resuscitate the old debate during the 1787 Constitutional Convention about large states overpowering small states. But as pointed out earlier, that is a bogus argument: A strong difference of opinion between large and small states has never been a decisive factor in any US Presidential election. We have had differences between regions, between parties, between personalities, and between ideologies; but we have never had differences because all the large states gathered in one corner and all the small states gathered in the opposite corner – it just never happened.

If Americans decide not to amend our Constitution, then this author endorses the LSN Solution as the preferred alternative.

Challenge 2. U.S. Senate Fix

Article V Provision

If Americans decided to change the Senate from a body that represents states (two Senators per state) to a representative body (on the principle of "one citizen one vote", while also representing states), it's not as simple as adopting a constitutional amendment to modify Article I Section 3, which specifies that the Senate will be composed of two Senators per state. This is because Article V, which delineates the procedures and rules for amending the Constitution, specifies that no state will be denied equal suffrage in the Senate without its consent. Faced with this intentional roadblock to changing the makeup of the Senate, we are left with the following possibilities:

1. We could propose an amendment to change the makeup of the Senate, and get every one of the 50 states to adopt it – probably an impossible hurdle, since at least one state with a small population would almost certainly object, and an objection from any single state would nullify this approach.

2. We could amend the Constitution to reduce the powers of the Senate, so that, even as the Senate remained unrepresentative, this wouldn't matter so much. For example, rather than requiring the Senate to pass all legislation before it becomes law, we could give the Senate only the power to block a law passed by the House, provided that the Senate rejects that law by a 2/3 majority within 30 days after it is passed by the House. Many other similar measures could be used to reduce the Senate's role. (This was the type of change the British used to reduce the power of the very unrepresentative House of Lords.) While this approach has merit, we might end up with a unicameral legislature, with none of the checks and balances which a bicameral legislature provides.

3. We could eliminate the Senate altogether. This is cleaner than method 2 but still leaves us with a unicameral legislature, subject to the whims of the voters every two years, and without the benefits of a bicameral legislature. Having two chambers, one designed to change laws quickly in response to public opinion, the other designed to operate more slowly and carefully, is probably a good feature of the American system.

4. We could accomplish our objective in two steps, which is the process I recommend:

    Step 1. Replace Article V, rewriting the procedures for amending the Constitution (see Big Fix 3 above).

    Step 2. After that amendment is adopted, we could then proceed to adopt another amendment to change the makeup of the Senate. In this new configuration, each Senator will represent BOTH the people of the state and the state itself. The reconfiguration of the Senate could be combined with the replacement of the position of Vice President of the United States with the new position of Chancellor of the Senate.

Proposed Makeup of the New Senate

To clarify the discussion in this section, I use the term "Original Senate" to refer to the existing Senate as prescribed by the 1787 Constitution, and the term "New Senate" to describe the reconstituted Senate suggested here.

The New Senate will be a representative body, made up of Senators elected for six-year terms. The number of Senators for each state equals the number of that state's Representatives divided by five, with fractions always rounded up. Thus states with one to five Representatives in the House get one Senator; states with six to ten Representatives get two Senators; those with 11 to 15 Representatives get three Senators; and so on. However, the maximum number of Senators for any state is six.

The rationale for fixing the maximum number of Senators for any state at six comes from the election procedure for Senators. Each Senator represents an entire state, and so all voters in the state should help select each of its Senators. With staggered elections for six year terms held every two years, a state with six Senators could elect two of them in each election cycle. This seems manageable, as we have held many simultaneous elections for two Senators in the same state, in which one election is called to fill an unexpired term of two years or four years. But electing three or more at a time feels unwieldy, especially as a steady diet.

The following table shows the allocation of Senators in the New Senate to the 50 states, based on the apportionment of Representatives following the 2010 Census. It also shows the ratio of power between the citizens of this state and the citizens of the state with the least power – the Ratio of Power Per Person, or RP/PP. Note that the maximum-of-six-Senators rule would only affect California and Texas, which would otherwise qualify for 11 and 8 Senators respectively. The least powerful citizens reside in the state with the highest number of people per Senator (that is, California), so their relative power is defined as 1.0. Finally, the table shows that the New Senate would have 103 Senators, not much different from the Original Senate, which has 100 Senators at present :

Apportioning Seats in the New Senate		
	Seats	

State	House	Senate	RP/PP
Alabama	7	2	2.6
Alaska	1	1	8.6
Arizona	9	2	1.9
Arkansas	4	1	2.1
California	53	6	1.0
Colorado	7	2	2.5
Connecticut	5	1	1.7
Delaware	1	1	6.9
Florida*	27	6	2.0
Georgia	14	3	1.9
Hawaii	2	1	4.6
Idaho	2	1	4.0
Illinois	18	4	1.9
Indiana	9	2	1.9
Iowa	4	1	2.0
Kansas	4	1	2.2
Kentucky	6	2	2.9
Louisiana	6	2	2.7
Maine	2	1	4.7

Maryland	8	2	2.1
Massachusetts	9	2	1.9
Michigan	14	3	1.9
Minnesota	8	2	2.3
Mississippi	4	1	2.1
Missouri	8	2	2.1
Montana	1	1	6.3
Nebraska	3	1	3.4
Nevada	4	1	2.3
New Hampshire	2	1	4.7
New Jersey	12	3	2.1
New Mexico	3	1	3.0
New York	27	6	1.9
North Carolina	13	3	2.0
North Dakota	1	1	9.2
Ohio	16	4	2.2
Oklahoma	5	1	1.7
Oregon	5	1	1.6
Pennsylvania	18	4	2.0

Rhode Island	2	1	5.9
South Carolina	7	2	2.7
South Dakota	1	1	7.6
Tennessee	9	2	2.0
Texas*	36	6	1.5
Utah	4	1	2.2
Vermont	1	1	9.9
Virginia	11	3	2.3
Washington	10	2	1.8
West Virginia	3	1	3.3
Wisconsin	8	2	2.2
Wyoming	1	1	11.0
Totals	435	103	

The power inequalities of the Original Senate have been largely corrected in this suggested makeup of the New Senate. Rather than a worst case of 66 to 1 (the exorbitant relative power of voters in Wyoming to voters in California in the Original Senate), the worst case in the New Senate would be 11to 1 (still Wyoming to California).

Terms of Office for the New Senate

One of the purposes of the Original Senate, as established by the Founding Fathers, was to be a more deliberative body, as a counterweight to the House, which was expected to be elected directly by the people every two years and thus to be more responsive to the changing views of the citizenry. For this reason, Original Senate terms were fixed at six years, with a third of the Senate elected every two years. Change would therefore come to the Senate more slowly than to the House.

The New Senate should follow exactly the same scheme, with a third of the Senators elected every two years, and with staggered elections for Senators from the same state. The only issue occurs when a state gains or loses a Senator as a result of the decennial census. This can be easily handled as follows:

- When a state loses a Senator as a result of reapportionment, the Senator whose term of office next expires simply is not replaced.
- When a state gains a Senator, the additional seat is filled at the next biennial election, and the term of office for the new Senator is either two, four, or six years, depending on how it fits into the scheme of staggered terms for the Senators within a state.

It should be noted that few changes in the number of Senators apportioned to a state can be expected. For example, if this system had been in place beginning in 2000, then only Florida would have seen an increase of one Senator as a result of the 2010 reapportionment, and no state would have experienced a decrease. Therefore, this system is rather stable.

Conclusion

The makeup of the Original Senate, as prescribed in Article I of the Constitution, is far from representative. In a representative democracy we should not forever retain a construct in which half of the national legislature fails to properly represent the American population. Many solutions to this problem present themselves, but only a structural solution such as replacing Article V concerning the procedure for amending the Constitution combined with the New Senate proposed here solves the challenge of the Article V provision concerning the Senate as well as the challenge of the non-representative makeup of the Original Senate. The advantage of this proposal is that it builds on and largely retains many features of the Original Senate, including its continued dependence on state elections held at large and six-year terms of office, while also accommodating future population shifts as reflected in the census. We should carefully consider potential solutions and move forward on one of them.

Challenge 3. Gerrymander Fix

An old saying is most relevant here: "Perfection is the enemy of the good." I do not claim that this solution is perfect, that it meets every conceivable objective of redistricting reform, or that it is the very best way to draw election districts. I do claim that it is far preferable to the system we have now. Further, it is achievable on a state-by-state basis or, preferably, through national legislation or a constitutional amendment.

Redistricting Principles

We need a completely mechanical, replicable, transparent, uniform-across-all-states, and (especially) non-partisan process for redistricting.

Seven states have only one seat in the House, so this discussion pertains to the 43 states that have more than one House seat. However, the problem of gerrymandering may be even more pronounced with respect to drawing election districts for state legislatures. The solution recommended here for Congress can be applied to legislative districts in all 50 states as well.

Most observers would agree that the optimal solution to this problem is to 1) remove redistricting from the control of politicians and 2) adopt a rule-based process to make redistricting easy and automatic. The solution proposed herein satisfies both of those criteria. This section explains the proposed redistricting solution as a manual process, which lends itself to automation.

PRELIMINARILY we should all agree on the basic objectives for any non-partisan redistricting scheme:

- Equalize the population per House seat within a state,

- Keep neighbors together in the same congressional district, and

- Ignore all other considerations.

Equalize population per House seat: The first of these objectives, equalizing the population per House seat, reflects basic fairness, the time-honored notion of "one person – one vote".

Keep neighbors together: The second objective is intuitively obvious to Americans, but geography is not necessarily the only criterion that could be used. In Florence in the Middle Ages, representatives to the city Senate were chosen by occupation: construction trades elected one rep, farmers another, merchants another, and so on. We could use religion: Catholics elect their representatives and all other denominations theirs. We could use age: everyone 18 to 30 elects their reps, those 30 to 55 elect theirs, and so on. We could divide ourselves by social class, as France did before the French Revolution: churchmen in the First Estate, noblemen and aristocrats in the Second Estate, and the bourgeoisie in the Third Estate.[16] We could do it by income or net worth: Starting at the top, the wealthiest 710,000 residents of a state elect one congressperson, then the next wealthiest 710,000 elect the second congressperson, on down to the poorest who elect the last. We could also just let a computer randomly assign each voter to a congressional district. But having said all that, we in this country still have some affinity for geographic proximity as a basis for deciding which folks belong in the same election district. Hence a rule-based solution to redistricting must consider neighborhoods.

The rule proposed here is that each congressional district should occupy a contiguous and compact land mass, incorporate whole counties whenever possible, and, when one county needs to be partitioned in order to complete a CD with the

---

[16] When we describe journalists as "members of the Fourth Estate", that is actually a reference to the Three Estates in pre-revolutionary France.

requisite population, keep together everyone who lives in the same Zip Code Tabulation Area (ZCTA, defined later).

We should also admit that both natural and man-made barriers affect the formation of communities. Buda and Pest were separate towns on opposite sides of the Danube River until bridges appeared, allowing Budapest to form. Boundaries between Swiss cantons often consist of a high Alpine ridge, impassable for half the year. These and countless other examples demonstrate the importance of geography. But we also observe that the resulting communities – on either side of a river or mountain pass or large lake or ravine – are often in separate counties and almost always in separate zip codes since the postman does not want to cross a river or ravine either, so that keeping zip codes together largely addresses the issue of natural geographic boundaries.

I would like also to posit that the notion of keeping neighbors in the same CD is sufficiently important that fidelity to this standard affords some relaxation in the rule to equalize populations. I do not know the magic number or percentage here, but in this proposal I am using 5% as the norm: I allow a CD to have up to 5% more or 5% less than the requisite population of a CD if doing so allows an entire county or an entire ZCTA to stay in the same CD. (When a ZCTA needs to be partitioned, it can be divided into census tracts (also explained later).)

Ignore all other considerations: Many state statutes, some federal statues, and countless court cases have addressed the allowable criteria in drawing election districts. Laws and courts have mandated equal populations in each district as well as geographic compactness. Some redistricting plans consider race or other demographic factors to ensure that the redistricting scheme does not unfairly disadvantage any protected class. Those responsible for drawing district boundaries have also considered (whether openly or secretly) party registrations, previous voting patterns, and wealth, among other criteria. Since the 1960s, the major debates have centered on race, socio-economic status, political affiliation, and previous voting history. It appears that every redistricting plan from every state has been subject to litigation; and courts have had a devil of a time trying to sort out these competing interests in order to decide what is legal, fair, and reasonable. After the last round of redistricting based on the 2010 Census, 38 of the 43 state redistricting plans faced legal challenges.

The many objections to redistricting plans all seem to relate to the perceived misuse of redistricting as a method to achieve partisan political objectives rather than the need to ensure fair and free elections. Yet if we remove politicians from the process and focus only on the twin objectives of equalizing population and geographic proximity, we will eliminate the need for all other criteria. This proposed plan does exactly that.

NEXT, we should agree that a non-partisan redistricting solution should satisfy these guidelines:

- Avoid human decisions concerning any particular election district boundary;

- Adopt a completely rule-governed process;

- Follow the same process in every state;

- Make the process transparent to and replicable by anyone so interested.

Avoid human decisions: Most published proposals for redistricting have included some kind of state-level commission to oversee the process in each state. Some plans specify a completely non-partisan body. Other plans specify a commission balanced between the major political parties, perhaps with a third group of independents or non-partisan participants. The problem with all of these proposals is that politicians, lobbyists, or other influence peddlers can manipulate or control any such commission. Then the task of guarding against such corruptions becomes a permanent feature of the political landscape. Furthermore, in all of these schemes the state commissions, legislatures, and courts still spend a considerable amount of time and effort drawing election district boundaries. A better system would make the redistricting process automatic, so we could spend our time discussing substantive issues rather than focusing on process.

In a democracy, people get to choose their representatives; the representatives do not get to choose their constituents. Anytime politicians draw the election districts, we tend toward a system where the representatives choose the voters rather than the reverse. Therefore, a truly non-partisan redistricting system should remove humans from making any election district boundary decisions. Full Stop.

Rule-Governed Process: Any proposed process should be governed by specific rules that spell out precisely how to draw the election districts. The process must work for any jurisdiction in the country subdivided into any number of election districts, again maintaining allegiance only to the two principles of equalization of population and geographic proximity. Such a mechanical process could be automated. The Federal Elections Commission should publish the resulting computer program and make it freely available.

Uniform in Every State: The U.S. Constitution, Article I, Section 4 Elections, Meetings grants Congress power to regulate elections for members of Congress should Congress choose to do so:

> *The Times, Places and Manner of holding Elections for Senators and Representatives, shall be prescribed in each State by the Legislature thereof; but the Congress may at any time by Law make or alter such Regulations, except as to the Place of Chusing [sic] Senators.*

Based on that paragraph, in 1845 Congress established a uniform day for holding the national elections. Before that law was passed, each state chose when to conduct its election. Today we take it for granted that all our national elections take place on the same day, but it was not always so. Based on the same Constitutional authority, in 1965 Congress mandated single-seat election districts. Similarly, Congress has the authority to determine how congressional districts are drawn since this is very much a part of the "Manner" of holding elections.

The reason for Congressional action with regard to gerrymandering is obvious. If Party A dominates one state and has gerrymandered its congressional districts while Party B dominates another state and has likewise gerrymandered its districts, why would either state unilaterally disarm? The only viable and long-lasting solution is one that applies equally to every state.

Transparent and Replicable: Drawing election districts should not be rocket science – one should not need an engineering or math degree to do it. The process only becomes complicated when we introduce objectives and criteria which ought to be irrelevant such as race, wealth, or political affiliation. Therefore, a process that eliminates those irrelevant factors should be something any citizen can comprehend and any citizen with the desire to do so can replicate.

The actual physical process of drawing boundaries for congressional districts should be straight-forward, uncomplicated, easy to understand, completely non-political, and (ideally) fully automated. Since the computer software to do this has not yet been created, I will explain the process in narrative form. Once we have come to agreement on the process, computer programmers will then be able to write the computer software to do this automatically.

Proposed Redistricting Process Summary

I propose to end all the debate and all the litigation. This solution is not perfect, but it's far better than any other I've encountered to date. I'm not wedded to this particular solution just because I came up with it. Any solution that satisfies the aforementioned principles should be considered. But let me put this one on the table, and then we can all discuss this proposal and any others that may also fit the bill. What follows here is a broad summary of the process and maps of several sample states. (The details of the proposed scheme appear in Appendix 1.)

This process centers on the boundaries of counties (or similar political subdivision used by a state) and of Zip Code Tabulation Areas (ZCTAs). The U.S. Census Bureau developed ZCTAs from the US Postal Service's 5-digit zip codes. Think of a ZCTA as a zip code with geographic boundaries. Everyone resides within a ZCTA, even if your mailing address is a P.O. Box and even if your house is not on any mail delivery route. Therefore, we begin with a map of a given state's counties and the ZCTAs within each county, along with the population of each county and each ZCTA.

We will draw each CD by selecting a Starting Point for the current CD according to a simple rule and then assigning to that CD the counties closest to the Starting Point. To achieve the correct population for a CD in the state, we may need to partition LAST COUNTY into ZCTAs and even LAST ZCTA (if it is exceedingly populous) into census tracts.

Starting Point (S) Selection Rule: If the height of the UNASSIGNED AREA (UA) (the portion of a state not yet assigned to a CD) exceeds its width, then S is the northernmost point in UA; otherwise, S is the westernmost point.

Use a compass to draw ever-widening arcs around S, assigning all of each county as it is encountered to the current CD. Stop adding whole counties when one more county (termed LAST COUNTY (LC)) would cause the CD population to exceed its TARGET. LC may be either omitted from the CD or included wholly within it, provided the resulting CD population would remain within the allowable variation from its target. If LC can be neither wholly omitted nor wholly included, then it must be partitioned into ZCTAs, assigning to the current CD those ZCTAs nearest to S.

The following images show the construction of CDs for an imaginary state with four Congressional Districts divided into 28 counties.

Imaginary State CD 1

The state is wider than high, so the Starting Point (S on the map) is the westernmost point. The arc touches eight counties wholly included in CD 1. The arc encounters a ninth county, LAST COUNTY (L on the map), but here we assume that the CD population is close enough to TARGET without L, so L is omitted.

Imaginary State CD 2

Since UA is still wider than high, S is again the westernmost point in UA. The arc again touches a total of nine counties, but this time LAST COUNTY (L) can be included in CD 2, while the total population for CDs 1 and 2 is within the allowable variation.

Imaginary State CD 3

For this CD, the height of UA is greater than its width, so S is the northernmost point within UA. The arc touches six counties that are wholly included in CD 3. We are assuming that the seventh county (L) can be neither wholly included nor excluded, and so it must be partitioned. Hence we draw a second arc through LAST COUNTY, adding ZCTAs until the TARGET population for CDs 1, 2, and 3 is reached.

Imaginary State CD 4

After we have created all CDs save one, that last CD must contain everything left over, so we do not need S, an ARC, or L.

Here is a review of the proposed process for drawing congressional districts in every state:

1. Follow the rule to determine the Starting Point (S) at the westernmost or northernmost point of the UNASSIGNED AREA (UA).

2. Using a compass, draw an ever-widening ARC around S through UA.

3. Add each county touched by ARC to the current CD, stopping only when one more county (LAST COUNTY (L)) would put too many people in the CD.

4. Omit, include, or partition L, according to the rule.

5. If L is partitioned, continue ARC through L, adding each touched ZCTA to the current CD until TARGET is reached.

6. Repeat these steps until all CDs for the state are created

Sample Congressional Districts

CD Boundaries in Maryland (8 CDs), North Carolina (14 CDs), and Pennsylvania (18 CDs)

Here are three examples based on this proposed scheme, showing the approximate congressional districts which would have resulted from the 2020 Census in Maryland and North Carolina and from the 2010 census in Pennsylvania.

Note that the CD boundaries within partitioned counties are approximations, not the actual CD boundaries. In reality, the edges of ZCTAs form a jagged line rather than an even arc, so the boundary lines in these examples represent the approximate locations of the CD boundaries. Consider these as a proof of concept rather than as definitive solutions.

MARYLAND

Note that, in the 2020 apportionment, North Carolina gained a seat and now has 14 Congressional Districts.

NORTH CAROLINA

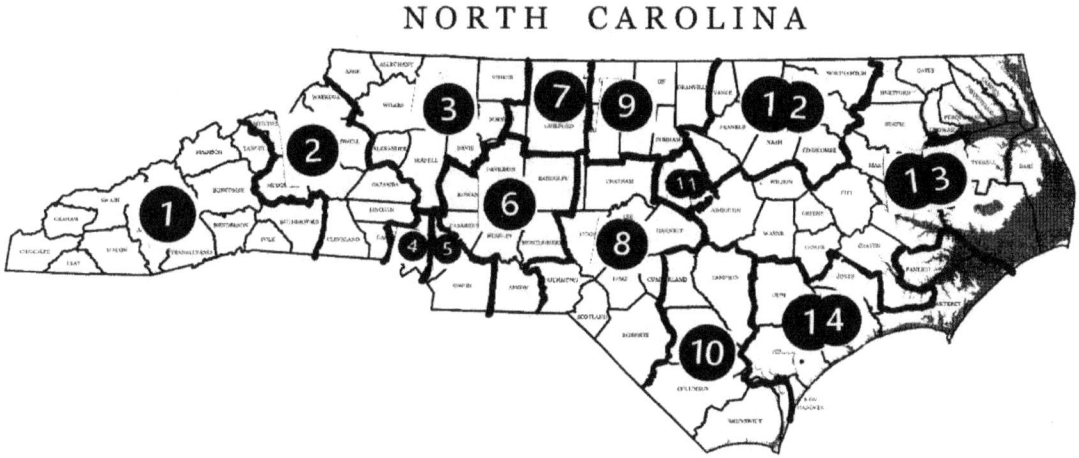

PENNSYLVANIA (based on the 2010 Census)

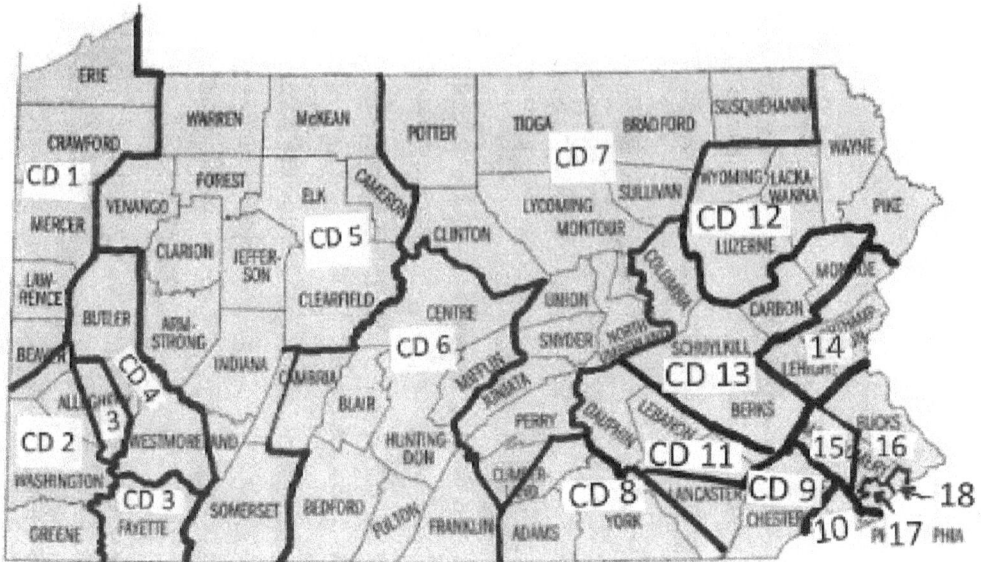

Political Results in Maryland and North Carolina

Of course, everyone reading this wants to know how this might affect ME. Let's examine the implications of the proposed scheme on the political fortunes of Republicans and Democrats in Maryland and in North Carolina. While no one can predict how people will vote in future elections, we can get a hint of expected results by examining the voting patterns of the areas that make up each of the proposed CDs. We will use the results of the 2020 elections for the House of Representatives for this comparison. This analysis considers only how each major party fared in each county. It does not consider other factors, such as the characteristics of each candidate.

Maryland 2020 Elections for the House

As a starting point, registered Democrats outnumber registered Republicans about two to one, but many voters are unaffiliated or "Independent". These are the actual numbers and percentages of registered voters in Maryland by party affiliation as of October 2020 (just before the 2020 election):

REGISTERED VOTERS	Number	Percentage
Democratic	2,284,607	55%
Republican	1,026,114	25%
Third Party & Other	64,817	1%
Unaffiliated	781,228	19%
Total	4.156.766	100%

In this state, gerrymandered to favor Democrats, Maryland voters elected seven Dems and one Repub to the House in each of the last three elections. None of the third party, independent, or write-in candidates moved the needle in any of these elections, so I decided to tabulate only the votes for Republicans and for Democrats.

To get a hint at expected political results using the CD boundaries proposed herein, I added up the votes cast in the general elections for the House of Representatives in 2020 in each county. If a county is wholly within one proposed CD, I added all the votes from that county to the totals for that CD. If only a percentage of a county lies within a CD, I multiplied the total county votes by the percentage of the county population that lies within that CD. Here are the results:

2020 House Voting Results
Applied to Proposed CDs

CD #	%Dem	%Rep	%
CD 1	45%	54%	
CD 2	62%	38%	
CD 3	42%	58%	
CD 4	76%	23%	
CD 5	73%	27%	
CD 6	81%	18%	
CD 7	66%	34%	
CD 8	77%	23%	

2020 House Voting Results Applied to Proposed CDs

As expected, in the 2020 Congressional elections in Maryland, Democrats got 65% of the vote for major party candidates, and Republicans got 35%. Based on the proposed CD boundaries, Democrats would have won six of Maryland's eight seats in the House. None of these elections would have been close.

North Carolina 2020 Elections for the House

In North Carolina, the starting point again is the actual result. Of the total vote for major party candidates in 2020, Democrats had a slight majority of 50.3% to the Republicans 49.7%. Republican candidates won 8 of the 13 House seats in North Carolina.

In the re-apportionment after the 2020 census, North Carolina gained a seat and now has 14. As with Maryland, I simulated the results in North Carolina by adding whole and partial county votes to the Republican and Democratic columns in each proposed CD. As you can see from the table and chart, Republicans would have won 8 seats and the Dems would have won 6:

CD#	Dem%	Rep%	W
1	45%	**55%**	R
2	31%	**69%**	R
3	35%	**65%**	R
4	**79%**	21%	D
5	**67%**	33%	D
6	32%	**68%**	R
7	**58%**	42%	D
8	45%	**55%**	R
9	**67%**	33%	D
10	47%	**53%**	R
11	**63%**	37%	D
12	**59%**	41%	D
13	45%	**55%**	R
14	37%	**63%**	R

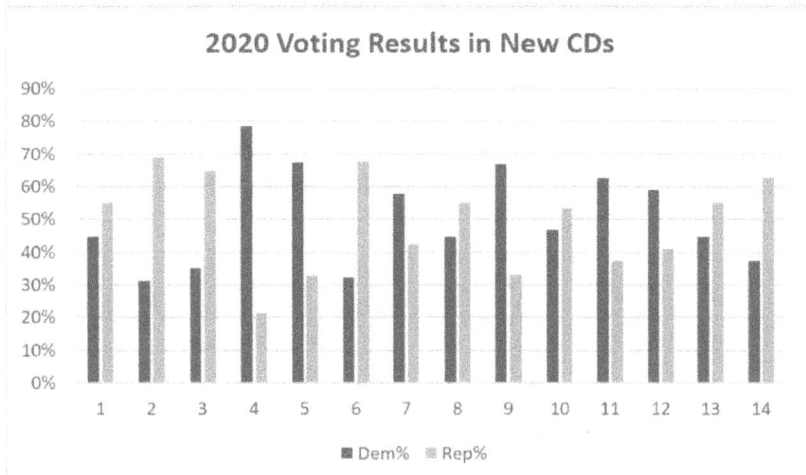

2020 Voting Results in New CDs

■ Dem% ▨ Rep%

Racial Profile in Maryland

Ever since a Boston cartoonist in 1812 introduced the term "gerrymander" to the American political lexicon, Americans have argued about unfair influences on drawing election district boundaries. Editorials and lawsuits abound concerning the "unfair" influence of race, religion, party registrations, age, income, education, and rural-versus-urban constituents. Of all these characteristics, the one factor that always seems to dominate such discussions is race. A major attraction of my proposal is that neither race nor any of these other characteristics factor in drawing election district boundaries.

The chart below, based on the 2020 Census, shows the percentage of residents in each proposed CD in Maryland who identify with each race. Overall, the state is 56% white, 30% black, and 7% Asian. 11% are Hispanic, who may be of any race. White residents constitute an outright majority in CDs 1, 2, 3, and 5, and a plurality in CDs 6 and 7. Blacks are the majority in CD 4 and a plurality in CD 8.

New CDs by Race - Maryland

	white	black	hispanic	asian
CD 1	81%	9%	6%	4%
CD 2	61%	28%	5%	6%
CD 3	76%	17%	4%	2%
CD 4	38%	54%	5%	3%
CD 5	52%	19%	13%	16%
CD 6	38%	32%	18%	12%
CD 7	47%	38%	11%	4%
CD 8	39%	47%	11%	4%

Racial Data for New CDs in Maryland

Redistricting Process Details

I recognize that cartography (map-making) is not everyone's cup of tea. Many readers may find this subject confusing or tedious or both. For that reason, I have placed the detailed explanations of the process in appendices:

- Appendix 1. Detailed Redistricting Procedures
- Appendix 2. Maryland Redistricting
- Appendix 3. North Carolina Redistricting

I'd love to see examples from additional states. Should you care to create CD boundaries for another state, please follow the guidelines in Appendix 1 and refer to the detailed examples in Appendices 2 and 3. You can email the results to me at bob_spear@hotmail.com, and I will post them on my blog at 21CommonSense.org.

Two Alternative Solutions

Though I have opted for the "whole counties" redistricting scheme presented in the foregoing pages, two alternative schemes also merit serious consideration. I will briefly describe each of these and summarize the pro and con arguments for each. One solution follows my preferred methodology of drawing arcs around a starting point but uses only ZCTAs; the second involves the creation of multi-seat CDs.

Alternative 1: Redistricting only with ZCTAs

We could use the same redistricting scheme proposed herein but use only ZCTAs instead of entire counties. We start each CD by designating a Starting Point in the same way we have proposed. We then draw ever-widening arcs around that starting point, adding ZCTAs as they are encountered. We stop adding ZCTAs when Target is reached.

Here is a rough approximation of the resulting CD maps for Maryland and North Carolina:

Maryland (8 Congressional Districts) (2020 census)

North Carolina (13 Congressional Districts) (2010 census)

This example used straight borders perpendicular to the Starting Point rather than arcs around the Starting Point.

NC CD 12 complete
NC CD 13 complete

All NC CDs complete

Pros: This seems the most fair, as it eliminates county borders which are themselves often the product of the same unfortunate manipulations that underlie gerrymandering. Examples from many states show the evolution of counties, whose boundaries have shifted to follow the racial or economic makeup of the constituent neighborhoods. Hence, if we now build CDs based on the existing county boundaries, we are perpetuating systems that are inherently undemocratic.

126

Using only ZCTAs avoids this bias. Another benefit of the ZCTA-only solution is that this solution will likely result in fewer "islands" (non-contiguous areas that cannot easily attach to a CD).

Cons: Many current state constitutions, laws, regulations, and traditional practices require that county boundaries be respected when CD boundaries are drawn. Some modern political science research suggests that citizens of counties lying wholly within one CD are more politically aware and engaged than are citizens of counties that belong to multiple CDs.[17]

Alternative 2: Multi-Seat Districts with RCV

This solution is based on the creation of 3-seat CDs, combined with Ranked Choice Voting (RCV) adapted for multi-winner elections.

States are subdivided into as many 3-seat districts as mathematically possible (thereby leaving 0, 1, or 2 seats for an additional 1- or 2-seat CD if needed). District boundaries are drawn using the same procedure as that proposed for single-seat districts.

Here are the CD maps for two sample states using this scheme:

Louisiana (6 seats, hence 2 CDs of 3 seats each)

---

[17] Curiel, J. and T. Steelman, "How to measure the impact of partisan gerrymandering", *op. cit.*

Minnesota (8 seats, hence 2 CDs of 3 seats each plus one CD with 2 seats)

Multi-seat CDs enhance democracy only when combined with open primaries and a proportional voting scheme, in which the majority opinion wins the majority of seats but not all seats, and opinions held by a significant minority also win some seats.

This is the RCV procedure I suggest for use in multi-seat elections: Voters select a 1st, 2nd, and 3rd choice, as in all RCV elections. To count votes, a weighted vote-counting scheme is followed. Each candidate's total weighted vote = 3 X that candidate's 1st choice votes + 2 X the 2nd choice votes + the 3rd choice votes. In the primary, the number of successful candidates = the number of seats being contested + 2, while in the general election the number of winners = the number of seats being elected.

Pros: If Party A gains 51% of the votes in each of three adjoining single-seat districts, Party A's candidates will win all three, and Party B is shut out – hardly a fair result for a party that wins nearly half the votes. But if we use RCV procedures in a three-seat district instead, Party A will win two seats and Party B will win one, a much more democratic result and much more in alignment with the views of the voters.

Cons: Many's the slip twixt spoon and mouth. We have not used multi-seat districts in this country for many years, and when we did, its intent was to inhibit democracy rather than expand it. Further, we have never used a Ranked Choice Voting procedure for multi-seat districts in federal elections. So the legitimate fear is that anti-democratic forces will find a way to bastardize the process regardless of reformers' intent.

General Response to Alternative Solutions

In designing reforms to our political system, I have endeavored to respect existing practices where these do not materially conflict with the expansion of democracy. Further, I am a bit chary of experimental solutions unless the anticipated benefits clearly outweigh the risks. Though both of these alternatives have merit, I finally reject the first because of respect for the widespread practice of using existing county borders when drawing CDs, and I reject the second because the risk of unanticipated consequences outweighs the anticipated benefit.

Conclusion *and next steps*

When it comes to re-drawing legislative boundaries, gerrymandering is a significant impediment to our "Forming a More Perfect Union". Until now, the technical challenge is that the process itself has been tedious and complicated. The political challenge is that those who stand to benefit from the results of the process have overseen the process.

Gerrymandering can be solved if we simply decide to do it, and it's not all that hard to accomplish. It only becomes hard when we take into consideration factors other than population and geographic proximity. If we implement redistricting based solely on these two factors, we can pretty well lick the gerrymandering problem in one reapportionment cycle. Furthermore, if we adopt the rule-based solution proposed herein, we can automate it.

Finally, let me again stipulate that this solution is less than perfect. But it's much better than the disparate and woefully undemocratic systems now in place, better than systems that use citizen commissions who then become targets for manipulation, and easier to implement nationally than the other solutions currently on the table.

Challenge 4. Other Election System Fixes

Fixes Previously Addressed

Several of the challenges and fixes in this volume overlap, and several fixes have already been discussed, so we will not belabor those details again. These include

- Manner of choosing the President,
- Compressed election schedule,
- Ranked Choice Voting (RCV),
- Open primaries for all federal elected offices,
- Amending the Constitution,
- Replacing the Vice President with a Chancellor of the Senate,
- Reconstitution of the US Senate as a representative body, and
- Redistricting for the House of Representatives through a rule-based process with no human decision-making.

Some items remain to be discussed in this chapter, including

- Voting rights, voting registration, and election procedures;
- Campaign finance reform; and
- Candidates and elected officials: Financial disclosures, transparency, and nepotism.

Voting Rights

Let Everyone Vote!

From South Africa to Nigeria to Egypt, universal suffrage swept across the African continent in the latter half of the 20th century and became a hallmark of the post-Colonial landscape. Americans watched their televisions with fascination as urbanites and villagers alike waited in long lines to be able to vote for the first time.

Yet in our own country, many citizens still struggle to secure their right to vote. Many citizens, discouraged at their perceived lack of political power, fail to try to vote at all.

The preface to this work laid out what needs to be our underlying principle: Democracy works best if all participate. If we wish to build and maintain a vibrant democracy, we must work diligently to make universal suffrage in America a reality rather than merely an idealistic but unachievable dream, or, what's worse, a principle to which we give lip service but do not really wish to achieve.

Some of the improvements that voting rights proponents need to champion include:

- The Constitution should guarantee that all citizens have the right to vote as soon as they reach their 18th birthday. This is a fundamental right that should not be left to the discretion of each state.
- Everyone should vote. No government should have the right to take away any citizen's voting rights for any reason.
- We should consider the notion of compulsory voting. After all, this is the practice in Australia, a country known for its uncompromising protection of individual rights.
- Automatic registration of all citizens upon their 18th birthday should become our normal practice. What plausible argument can be offered in opposition to this idea? Potential voter fraud is not credible: few 18-year-olds are credible fraudsters.
- Automatic voter registration when a citizen interacts with government for any reason should also become normal practice: filing taxes, filing for Medicaid or welfare, recording a real estate transaction, enrolling at a public school or college, as well as showing up to vote. Again, why not?
- Voting authorities must mail paper ballots to all registered voters automatically.
- Mail-in ballots and a two-week voting window must become the universal norm. The argument for voting only on the first Tuesday in November was based on an agricultural society, which no longer obtains.

Various organizations are involved in efforts to bring about voting reforms, including the League of Women Voters (http://lwv.org/issues/protecting-voters), Common Cause (http://www.commoncause.org/issues/voting-and-elections/), and Fair Vote (http://www.fairvote.org/).

One recommendation deserves special consideration, namely, universal automatic voter registration along with a national, permanent Voter-ID, issued through a National Voter Registration Authority. Americans have long resisted any form of national identification card, and this idea smacks of a national ID card. You might recall the vigorous debate concerning the growing use of the Social Security Number as an ID number by various entities, both public and private. That debate ended with federal legislation forbidding the use of SSNs for anything other than paying taxes and tax-related transactions. States, for example, could no longer use the SSN on drivers licenses, and the Feds quit using the SSN as a Medicare ID. Congress was responding to the public's perception that the ever-expanding use of a person's SSN reflected Big Government intruding on our personal privacy.

Fast forward 20 years, and the problem today is that the public does not yet recognize that personal privacy in any sphere is largely a thing of the past. When a terrorist bomb explodes in an urban area, police have video surveillance of nearly every person and nearly every square foot of the impacted area for the hours before the attack, and law enforcement has this information very quickly after the attack occurs. When you pass through a toll booth on the highway, a camera captures your license plate and a snapshot of the driver. Google knows of your travels through the GPS in your vehicle, Apple knows where you've been and who you've been talking to through your use of your iPhone, Bank of America knows your every use of an ATM, Amazon knows what you like to buy and when and to whom you ship it, and every retailer who accepts a credit/debit card knows what you purchased and when you were in the store, Websites track your visits, and your Internet Service Provider knows all the places you go on the Web. This is only the beginning of the list of large data collection agents who have built and continue to amass an amazingly extensive record of your life. Furthermore, these data can be subpoenaed by a court, and the private entities who have collected the data can be required to reveal it. All this is occurring even before we consider what the federal government is collecting directly or inadvertently, from NSA or FBI captures of telephone or Internet traffic to background checks for getting a government job or obtaining a security clearance or qualifying for a government-insured loan. It really is high time that the public realize that having a national Voter ID does not compromise your privacy – you've lost that a long time ago through disparate aspects of modern life. Please believe me about this – I have been involved in the cybersecurity world for many years, and I can testify that this list is only the beginning of the information about you that is readily available to the government in cyberspace. The very last thing you need to worry about with respect to your privacy is the potential loss of that privacy through a national voter database.

So what are the Pros and Cons of having a national Voter-ID? First, we should mention that Congress could and should restrict its use only for voting. Just like the SSN, we should not start using your Voter ID as your universal identification every time you want to borrow a book from the library. So, the Pros are as follows:1) we can expand the voter rolls to include every single American citizen upon reaching age 18 or upon interacting with government at any level at any time or when proactively registering to vote; 2) we can eliminate duplicate registrations for the same person in multiple jurisdictions, because as soon as your eligibility in a new location is recorded, your eligibility in the former location will be automatically canceled; 3) the same system which automatically registers new voters will also purge voters who have died; 4) as a result, voter fraud, already a minuscule problem as every serious study of this subject has demonstrated, will practically cease to exist; and 5) states can save all the money currently spent on voter fraud investigations and on maintaining and purging voter rolls. The Cons of the national voter database are that, like any database, it could be hacked and/or abused. In the grand scheme of things, this risk is minimal. The Pros vastly outweigh the Cons.

Campaign Finance Reform

Congress outlawed campaign contributions from corporations and passed restrictions on unlimited contributions to political parties, political campaigns, and individual candidates, as well as rules requiring public disclosure of people and organizations making such contributions. The core legislation is called the McCain-Feingold law, after its principal sponsors, Senators Russ Feingold (D-Wisconsin) and John McCain (R-Arizona). In the *Citizens United v. Federal Elections Commission* case, the Supreme Court threw out many of the significant provisions of the McCain-Feingold law, especially the provisions dealing with corporate contributions and with disclosure.

While Americans hold their First Amendment rights very dear, we need also to protect our democracy from domination by Big Money. For this reason, we must overturn *Citizens United* -- either by legislation that passes constitutional muster or by new justices on the Supreme Court or by a constitutional amendment. Public financing of all federal election campaigns could also do the trick and, whatever the cost, would be a small price to pay for a Congress that could not be bought and sold.

So, in sum, campaign finance reform has these components:

- Limits on who can contribute to political campaigns,
- Limits on when campaign contributions can be made,
- Limits on the amounts that can be contributed to one campaign, to one party, or in one election cycle,
- Limits on candidates soliciting campaign contributions,
- Disclosure of all campaign contributions, and
- Public financing of political campaigns.

Several grassroots organizations are working on this problem, including Wolf-PAC (http://www.wolf-pac.com/), EveryVoice.org (http://everyvoice.org/), End Citizens United (http://endcitizensunited.org/), Common Cause (http://www.commoncause.org/issues/money-in-politics/), League of Women Voters (https://www.lwv.org/voting-rights/money-politics), MoveToAmend.org (https://movetoamend.org/), and MAYDAY.US (https://mayday.us/). Follow the links to these organizations and their campaigns to find out more, join, volunteer, and contribute.

Advocates for campaign finance reform have already written a ton about the need to reduce the influence of money on politics and on political campaigns, and I have nothing new to contribute to this debate. I'll only say that I believe strongly in this cause, and I have contributed to each of these grassroots organizations.

Candidates and Elected Officials: Financial Disclosures, Transparency, and Nepotism

We must demand that all candidates for federal office from President on down, as a condition for appearing on a general election ballot, release their own and their spouse's personal tax returns and disclose their personal finances, including assets, income, transactions, and liabilities as well as details concerning creditors, investors, and customers. We must require all federal elected officials to continue to do this annually. We must also forbid elected officials from nominating or appointing members of their immediate family to any post in the Government.

Summary of Electoral Fixes by Method of Realization

This paper has presented quite a few fixes to the way we choose our federal office-holders. We can achieve some of these fixes through new or amended state or federal statutes, while others require a constitutional amendment. For many of these fixes to really take hold, we need a cultural shift. Here is a summary of the suggested improvements broken down into these four categories: state law, federal law, constitutional amendment, and cultural change. This discussion does not repeat the thrust of the arguments in favor of each reform but rather presents the possibility of achieving the reform through each method of realization.

Fixes Through State Laws

We can implement some fixes through state laws, but such laws would be effective only if all or most of the states passed those laws. Gerrymandering is a good example. In some states a grassroots citizens' movement has fought to remove politics from Congressional redistricting. But the politicians in each state's majority party ask,

> Why should we unilaterally disarm? If we get rid of gerrymandering
> in our state, the minority party in our state will gain more members
> in Congress. But I do not see their party getting rid of
> gerrymandering in the states their party controls – so the result
> would be that our party loses. Sure, we favor reforming the system
> but only if everyone does it together.

This then becomes an argument for the status quo.

One solution to this conundrum could be a compact among states, all agreeing to adopt the same reform when other states agree to do likewise. Of course, this type of solution only works if the argument about "unilateral disarmament" is the real objection to reform and not just an obstructionist tactic. To improve its chances of success, groups of states could adopt it. For example, Rep. Jamie Raskin (D-MD), when he was still a Maryland State Senator, introduced legislation to eliminate gerrymandering simultaneously in Maryland and Virginia.[18] The two states are good candidates for this type of deal because they are mirror images of each other politically. Maryland, with a Republican governor but Democratic legislature, is heavily gerrymandered to favor Democrats, resulting in 7 Democrats and only 1 Republican in Congress. Virginia is the opposite: With a Democratic governor but Republican state legislature, the state is heavily gerrymandered to favor Republicans, who hold an 8-3 majority in Congress. If both states drew district boundaries without partisan considerations, the expected results in each state would more fairly represent their electorates, but the total number of Congresspersons from each party would probably remain about the same. Repubs might pick up 1 or 2 seats in Maryland; Dems would do likewise in Virginia.

Reformers might be able to identify similar groupings of states all across the country.

Like all solutions implemented by state statute, what lawmakers enact today they can repeal tomorrow. So one approach, that of amending state constitutions, is a considerable improvement over a simple state statute.

Manner of choosing the President

Local-State-National Interstate Compact (LSNIC): States could pass laws binding themselves to cast all their electoral votes for the winner of the election according

---

[18]   http://www.baltimoresun.com/news/maryland/politics/blog/bal-senator-proposes-twostate-solution-on-redistricting-reform-20160209-story.html. [Accessed July 25, 2017.]

to the LSN vote counting scheme. These state laws would become effective as soon as enough states pass it so as to constitute a majority of all electoral votes.

Ranked Choice Voting:

In the 2016 election, Maine became the first state to adopt Ranked Choice Voting for most of its elections. The good folks at FairVote.org believe that this Maine victory may be a harbinger of the future and that more states and other jurisdictions around the country will also begin to adopt RCV.

Although Congress can and should mandate RCV for elections to federal offices, states are responsible for elections for their own Governors, other state-wide offices, and state legislatures. Therefore, every state should adopt Ranked Choice Voting for all the elections it controls. This should include the state's elections for federal offices if Congress fails to act.

Solutions to gerrymandering for state legislatures as well as Congress

While the best solution to the gerrymander challenge is a Federal law mandating a uniform rule-based process without human decision making for all states, individual states can adopt that same process until Congress acts.

A similar redistricting plan as that proposed for Congress might offer the best option for solving the gerrymandering challenge for state legislatures. Specifically, we can select a Starting Point for each district as previously described, and then we can add whole ZCTAs (rather than whole counties) to build each legislative district. In some states, certain ZCTAs might be home to too many people for state legislative districts, representing much smaller populations than Congressional Districts. In such cases, we can partition LAST ZCTA into the Census Bureau's census tracts, which contain ~4000 people each.

If a state finds the fully mechanical solution infeasible for some reason, it could still adopt a non-partisan redistricting commission, assisted by appropriate technology, and charged only with drawing election districts based on geographic proximity, roughly equal populations, and no other considerations.

Automatic voter registration

While the best solution in this matter might be a federal statute or constitutional amendment, individual states can achieve this for their own citizens. States could automatically register voters when they reach their 18th birthday (most of them are in school and therefore a captive audience, making this easy enough to implement). States can also verify a citizen's voter registration status and then automatically register them if necessary whenever the citizen interacts with state or local government in any way – getting a driver's license, purchasing and registering a vehicle or a boat, engaging in any real estate transaction, paying taxes, registering for a public college, applying for welfare or unemployment compensation or Medicaid, perhaps even paying for a parking ticket.

Just as an aside, high schools should require every high school student to "vote" in a mock election, using the same ballot that their parents are using in the real election and at the same time. This will help our young people get into the habit of voting.

Convenient voting procedures

Every state can adopt welcoming rather than restrictive voting rules: mail paper ballots to all registered voters two weeks before the voting window begins; provide a two-week voting window; receive all ballots by mail and drop-off boxes.

Fixes Through Federal Laws

For our national fixes to be most effective, we must adopt them nationally – which means either a federal statute or an amendment to the US Constitution. However, federal statutes sometimes run afoul of the Constitution itself. The Constitution contains two provisions which often appear in conflict with each other:

- Article I Section 8 lists the powers of Congress, and then contains this final power: "To make all Laws which shall be necessary and proper for carrying into Execution the foregoing Powers, and all other Powers vested by this Constitution in the Government of the United States, or in any Department or Officer thereof."

- Amendment 10 states, "The powers not delegated to the United States by the Constitution, nor prohibited by it to the states, are reserved to the states respectively, or to the people."

In practice, when Congress proposes a law concerning an issue not expressly within Congress's authority, proponents argue that Congress's power to act on this issue is implied by its express powers. Those who oppose the law disagree, contending that the 10th Amendment supersedes, so the issue must be left to the states or the people. In some cases Congress goes ahead and passes the proposed law. Then someone files suit against it, claiming that the law violates the 10th Amendment. Sometimes the Supreme Court agrees with the opponents and determines that the law is unconstitutional, while in other instances the Court allows the law to stand.

Thus the question of constitutional limits on Congress's power is clearly an issue concerning many of the fixes suggested in this volume. For example, concerning the time when elections take place, Article I Section 4 states, "The Times, Places and Manner of holding Elections for Senators and Representatives, shall be prescribed in each state by the Legislature thereof; but the Congress may at any time by Law make or alter such Regulations". Originally, every state selected the date of the general election as it saw fit, but in 1845 a federal statute fixed the date of the general election as the first Tuesday after the first Monday in November. So Congress clearly has the authority to fix the date of the general election for Congress. But what about the general election for the electoral college? And what about primaries? When the Constitution was written, primary elections did not exist. Some might argue that Congress's authority to set the date of the general election for Congress implies that it has the authority to also set the dates of primaries. Actually, the Constitution does not distinguish between primary and general elections – it just refers to "elections".

One solution to the question of federal versus state authority has had some success over the years and could be used as a model for wider application. This solution is the use of block grants in which Congress allocates sums of money to individual states, based on the varying needs of each state. Each state then has the authority to spend the block grant funds as it sees fit within the broad parameters of the purposes of the block grant. Congress has used block grants for education assistance programs (clearly a state matter), healthcare (Medicaid, administered by the states), emergency relief from natural disasters, and infrastructure projects. The federal government can sometimes smooth out differences between the states based on the relative wealth of each state, while in other cases state needs differ widely. Landlocked states do not need money for ports, for example, while other states never suffer earthquakes. In all these cases, governmental assistance may be necessary to give each citizen the right to "life, liberty, and the pursuit of happiness", but the Feds are not always the best source for that assistance.

Ranked Choice Voting

The Constitution explicitly gives Congress the power to fix the "manner of elections" for Senators and Representatives; and implicitly, Congress probably also has the power to fix the "manner of elections" for President and Vice President. While state laws can implement RCV on a state-by-state basis, it would be far preferable, quicker, and more effective for Congress to mandate RCV in all federal elections.

National Presidential Primary

Because Congress can fix the "manner of elections" for Senators and Representatives, Congress can certainly fix both primary and general election dates for members of Congress. We can debate whether or not Congress has the constitutional authority to mandate a National Presidential Primary. If Congress same, the Supreme Court might rule it unconstitutional. Were that to happen, then we would need a constitutional amendment to. But we're not at that point yet, so a federal law instituting a National Presidential Primary is certainly worth a try.

Congressional Redistricting Solution

Congress can mandate this; a constitutional amendment can solve it more permanently; but if the fix does not work well or leads to other challenges, a federal statute is easier to replace than a constitutional amendment. Perhaps the best approach would be to adopt a federal statute first, try it out for a few election cycles, and then initiate a constitutional amendment when we have determined that this is a good permanent solution.

A compressed election season schedule

Congress can fix the dates of primary and general elections for members of Congress, and probably also for President and Vice President – after all, in 1845 Congress mandated the date of the general election for all federal offices as the first Tuesday after the first Monday in November. Congress can choose to adjourn whenever it pleases. Hence, Congress could eliminate the lame duck session of Congress and greatly shorten the transition period for the office of President.

Convenient voting procedures

The argument that Congress has the power to effectuate these reforms is based on the same constitutional provision as other congressional election reforms, namely, the first clause of Article I Section 4, giving Congress the power to determine the manner of holding elections for the Congress. If a federal law in this area is determined not to be constitutional, then a constitutional amendment giving Congress the power to establish such regulations might be in order.

Automatic, universal voter registration

Congress already has the authority to implement laws ensuring the voting rights of all citizens (Amendment 14), regardless of race (Amendment 15), religion

(Amendment 1), sex (Amendment 19), or age (for anyone at least 18 years old) (Amendment 26). A federal law providing universal, automatic voter registration for all adult citizens would be a fine way to exercise that authority and would likely pass constitutional muster. Again, if not, then a constitutional amendment is the alternative.

Campaign finance reform

There are several parts to campaign finance reform, each amenable to different solutions:

- Concerning campaign contributions, Congress could try to pass new campaign finance reform laws, avoiding the elements that the Supreme Court found unconstitutional in the *Citizens United* case.
- The President, with the advice and consent of the Senate, could appoint new Supreme Court justices, who could overturn the *Citizens United* decision.
- Congress could legislate public financing of all federal political campaigns.

Candidates and elected officials: Financial disclosures, transparency, and nepotism

Congress could pass federal laws that require candidates and elected officials to disclose their tax returns and their assets and other financial interests. We already have laws preventing nepotism, but the President is exempt from that law; we should fix that; the President and Vice President should be subject to the same law as our legislators. However, it's unclear whether courts would consider such laws constitutional.

Fixes Through Constitutional Amendments

Some fixes require a constitutional amendment, an exceedingly high bar to pass.

Article V of the Constitution provides two methods for proposing amendments to the Constitution:

- Congress, by a two-thirds vote in both chambers, can propose an amendment. This is the only method that has been used so far.

- Two-thirds of the state legislatures can also request Congress to call for a constitutional convention for the purpose of proposing constitutional amendments. This method has not yet been used.

To become part of the Constitution, a proposed amendment must be ratified by three-fourths of the state legislatures or three-fourths of state conventions, whichever mode of ratification is specified by Congress.

Amending the Constitution is difficult. In the 233 years since the Constitutional Convention of 1787, we have only managed to adopt 27 amendments.

A constitutional amendment is a most desirable fix, precisely because it is so difficult to undo; but for exactly the same reason, it is also the most difficult to achieve.

Amending the Constitution

We need to replace the amendment process itself. Though this is not an election system fix *per se*, its adoption will greatly facilitate the other proposed constitutional changes, including an entirely rewritten constitution.

Manner of choosing the President

A constitutional amendment to adopt the direct election of the President is much better than the Local-State-National Interstate Compact for two reasons: 1) A significant majority of Americans favor direct election of the President. Simply put, Americans believe that the candidate receiving the most votes should win. 2) Most importantly, a constitutional amendment is preferred precisely because no state can undo it

New Senate to replace the Original Senate

Even one or more constitutional amendments may not bring about this fix, but clearly the constitutional amendment route or a brand new Constitution are the only fixes available.

Replace the Vice President with the Chancellor of the Senate

The only way to effect this change is through a constitutional amendment. This change could be combined with an amendment to reconstitute the Senate.

Apportion House seats based on voting rather than population

In counting the population of each state in order to apportion seats in the House of Representatives, Article I Section 2 of the 1787 Constitution counted 3/5 of all slaves and did not count Indians at all. The 1787 Constitution also specified the number of seats apportioned to each of the thirteen original states. A law passed in 1913 (when the US population stood at 92 million) set the total number of seats at the current 435. With a population of 330 million today, it might be advisable to revisit the total number of seats. The new number proposed herein is 501 seats in the House. Obviously, we should remove the enumeration of particular states from the Constitution.

We should also provide for representation in Congress for American citizens who do not reside in any state. These citizens should vote for all federal offices in a new Non-State Election District. (This would follow the French model.)

Following each decennial census, we should apportion House seats among the several states based on the average number of votes cast in each state in the two most recent Presidential elections (rather than the population of each state, as at present). However, for drawing the boundaries between election districts within a state, we must still use population figures.

The idea of basing reapportionment, not on population, but rather on the number of people who voted, serves several purposes: 1) this provision encourages citizens to vote, because more voters means more Representatives in the House; 2) similarly, this provision encourages states to design election procedures that will maximize voter turnout, rather than intentionally discouraging certain kinds of voters from exercising their franchise; and 3) the numbers cannot be easily fudged, since the number of votes cast in every election are publicly announced and readily available. Also, the notion that the number of qualified voters (called "electors" in the 1787 Constitution) is a relevant factor in composing the House is adapted from the 1787 Constitution, Article I, Section 2, which states: "The House of Representatives shall be composed of Members chosen every second Year by the people of the several states, and the Electors in each state shall have the Qualifications requisite for Electors of the most numerous Branch of the state Legislature."

Candidates and elected officials: Financial disclosures, transparency, and nepotism

This amendment would require full financial disclosure by all federal general election nominees and all federal elected officials It would also prohibit nepotism by any elected official. Because of Supreme Court decisions that have expanded Presidential powers and have restricted the ability of Congress to rein in those expanded powers, it could be that a constitutional amendment is the only way to effect this reform

Comprehensive constitutional amendment on electoral reform

For all the electoral reforms proposed in Part II, a single constitutional amendment might be best. The proposed amendment would cover both the principles and the procedures of all federal elections. For safety's sake, it should also give Congress the power to modify procedures that turned out not to work as intended.

Chances for adoption of this single constitutional amendment concerning elections will be greatly enhanced if we are able to first adopt the Amendment on Amendments.

The single amendment on elections (The Amendment on Elections below) will
- change the basis for reapportioning seats in the House;
- reconstitute the Senate as a representative body;
- replace the position of Vice President with the new position of Chancellor;
- require Ranked Choice Voting;
- institute a uniform and rule-based process for drawing election district boundaries in every state based only on population and geographic proximity;
- establish the election schedule for all federal primary and general elections, including a National Primary for all federal elected positions;
- require open primaries, with all candidates for a given office competing against each other in a single primary, without regard to political party;
- establish paper, mail-in ballots for all elections, and a uniform fifteen day voting window;

- provide for direct election of the President and the Chancellor, eliminating the electoral college;
- establish a National Voter Registration Authority to provide universal, automatic voter registration, a permanent Voter Identifier for every eligible citizen, and a national database of registered voters;
- remove political parties from all election laws and regulations;
- allow Congress to modify any election procedure which turns out to have been ill-advised.

Fixes Through Cultural Change

Many of the fixes proposed in this paper will only become useful improvements to our democracy when people believe in them and act accordingly. That will require a cultural change. Let me recite a few examples:

- Ranked Choice Voting only really works if voters mark their ballots with more than one choice for each office. Even if RCV is the legal voting procedure, if few voters vote for more than their 1st choice, then the candidate with a plurality after round 1 will always end up the winner as other candidates are progressively eliminated. So we will need a significant public education effort to encourage voters to understand their enhanced voting power. And then we will need the voters to actually use that power.

- We can establish an official season for electioneering that begins on July 4, but because of our First Amendment freedoms, candidates can say anything they want at any time. Therefore the public's recourse is to discourage media outlets from giving free coverage to political campaigning outside the approved season and to punish at the polls those candidates who violate the agreed-upon conventions.

- Many Americans have become apathetic about politics, disengaged from political discourse altogether. Compared to other Western democracies, America's voter participation is abysmal. A significant percentage of our fellow citizens have become completely disenchanted with Congress (which garners an 11% approval rating from the public), and we have turned away from the two major political parties: for twenty years, new voters are opting more and more to register as independents, if they even register to vote at all. The various fixes proposed in this paper could motivate uninvolved citizens to re-engage in the political process. When we empower people more than parties, when independents can participate in primaries, when every vote counts equally, when people see that they can have more opportunities to contribute and more leverage to affect the outcome, then and only then can we entertain the hope that the new cultural norm will favor engagement over apathy.

- To encourage greater voter participation, every student in grades 9 through 12 in the country should vote in every election, using a sample or specimen ballot. The ballot itself can be the actual ballot for the precinct where the school is located. We should give awards to schools with the highest participation rates. In this way, every high school graduate will have participated in one Presidential and one mid-term election while in school.

Portrait of Future Congressional Elections

Putting this all together, here is a snapshot of future Congressional elections if all these proposals are adopted by the year 2021:

- We will have adopted Ranked Choice Voting (RCV) for all federal elections.

- After the 2020 Census is complete, apportionment of House seats will occur, based on the number of ballots cast in the two most recent Presidential elections. Based on the number of House seats in each state, apportionment of seats in the New Senate will be automatic.

- Congressional redistricting will occur according to the rules for redistricting without human intervention described in this document. We will create computer software to automate this process. CD boundaries will remain in effect until the next decennial census.

- Primary Rules:

  o Any citizen can become a candidate for the House or Senate, according to the rules of that state.

  o All candidates will appear on the singular primary ballot. The ballot will indicate the party affiliation of each candidate.

  o All registered voters may vote in the primary.

- o RCV procedures apply to voting (that is, voters will rank order their selected candidates) and to the counting of ballots.

- o The number of successful candidates in the primary is 3.

- General Election Rules:

  - o The general election ballot will contain the names of only those candidates who were successful in the primary.

  - o All registered voters may vote in the general election.

  - o RCV procedures apply to voting (that is, voters will rank order their selected candidate) and to the counting of ballots.

- Election Season Rules:

  - o In even-numbered years, Congress adjourns *sine die* before Independence Day, and campaigning begins.

  - o The National Primary Election window for receiving and counting ballots is from October 1 to October 15.

  - o The General Election window for receiving and counting ballots is from December 1 to December 15

  - o The New Congress convenes in January. (Note: No lame-duck session occurs.)

- Political Parties:

  - o Political parties, like any benevolent association, at their own expense, may hold caucuses, conventions, polls, and elections for party officials. They may endorse candidates, raise funds, articulate positions, advertise, and lobby.

  - o None of these activities have any legal standing or bearing on elections.

Single Constitutional Amendment Concerning Federal Elections

Here is a draft of a single constitutional amendment that addresses all the federal electoral reforms recommended in this volume.

Note that this amendment reconstitutes the U.S. Senate. Therefore we need to replace Article V with the Amendment on Amendments before considering the following Amendment on Elections.

Amendment on Federal Elections

Section 1. Composition of the Legislature.

Article I Sections 1, 2, and 3 are repealed and replaced as specified in 1.1, 1.2, and 1.3 of this section of this amendment.

1.1   The Legislature

All legislative Powers herein granted shall be vested in a Congress of the United States, which shall consist of a lower chamber called the House of Representatives and an upper chamber called the Senate.

1.2   The House of Representatives

The House of Representatives shall be composed of 501 Members chosen every second year. Congress may modify the number of members by law.

500 seats in the House of Representatives shall be apportioned among the states during the first year of each new decade, based on the average number of voters who voted in each state in the two most recent Presidential general elections: but each state shall have at least one Representative, and each Representative shall have one vote.

1 additional seat in the House shall be chosen by American citizens who live outside any of the several states.

When he/she takes office, a Member of the House of Representative must be

- At least 25 years old;
- At least 7 years a citizen of the United States;
- Less than 19 years a Member of the House of Representatives;[19] and
- A resident of the state from which he/she shall have been chosen.

The House of Representatives shall choose their Speaker and other Officers; and shall have the sole Power of Impeachment.

1.3   The Senate

The Senate of the United States shall be composed of Senators from each state, chosen at large by the voters for a six-year term of office; and each Senator shall have one vote. The number of Senators from each state is determined automatically by the number of Representatives apportioned to each state, according to this table:[20]

---

[19] This provision implements term limits for the House. Ten 2-year terms is specified as the maximum amount of time a member may remain in the House.

Representatives	Senators
1 to 5	1
6 to 10	2
11 to 15	3
16 to 20	4
21 to 25	5
26+	6

1 additional seat in the Senate shall be chosen by American citizens who live outside any of the several states.

Seats in the Senate shall be divided as equally as they may be into three classes (Class I, Class II, and Class III). For any state, the number of seats assigned to each Class shall be the same, as nearly as possible. One Class shall be elected every two years. Thus one-third of the total Senate, and one-third of the seats in the Senate from each state, shall be elected every two years. Whenever a state elects more than one Senator in a given election cycle, a separate election shall be held for each Senate seat.

When, due to the decennial Congressional reapportionment, the number of Senators for any state is decreased, the next Senator from that state whose term of office is expiring shall not be replaced after his term expires. When the number of Senators from any state is increased, a new Senator from that state shall be elected

---

[20] That is, a state with 1 to 5 House seats will have one Senator; a state with 6 to 10 House seats will have two Senators; a state with 11 to 15 House seats will have three Senators; and so on. This provision mandates that every state shall have from one to six Senators. This scheme still gives more power to states with small populations than is strictly justified based on population alone, but it is vastly fairer than the current scheme of two Senators per state regardless of population, and it is much easier to implement than a scheme based only on population, which would require election districts that cross state boundaries.

at the next election, and that seat will be assigned to Class 1, 2, or 3, so that, as far as possible, one third of the Senate remains elected every two years, and one third of the Senators from each state remains elected every two years.[21]

Voters will elect senators to Class I Senate seats in 2024 and every 6 years thereafter; to Class II Senate seats in 2026 and every 6 years thereafter; and to Class III Senate seats in 2022 and every 6 years thereafter.[22]

The first election cycle following reapportionment will include separate primary and general elections for all three Senate classes. This will include elections for 6-year terms for all the seats in the class normally scheduled for elections that year, as well as elections for 4-year terms and for 2-year terms for those seats in the other two classes which do not have an incumbent.

When he/she takes office, a Senator must be

- At least 30 years old;
- At least 9 years a citizen of the United States;
- Less than 17 years a Senator;[23] and
- A resident of the state from which he/she shall have been chosen.

1.4 Chancellor of the Senate

In accordance with Section 3 of this amendment, voters shall elect a Chancellor to a four-year term of office in even-numbered years not evenly divisible by four. The Chancellor shall preside over the Senate. The Chancellor shall have no vote unless the Senate be equally divided. The Chancellor shall appoint a Chancellor Pro Tempore, with the concurrence of the Senate. The Chancellor Pro Tempore shall preside over the Senate in the absence of the Chancellor, or when the Chancellor shall exercise the office of President of the United States.

---

[21] This provision could result in the election of a Senator to a newly-created seat for a term of only two years or four years, that is, until such time as that seat's class next comes up for election.

[22] This continues the Senate Class assignments under the 1787 Constitution.

[23] This provision implements term limits for the Senate. Three 6-year terms is specified as the maximum amount of time a member may remain as a Senator.

The Chancellor[24] (but not the Chancellor Pro Tempore) shall have power to nominate and, by and with the advice and consent of the Senate, shall appoint Associate Justices of the Supreme Court and federal judges of inferior courts. The term of office for all federal judges is16 years from the date of appointment.[25] The Chancellor may appoint no more than three Associate Justices in any one year and no more than eight Associate Justices during the Chancellor's four-year term of office.

Any current or former federal judge is eligible to be nominated to serve as an Associate Justice of the Supreme Court. When the position of Chief Justice of the United States becomes vacant, the sitting Associate Justices shall select one of their own number as the next Chief Justice.[26] The newly-selected Chief Justice will then begin a 16-year term of office.

In all cases of Chancellor judicial nominations and Presidential executive branch nominations, if the Senate fails to approve or disapprove a nomination within 60 calendar days after the Chancellor/President has made the nomination, unanimous consent of the Senate shall be recorded.

The Senate shall have the sole power to try all impeachments. When sitting for that purpose, they shall be on oath or affirmation. When the President of the United States or the Chancellor of the Senate[27] is tried, the Chief Justice shall preside: And no person shall be convicted without the concurrence of two-thirds of the members present. Upon conviction, the convicted person shall be immediately removed from office and disqualified to hold and enjoy any office of honor, trust or profit under the United States: but the party convicted shall nevertheless be liable and subject to indictment, trial, judgment, and punishment, according to law.

---

[24] An important change in Constitution II is that the Chancellor, rather than the President, makes all judicial appointments.

[25] The 16-year term of office provides a new check on the unfettered power of federal judges, especially those of the Supreme Court.

[26] The purpose of this provision is to encourage comity among the Justices. They will be more likely to work well together if their leader is chosen by them.

[27] The Chancellor, as the presiding officer of the Senate, were he/she impeached by the House, should not preside over his/her own trial. Therefore, the Chief Justice should carry that responsibility.

Section 2. General Provisions on Federal Elections

2.1 Voter Eligibility

All citizens who have attained the age of 18 are eligible to vote in all federal and state elections and in the state in which they reside. Citizens who reside outside the jurisdiction of any state are eligible to vote in the Non-State Election District.

2.2 Automatic Voter Registration

Congress shall establish a National Voter Registration Authority, which will

- create a national database of registered voters, to be shared with all jurisdictions that conduct elections,
- prevent the national database of registered voters from unauthorized disclosure or access from unauthorized entities,
- ensure that the national database of registered voters is used for no other purpose than voter registration, authentication, and authorization,
- assign to each voter a unique Voter Identifier which remains with that voter for life,
- maintain for each voter both their legal (voting) address and current contact information,
- accept and process voter registration applications from all eligible citizens,
- automatically register each citizen to vote upon their 18th birthday,
- automatically register each citizen to vote, or verify his/her earlier registration, whenever a citizen interacts with a state or federal government entity,
- remove a voter who has deceased, and
- establish appropriate means of voter authentication and authorization to vote.

2.3 Ranked Choice Voting

Ranked Choice Voting (RCV) is mandatory for all federal elections.

VOTING: For primary elections, for each office being contested, voters will be able to rank their choices, selecting a 1st choice, a 2nd choice, and a 3rd choice. For general elections, with only three names on the ballot, voters will be able to select a 1st choice and a 2nd choice.

COUNTING BALLOTS:

- For each primary election, follow this procedure to determine the three primary winners who qualify for the general election.:

  1. Count the 1st choice votes for each candidate, and rank order the results. Repeat steps 2 through 4 until only three candidates remain or until three candidates each exceed 25% of the 1st choice votes.

  2. Eliminate the candidate with the fewest votes.

  3. Reassign each vote for the eliminated candidate to each voter's next highest choice for a candidate not yet eliminated.

  4. If a ballot for the eliminated candidate contains no choice for a candidate not yet eliminated, then that ballot is exhausted and is no longer counted as part of the total vote.

- For a general election, follow this procedure to determine the winner:

  1. Count the 1st choice votes for each candidate, and rank order the results. If the leading candidate has less than a majority, then eliminate the candidate that came in third, and reassign each vote for the eliminated candidate to each voter's 2nd choice

  2. If a ballot for the eliminated candidate contains no 2nd choice, then that ballot is exhausted and is no longer counted as part of the total vote.

Congress shall have the power to refine the above RCV procedures.

2.4 Voting Procedures

All regular elections for federal offices occur in even-numbered years. Primary elections take place in September, and each primary election has three winners. Those three primary winners are the only candidates in the general election, which is held in December. When a vacancy occurs in any state's representation in the Senate or the House, the executive authority of that state shall issue a Writ of Special Election to fill that vacancy.

States conduct all elections[28] but the Secretary of State shall conduct elections in the one Non-State Election District. A secret ballot is guaranteed. Voters record their votes on paper ballots, which states must retain for ten years. Voters submit completed ballots either by mail or by delivering them to ballot collection boxes. By law, Congress may authorize other methods of voting.

The "voting window" – the period when received ballots are processed and counted – lasts for fifteen days in every election. For the National Primary Election, the voting window is from October 1 to 15; for the General Election, the voting window is from December 1 to 15; for Special Elections, the Writ for Special Election shall specify both fifteen day voting windows. Votes must be received by the last day of the voting window.

Election officials shall announce the first-choice results of every election each day during the last five days of the voting window. After the voting window closes, election officials shall apply Ranked Choice Voting procedures to each election and shall then announce and certify election results as soon as they are known.

Open primaries are mandatory for all federal elections (for President, Chancellor, and both chambers of Congress). All registered voters are eligible to vote in every primary and general election within the jurisdiction where they legally reside.

Any eligible candidate may compete in any primary, subject to state rules for qualifying for the ballot. The party affiliation of a candidate, if any, will be indicated on the ballot. Each primary has three winners, and these are the only candidates that appear on the general election ballot. A primary winner may withdraw within one week after being certified to appear on the general election ballot.

No candidate for Federal office may engage in fundraising while Congress is in session.

To appear on a primary ballot, a candidate must authorize the US Treasury to release, two weeks after the primary election, the five most recent tax returns of that candidate and his or her spouse, if that candidate qualifies for the general election, and if that candidate does not withdraw as a candidate before such tax returns are released. Each general election candidate must also release, on the same

---

[28] The current, well-established system gives the responsibility for conducting elections to the states. There is no compelling reason to change this.

schedule, a statement of net worth, showing his/her complete assets and liabilities and those of his/her spouse.[29]

2.5 Consolidated Election Schedule

- In even-numbered years, Congress adjourns *sine die* before July 4.
- September 15: States mail primary ballots to all registered voters.
- October 1 – 15: Voting window for National Primary Election.
- October 22: Each of the three successful presidential candidates must announce his/her vice presidential running mate. [Delete this clause if the position of Chancellor has replaced the Vice President.]
- November 15: States mail general election ballots to all registered voters.
- December 1 – 15: Voting window for National General Election.
- Noon on the 1st Sunday in January: Congress convenes. Inauguration of the newly elected chancellor
- Noon on the 2nd Sunday in January: Inauguration of the newly elected president.

Section 3. Elections for President and for Chancellor

The President and the Chancellor shall be elected directly by the voters. The President shall be elected for a four-year term of office in years evenly divisible by 4. The Chancellor shall be elected for a four-year term of office in even-numbered years not evenly divisible by 4.

Any candidate who withdraws as a Presidential or Chancellor candidate by September 1 may become a candidate for the Senate or for the House in the same election cycle. A person can be a candidate for only one federal office at a time.

Congress shall establish a National Vote Tabulation Authority, whose responsibility is to collect from the states the 1st choice results of the primary and general elections for President and for Chancellor, to apply RCV counting procedures on a nationwide basis and collect updated 1st choice results from the

---

[29] This provision requires all general election candidates to be completely transparent with respect to their personal finances.

states as candidates are eliminated, to tabulate and summarize the results, and to announce the winners.

Section 4. Elections for Members of Congress

4.1 Election Districts

Following apportionment of House seats to each state, each state will be redistricted into the appropriate number of Congressional Districts (CDs). Voters in each CD will elect one Representative.

The objectives in drawing CDs are:

- Equalize populations among CDs within a state,
- Keep neighbors together, and
- Ignore all other considerations

4.2 Redistricting Principles

The redistricting procedure must satisfy these principles:

- Avoid human decisions concerning any particular CD boundary.

- Adopt a completely rule-governed process.

- Follow the same process in every state,

- Make the process transparent to and replicable by anyone so interested.

- Equalize the population of each CD within a state. (Each CD's population must fall within 5% (plus or minus) of the average population per seat in that state.)

- Without violating the 5% rule, assign an entire county to the same CD. When necessary to complete a CD while meeting the population criterion, partition one county into Zip Code Tabulation Areas (ZCTAs).

- A CD should consist of an entirely contiguous landmass. This is a desirable but not mandatory criterion.

- When redistricting for any state is complete, redistricting for that state will not be repeated until the redistricting required following the next decennial census.

4.3 Redistricting Procedure Summary

Repeat the following steps to create each CD within a state:

1. Select the Starting Point for drawing the current CD.

2. Assign to the current CD whole counties closest to the Starting Point.

3. When necessary, partition LAST COUNTY into ZCTAs in order to reach the population target for a CD.

4.4 Redistricting Procedure Details

Congress shall legislate a procedure to implement subsections 4.2 and 4.3 of this Amendment, including special cases and anomalies.[30]

Section 5. Continuance in Office

To continue in office, all federal elected officials, by October 1 of each year, must authorize the US Treasury to release the five most recent tax returns of that official and his or her spouse. Each official must also release, on the same schedule, a statement of net worth, showing his/her complete assets and liabilities and those of his/her spouse.

Every federal elected official is prohibited from hiring, nominating, or appointing any member of his/her immediate family to any position within the federal government.

Section 6. Transition to the Reconstituted Congress

The first Presidential and Congressional elections under this Amendment will take place in the first year evenly divisible by 4 which begins after this Amendment is adopted. The first elections for Chancellor will occur two years later. Beginning in January of the first Presidential election year, the last Vice President under the 1787 Constitution will become the Interim Chancellor and will continue to serve in that capacity until replaced by the first elected Chancellor. The Interim Chancellor will arrange for an orderly transition from the Congress under the 1787 Constitution to the Congress under this Amendment.

---

[30] The proposed detailed procedure appears in Appendix 1.

500 of the 501 seats in the House of Representatives shall be apportioned to the several states based on the average number of votes cast in each state in the two most recent Presidential general elections. One additional House seat is apportioned to the Non-State Election District. After the apportionment of seats in the House, apportionment of seats in the Senate is automatic.

All incumbent Senators will complete their six year terms. Those incumbent Senators' seats which continue to exist in the New Senate retain their current Class assignments The Chancellor will assign each additional seat in the New Senate to Class I, II, or III, in accordance with Section1.3 of this Amendment.

The first elections for the New Senate will follow the rules for elections following reapportionment, in accordance with Section 1.3 of this Amendment.

Upon ratification of this amendment, all incumbent federal judges, including Supreme Court Justices, will begin serving their new16 year terms.

After the completion of two Presidential election cycles under this Amendment, Congress may modify any of the provisions of this Amendment, provided two-thirds of both chambers concur.

Part III. A Revised Constitution

Ship of State II

Introduction to Part III

"It must be considered that there is nothing more difficult to carry out nor more doubtful of success nor more dangerous to handle than to initiate a new order of things; for the reformer has enemies in all those who profit by the old order, and only lukewarm defenders in all those who would profit by the new order; this lukewarmness arising partly from the incredulity of mankind who does not truly believe in anything new until they actually have experience of it."

Nicolo Machiavelli (1469 - 1527)
The Prince

Authority and Necessity

Why Do We Think We Have the Authority to Do This?

So you are telling me that we should keep a system that gives each voter in Wyoming 66 times more electoral power in the Senate than each voter in California? and the reason we should keep this system is because some Virginia plantation owners in 1787 wanted to ensure that their stranglehold on political power would not be diluted by the radicals in Massachusetts and New York who allowed nearly everybody to vote? Really? and this despite the fact that neither

Wyoming nor California was party to this "deal"? and you still want to call this a democracy?

Please.

Let me review the considered opinion of the "Father of the Constitution"[31]:

If there be a principle that ought not to be questioned within the United States, it is that every man has a right to abolish an old government and establish a new one. This principle is not only recorded in every public archive, written in every American heart, and sealed with the blood of American martyrs, but is the only lawful tenure by which the United States hold their existence as a nation.

> *James Madison*

The Articles of Confederation of 1781 permitted amendments to those articles, but only if the amendment was agreed to by Congress and then ratified by the legislatures of all 13 states. There were lots of shortcomings to the Articles of Confederation, not the least of which was this requirement for unanimous agreement by all the state legislatures to any changes.

Therefore, when the Constitutional Convention was held in 1787, the Framers of the Constitution quite simply ignored the method for amending the Articles of Confederation spelled out therein. In fact, if they had followed the Articles of Confederation's rules for making amendments, the whole effort would have been scuttled from the get-go, since the state of Rhode Island declined to even send a delegation. Rather, the Framers created a completely new form of government, and they announced that this new government would come into force in all the states that adopted it, as soon as 9 states had adopted it. (In the long run, all 13 states, even including Rhode Island, did ratify the 1787 Constitution.) Note that 9 is more than two-thirds but less than three-fourths of the 13 states.

---

[31] James Madison, Helvidius No. 3, September 7, 1793.

I feel now like the Framers did in 1787: There is no way that the existing system will be dramatically changed by all those who benefit from it. Therefore, it becomes necessary to go beyond the bounds of the existing constitution and create something very new.

Perhaps the Framers were on to something valuable as a precedent: We may not need to amend the 1787 Constitution by following the rules for amending the Constitution prescribed in Article V thereof. Rather, we can simply create an entirely new Constitution II, an entirely new Government, and adopt it with the consent of the governed. Who gives us the authority to do this? James Madison, of course – the guy who wrote the 1787 Constitution.

Why Do We <u>Need</u> to Do This?

Just look at the process for amending the Constitution, as spelled out in Article V: Congress can propose an amendment by a two-thirds majority in both Houses, or alternatively two-thirds of the state legislatures can call for a convention to propose an amendment; and the proposed amendment becomes part of the Constitution when ratified by three-fourths of the state legislatures. Note, first of all, that the people have no say whatsoever – it is entirely dependent on politicians in the Congress and in state legislatures. Maybe that was okay when the country was just starting out, at a time when even giving power to elected representatives was looked upon as somewhat radical. (In their previous model, the Framers had only England to look at, where power generally derived from the King.) In addition to the amendment process which shuts out the citizenry, look also at the protections built into the 1787 Constitution to ensure that the people would not really be able to affect any outcome: state legislatures chose US Senators; electors in the electoral college, beholden to nobody, selected the President; and even though the voters did elect members of the House, the role of the people was to play second fiddle at best.

Today, our modern American society is far more tolerant of the active participation of all citizens in our politics. Therefore, our new Constitution II should codify the empowerment of the people over the power of politicians.

Since we cannot depend on the existing Powers-That-Be to cede power to the people, it behooves us to assert that power ourselves. The premise of the "Constitution II Convention" – or whatever we choose to call it – is that **WE THE**

PEOPLE have the power to create our own democratic government, and we the people have the power to put a new/revised form of government into practice.

Guidelines for the Contents of Constitution II

The new thing we create must be far more democratic, far more subject to the will of the people. It must empower all Americans to play a role, to have a stake, and to have the ability to affect the outcome.

At the same time, we need not, indeed we should not, start over from scratch. As noted in Part I, what the Founding Fathers created was enormously creative, visionary, brave against all odds, and long-lasting. Most of their work retains these qualities. But many details remain incomplete, some provisions are outdated and no longer work as smoothly as intended, some are intentionally anti-democratic and continue to deny us a real democracy, and quite a few significant issues of our time could not have been foreseen when the Framers created the 1787 Constitution. Therefore, for those of us who would like our Constitution and basic form of government to keep working but also want to reform the parts that are broken and fill in the parts that are missing, we are left with two possible courses of action: 1) We could choose to introduce and fight for dozens of Individual constitutional amendments to fix every broken or missing part, including some which we know from the get-go have just about zero chance of ever gaining acceptance from the current power structure; or 2) we could opt for a substantial rewrite of the whole document.

In fact, that is essentially what Constitution II is all about: Keep the original wherever possible, incorporate all previously ratified Amendments, and also incorporate the fixes contained in Part II of this work. The structural changes in Constitution II include the replacement of the Original Senate by the New Senate as well as the replacement of the Vice President by a new Chancellor of the Senate.

Also consider the rather mundane question of language:

- The original 1787 Constitution contained 4490 words. Since ratification, we have adopted 27 Amendments containing a total of 3300 words, or 73% of the original length. The two dozen or so amendments suggested in Part II of this work would add about 3000 words, making the amendments longer than the original document.
- The previously adopted and newly proposed amendments modify or supersede numerous original provisions of the 1787 Constitution, scattered throughout the document, so that even just reading it

straight through and understanding how it all fits together is something of a challenge.

- The English language has also changed since 1787. Americans ought to be able to read their foundational document and understand what it means. We ought to be able to teach this in middle school, and pupils should be able to internalize its core concepts.

- The Model-T Ford was a fine machine in its day. If you still owned one in 2020 and wanted to modernize it, you could retrofit it to have an automatic transmission, a powerful engine, air conditioning, visible taillights, modern bumpers, and maybe even seatbelts and airbags; the result would be a patchwork quilt of alterations and make-do fixes and hardly recognizable as a derivative of the original. But inevitably there comes a point at which it's time for a new car, incorporating all the wonderful Model-T features that were novel at the time but also all the advances that have been invented since. That's where we are with our Constitution.

On the basis of language alone, it's time to replace the 1787 Constitution as written and amended with a new version, incorporating all the existing amendments into the body of the basic document and also incorporating our new provisions.

Therefore, Constitution II updates the document's English language usage, punctuation, and spelling. By incorporating all previous amendments into the constitution itself, the whole document becomes much more readable and understandable.

Additional Challenges and Fixes Addressed in Constitution II

The challenges and fixes discussed in Parts I and II of this discourse relate specifically to elections, representation, and voting. If we are going to replace the 1787 Constitution with Constitution II, then we probably ought to fix a number of other challenges which bear fixing at the same time. This section addresses challenges and fixes in two categories: those dealing with Congressional rules and those dealing with the Bill of rights.

Congressional Rules Challenge and Fixes

Arcane rules in both the Senate and the House combine with partisan intransigence to make our Congress woefully ineffective. (See Dems-Repubs, Yin-Yang[32])

Our Government was purposely designed to provide for competing interests, checks and balances, and representation of minority views. At its most basic level, this includes the federal system itself, in which governmental powers are divided between states and the federal government. Within the federal government, powers are divided among three co-equal branches – legislative, executive, and judicial, and each of these branches has a distinct role to play with respect to federal laws. The sole responsibility for making law is vested in a bicameral legislature, both chambers of which need to agree on a proposed law. The President also has a legislative role, in that he can either sign or veto a bill passed by both houses of Congress; but if he vetoes a law passed by Congress, the Congress can override that veto by a 2/3 vote in both chambers. Finally, the Supreme Court is the final review authority, as the Court can reject a law that it deems in violation of the Constitution.

---

[32] https://all-free-download.com/free-vector/yin-yang.html (adapted from original)

Given the many intentional, constitutional obstacles to passing a law, our Congress has nevertheless opted to adopt several additional obstacles, which are unnecessary from a constitutional standpoint and which serve to only further slowdown or block Congressional action. Inadvertently, these rules have also contributed significantly to the rise of the "imperial presidency". Proponents argue that these extra limits are necessary to protect minority rights (in the case of the Senate's filibuster and other procedural roadblocks) or a minority of the majority party (in the case of certain House rules). However, the simple fact is that our Congress has become muscle-bound and incapable of acting on even the most basic functions of governance.

When we hear that Americans are fed up with Congress, one of the principal complaints is that Congress cannot act, cannot actually do anything. Congress seems to spend all its time in endless arguing while legislating little of substance.

At the same time, often because Congress is unable or unwilling to act, Presidents of both parties have issued Executive Orders to accomplish things that Congress won't. Presidents will always claim that they are either acting within their constitutional authority or they are merely providing the necessary administrative details to implement laws that Congress has already passed. Be that as it may, we have witnessed the gradual accumulation of Presidential power and authority at the expense of Congress, with loud complaints by whichever political party does not currently hold the White House.

So the challenge for us is twofold: 1) change the rules of the House and Senate to force Congress to function or at least to reduce their many excuses for failing to function; and 2) restore some balance in the power of the President and that of Congress.

Even though Americans are disgusted by the performance of our Congress, we seem to have little stomach for doing anything about it. Many seem to think that Congress will ultimately work it out for themselves, or they seem to think that we the people are powerless.

We are misguided if we think that we can leave it to Congress to figure it out and fix it. Legislatures sometimes die of self-inflicted wounds. A most famous example occurred in the Sejm (Parliament) of Poland in the 17th and 18th centuries. The Sejm at that time had a rule called the *liberum veto* which allowed any single senator to veto and thus kill all the legislation passed by the Sejm in its current session, thereby causing its dissolution. Poland's kings needed to raise armies to fight invaders, but a single senator, sometimes bribed by foreign officials, nullified every Sejm session that attempted to pass the needed laws. As a result, Poland had no army to defend itself, the country was invaded and partitioned by its neighbors (Russia, Austria, and Prussia), and Poland ceased to exist as a separate nation from 1795 until the end of World War I. Throughout Europe, the term *Polish parliament* came to be a synonym for inept government. With no major legislation and very little legislation of any kind, our last Congress was about as inept as that 18th-century Polish parliament; and like the Sejm of that time, Congress better get its act together soon, before it just withers away into total irrelevance.

It's time that Americans demand that the Congress find the means to break through its own gridlock before we become an American version of the Polish Sejm, that is, before we too have a legislature known only for its inability to act. Find some *cajones*, you guys, and ACT to save your own institution before it crumbles into carping, name-calling, gotcha-moments, political theatre, and total incompetence. You have the power to fix this. Here are several specific proposals to accomplish just that.

Eliminate the Filibuster

Senate rules permit any senator to talk forever on any legislation under consideration. These rules also allow the senator who is speaking to pass the baton to any other senator, who can continue speaking without interruption until again passing the baton to someone else. In this way, a small group of senators can prevent any legislation from coming to a vote – they just keep speaking until the Senate leaders agree to withdraw the bill the minority doesn't like. It does not matter how important that legislation is – defending our country, paying our bills, whatever.

During the nineteenth century, Senate minorities perfected the rarely-used practice of talking a bill to death, which came to be known as filibustering. Unlimited debate continued in the Senate until 1917, when the Senate adopted a rule that permitted a two-thirds majority of senators present and voting to end debate on a bill, thus allowing the bill to come to the floor for an up-or-down vote. This device is called "invoking cloture" – that is, choking off further debate. With 100 senators, this meant that 67 votes were needed to invoke cloture. In 1975, the number of votes needed to invoke cloture was reduced to three-fifths, or 60 senators. So at present, 41 senators can kill any bill, even if 59 senators want to vote on it. In the filibuster's current form, it's not even necessary to mount the filibuster – just threatening to filibuster is enough to kill the proposed law: Senators do not need to actually filibuster; they can just declare their intention to do so, and the 60-vote majority is in effect.

Many Americans might be surprised to learn that the Constitution does not prescribe rules of debate for the Senate. The filibuster rules are only traditional practices adopted as Senate Rules of Order, which the Senate adopts anew as its first order of business whenever a new Congress convenes. The Senate has the authority to amend those rules by a two-thirds vote whenever it so chooses or by a simple majority vote at the beginning of a new Congress. Without any question, we should demand that the Senate change these rules. (You might be interested to learn that the original House of Representatives also had unlimited debate, but the increasing number of House members made the practice unwieldy, and so the House changed its rules – just like the Senate should do now.)

The Original Senate could eliminate the filibuster today by amending its own rules. Just in case that doesn't happen, Article II Section 5 of Constitution II eliminates the filibuster by mandating that decisions in both chambers will be taken by majority vote, and by providing further that any member may call a bill or nomination to the floor. Article II Section 7 provides further that the effective date of any law is July 1 of the year following the next general election, giving a new Congress the opportunity to change or repeal it. (The same section allows an earlier effective date of legislation, provided 3/5 of both chambers agree.)

Blocking Presidential Appointments

At present a single senator is often able to block a Presidential executive or judicial appointment indefinitely. Recent modifications to Senate rules have curtailed this practice to some extent, but the practice or tradition of blocking appointments through the actions of a single senator should be abandoned altogether. The new provision in Article II Section 5 of Constitution II allowing any Senator to call a nomination to the floor eliminates the ability of any one Senator to block a nomination permanently.

The President should also have the power to make executive department appointments when the Senate fails to act on a nomination. Article III Section 2 of Constitution II contains new wording concerning Presidential appointments, which provides for automatic, unanimous Senate confirmation for any nomination if the Senate fails to act on that nomination within 60 days. The same Senate confirmation procedure applies to judicial appointments made by the Chancellor of the Senate.

Rules for Bringing Legislation to the Floor of the House of Representatives

Both major political parties, at various times, have used their majority status in the House to prevent House consideration of legislation which might pass the whole

House with bipartisan support but which does not have enough support to pass the whole House within the majority party itself. From 2010 to 2018 this problem manifested itself as Republican obstructionism, but that is only because the Republicans were the majority party in the House of Representatives. Democrats are equally capable of these shenanigans.

Here is how this works: We have 435 members of the House, so 218 constitute a majority. In the Congress from 2016 to 2018, Republicans had 240 representatives, and 195 representatives were Democrats. Before any legislation came to the floor for a vote, it had to be passed by the House Republican Conference – that is, all the Republican representatives. But if a bill had the support of fewer than 218 Republicans within the Republican Conference, the leadership did not allow the bill to come to the floor of the whole House.

The purpose of this rule or practice was to block any legislation that would need votes from the minority party in order to become law. Thus it prevented the minority party from taking any credit. The real effect of this practice was to give any group of 23+ Republican representatives veto power over all legislation. It ruined the Speakership of Representative John Boehner and damaged that of Paul Ryan. It made governing extremely difficult if not impossible. It brought the US House of Representatives that much closer to becoming the Polish Sejm of the 18th century.

Fixing this could involve the following new House rules:

1. Any bill that has the support of a majority of the majority party in its conference will advance to the floor of the House.
2. Any representative may introduce a motion to bring any matter to the floor, including any pending legislation. If a majority of House members agree, that matter will become the first order of business on the next day that the House is in session.
3. As a most extreme solution, the Speaker of the House could become a non-partisan position, perhaps not even an elected politician or member of the House; or it could become a bipartisan position, in which the Speaker of the House must be approved by a majority of the members of both political parties. In either case, the job of Speaker should be to ensure the smooth functioning of the House and to bring to the floor any measure recommended by the leadership of the majority party or by a majority of all House members.

The same Article II Section 5 provision of Constitution II referenced earlier that allows any Member to call a bill to the floor with the approval of a majority of the House will solve this problem. If Members can cobble together a bipartisan majority of House Members, they can ensure that a bill will be brought to the floor for a vote by the full House.

Executive Orders

Congress should pass a law that requires the President to give Congress a 30-day warning before the effective date of any Executive Order. In addition, during that 30-day waiting period, either chamber by a majority vote can prevent that Executive Order from going into effect. (Of course, in the event of a national emergency, Congress could simply pass a law equal to the Executive Order, allowing it to go into effect immediately.)

The courts may find such a law to be an unconstitutional infringement on the authority of the executive under the 1787 Constitution. To circumvent any such finding, Article III Section 3 of Constitution II contains a new paragraph concerning Executive Orders. This provision gives either chamber of Congress 30 days to block an E.O. that it finds objectionable. Hence, if Congress allows an E.O. to go into effect, it must accept at least partial ownership of the result.

Congress also needs to amend the Emergency Powers Act, under which any President can declare a national emergency for any reason and thereby amass a plethora of additional power. At present, overriding the President's declaration of a national emergency requires a resolution passed by both chambers which the President can veto. A new version should make a Presidential declaration of a national emergency null and void if either chamber objects to it within 30 days – that is, the same Congressional power as we prescribe for an Executive Order.

Judicial Appointments

As explained previously, one of the key constitutional improvements in rebalancing the power between the Executive and Legislative branches will be the reassignment of the power of judicial appointments from the President of the United States to the Chancellor of the Senate.

Conclusion

In sum, we need an overhaul of the procedures that govern the way Congress operates. Americans deserve a Congress that serves the interests of the people. We do have the power to insist upon a functioning democracy. To achieve this fundamental goal, we will need to elect senators and representatives who actually want to govern and who want to work with all sides to arrive at solutions that work for all. We should also include specific provisions in Constitution II that will facilitate a functioning Congress.

Bill of Rights Challenge and Associated Fixes in Constitution II

Often bitter debates took place between the federalist and anti-federalist forces before the 1787 Constitution was ratified. Anti-federalists held that the Constitution as written failed in two major respects: it lacked sufficient protections for individual liberties, and it did not impose strong enough limitations on the power of the federal government. The anti-federalists finally gained assurances from those in favor of the new Constitution that, as soon as the new federal government became operative, the anti-federalists would be able to recommend the kinds of changes that they insisted on.

Accordingly, during the very first Congress elected under the newly-ratified Constitution, James Madison (who had been elected a member of the House of Representatives from Virginia) introduced a series of Amendments; the House approved 17 of these Amendments and sent them over to the Senate, who approved 12 of them and sent them to the states in August 1789. The states ratified 10 of these 12, which became effective in December 1791.

These first ten Amendments to the Constitution, which became known as the Bill of Rights, layout fundamental rights that the Constitution guarantees. Subsequent constitutional amendments guaranteed voting rights to former slaves, to women, and to all citizens over age 18.

Several Supreme Court decisions and federal laws have expanded on some of our basic rights. A few examples:

- A Supreme Court decision interpreted the 2nd Amendment as guaranteeing gun rights to individual citizens.

- Another Supreme Court decision interpreted the 1st, 3rd, 4th, 5th, and 9th Amendments as implicitly recognizing the right to privacy.

- A federal law, the Voting Rights Act, expanded voting rights for all citizens but especially for racial minorities.

However, Congress can alter laws. and court decisions can be overturned. Therefore, to secure these and other individual rights for present and future generations, we need to enshrine these fixes in the Constitution. The challenge lies in the fact that, without such constitutional guarantees, our Bill of Rights remains somewhat incomplete.

Several citizen rights exist in various states but not at the federal level, including Initiative, Referendum, and the right to amend the constitution. States do not have the right to supersede a federal statute or to secede from the Union.

Again, we must remember that in 1787 the authors of the Constitution had limited experience with the rights of individual persons or citizens, so we should not criticize them for not including some of these rights in the original document. They feared the tyranny of the mob almost as much as they feared the tyranny of a king, and with good reason. The Jacobite Rebellions in England (ending in 1746) were still fresh in their consciousness. Hence our Founding Fathers trusted Congress more than they trusted a President, and they trusted state legislatures more than they would ever trust the people to protect the freedom of all citizens and freedom from either form of tyranny.

We have come a long way since the 18th century. Today we have relatively more faith in the people though we retain a somewhat jaundiced view of government and especially of professional politicians. The trick is to devise a system of government that protects both individual and collective rights while limiting the ability of government to trample over those rights.

One principal piece of a solution is to divide governmental functions into three parts: make laws, enforce laws, and interpret laws; and then to assign these three basic functions to three co-equal branches of government – Congress, the President, and the Courts. A second piece is to divide power between the federal government and the state governments. The Framers implemented both of these pieces fairly well. But the third piece is to carve out a special role for the people, which the Framers did only in part.

We the people have been clamoring for more power ever since. For example, we campaigned for and obtained direct election of senators, and we insisted that voters select Presidential electors. We gained voting rights for women, for former slaves, and for all racial and ethnic minorities.

Though we have made significant progress, the task of "people empowerment" is not complete. All the items presented in the Bill of Rights Challenge relate in some way to the empowerment of people and of the states and/or to limiting the power of the federal government. These are all stated as "challenges" because none of them are fully realized in our Constitution. In this section, the discussion of each challenge ends by citing the provision of Constitution II that addresses that challenge.

Equality of Persons; Freedom from Discrimination; Freedom from Torture; Right to Privacy

- The Declaration of Independence states unequivocally:
    We hold these truths to be self-evident, that all men are created equal, that they are endowed by their Creator with certain unalienable Rights, that among these are Life, Liberty and the pursuit of Happiness.

    However, this fundamental assertion did not find its way into the Constitution.
- Congress has passed laws prohibiting discrimination on the basis of sex and sexual orientation, and it has outlawed age discrimination in employment after age 40. But these prohibitions are not in the Constitution. Other forms of discrimination are partially prohibited, such as discrimination based on race, ethnicity, religion, and national origin.

- While the 8th Amendment to the Constitution outlaws "cruel and unusual punishments", the Constitution does not forbid the use of torture for purposes other than punishment. Some have argued that torture used for the purpose of gaining information from a known or suspected traitor or spy or terrorist is not a punishment but rather an effective interrogation device justified by military necessity during war or by the need for public safety during periods of civil unrest or threatened terrorist activity. Others have argued that torture is always inhumane, reduces the government that practices torture to the same level as the terrorist, and furthermore is ineffective at gaining actionable intelligence. Social science research, testimony from victims of torture, and the historical record largely support the latter argument. Most modern societies have abjured the use of torture for any purpose whatsoever.
- In a landmark 1965 decision (Griswold v. Connecticut), the Supreme Court found a right to privacy implicit in the 1st, 3rd, 4th, 5th, and 9th Amendments. Subsequently the Court based several significant decisions at least in part on that 1965 decision including the right to an abortion (Roe v. Wade, 1973) and the ban on sodomy laws (Lawrence v. Texas, 2003).

The related fixes in Constitution II appear in:
- Article I, Section 2, ¶ 2.1 Equality of All Natural Persons
- Article I, Section 2, ¶ 2.3 Freedom from Discrimination
- Article I, Section 2, ¶ 2.5 Prohibition on Cruel and Unusual Punishment and on Torture
- Article I, Section 3, ¶ 3.4 Search and Seizure

Rights to Healthcare, Education, and the Necessities of Life

If we can argue that all of us have the right to "life, liberty, and the pursuit of happiness", then it follows that we as American citizens have the right to those basic necessities that sustain life and that allow us to pursue happiness. This includes at least the provision of healthcare, education, food, clothing, and shelter:

- Healthcare is needed to sustain life itself; without it, citizens die of disease prematurely and unnecessarily.
- Education is needed to prepare citizens for the pursuit of happiness; without it, a citizen's prospects are severely limited.
- Without food, citizens starve.
- Without clothing and shelter, citizens freeze, suffocate, or die from exposure.

There are limits to what governments can and should provide or guarantee. We do have a free-market economy, a capitalist economic system, which encourages entrepreneurship, investment, invention, creativity, risk-taking, and hard work. Those things deserve to be rewarded. However, the cards should not be so stacked against an individual, especially when the circumstances are beyond that individual's control, that "life, liberty, and the pursuit of happiness" are impossible.

Interestingly, the original Constitution does not mention capitalism, private property, or free markets. The term "private property" does appear in the 5th Amendment to the Constitution in the clause "nor shall private property be taken for public use, without just compensation." Article I Section 8 of the Constitution gives Congress the power to protect the rights of authors and inventors to benefit from their writings and discoveries, so this clause suggests a right to private property. Nevertheless, I find it most interesting that the foundational document of the greatest capitalist nation on earth does not discuss the role of free enterprise at all.

We need to also mention that our system of federalism allows us to construct a system of national, state, and mixed national-state programs that address these challenges. No one should assume, for example, that if a citizen has a constitutional right to something, the federal government must perforce provide it to everyone for free.

The related fixes in Constitution II appear in Article I, Section 3, ¶ 3.8 Healthcare, Education, and Necessities of Life

Clarification of 2nd Amendment

Here is the Second Amendment to the Constitution in its entirety: "A well-regulated Militia, being necessary to the security of a free State, the right of the people to keep and bear Arms, shall not be infringed." This Amendment became part of the original Bill of Rights when it was ratified in 1791.

The provenance of the 2nd Amendment is the English Bill of Rights of 1689, which explicitly forbade the Catholic monarch from forcibly disarming Protestants. The English Bill of Rights stated that the English king had no right to take away his subjects' means of defending themselves. In the US, the debate centered on the ability of states and citizens to protect themselves from forcible takeover by the federal government. The Framers argued that no federal standing army would be able to overcome resistance from a well-organized state militia. However, some also made the personal self-defense argument, harking back to the English Bill of Rights of 1689.

For 217 years, the Second Amendment was interpreted by federal courts as guaranteeing the right of each state to maintain its own militia (or national guard, as we now call it). But in 2008, in Heller v. District of Columbia, the Supreme Court held that the Second Amendment guaranteed each citizen the right to possess a firearm for traditionally lawful purposes, such as self-defense within the home. This decision invalidated a District of Columbia law that had outlawed handguns altogether. And interestingly, the Supreme Court based its decision at least in part on English Common Law and specifically on the English Bill of Rights of 1689.

People still argue vehemently over the Heller decision – from gun-rights advocates who argue that the Second Amendment prevents the government from imposing any limits whatsoever on personal weapons, to gun-control advocates who believe that Heller was wrongly decided and should be overturned, or that the Heller decision still allows regulation of firearms, just not their outright prohibition. The challenge here is to come up with a scheme that protects the right of each state to maintain a militia, the right of every individual to protect himself with a firearm, and the right of all citizens to protect themselves from totally unregulated firearms.

The related clarifications in Constitution II appear in:

- Article I, Section 3, ¶ 3.2 Right to Bear Arms and Article I, Section 4, ¶ 4.6 State Militia

Distinguish Between the Rights of Persons, of Citizens, and of States

We have entertained many arguments over constitutionally-guaranteed rights, not the least of which has been the argument over whether a particular constitutionally-guaranteed right pertains to all persons within the jurisdiction of the United States or only to citizens of the United States. For instance, do visitors to the US or permanent residents of the US have a right to free speech, free exercise of religion, and freedom of assembly? – or do those rights only attach to American citizens?

Can anyone in the country possess a firearm or only a citizen? Does anyone accused of a crime within the US get a jury trial or only citizens? The challenge is that the original Bill of Rights does not distinguish between citizens and other persons who fall within the jurisdiction of the US.

A similar challenge exists in delineating the rights of people versus the rights of states.

The clarification in Constitution II appears in Article I, Section1: Introduction to the Bill of Rights, which specifies that Constitution II establishes the rights of natural persons, citizens, and states. The subsequent sections of Article I specify the rights of Natural Persons, of Citizens, and of States.

Definition of Citizens, Natural-Born Versus Naturalized

Recent political controversies have centered on questions about the definition of citizens, and especially about the distinction between a natural-born citizen (born in the US or born of American parents while outside the US) and a naturalized citizen (an immigrant who subsequently obtained US citizenship). While the Constitution does not define any of these terms (citizen, natural-born citizen, or naturalized citizen), it does require that the President be a natural-born citizen. So the challenge is to clarify what those terms mean.

The related fix in Constitution II appears in Article I, Section 3, ¶ 3.1 Definition of Citizen

State and Local Rights and Responsibilities

States, localities, and individual citizens should have the right to act, alone or in consort with each other, on matters pertinent to their local interests. Gradually, too many rights of individuals and of states have been taken over by the federal government, usually with unsatisfactory results. Examples abound, but just a few will be cited here:

- In the natural order of things, K-12 education should be the responsibility of states, parents, and local school officials. It is difficult to argue that the federal government needs to be involved in K-12 curriculum, school policies, scheduling, financing, and so on. Does Washington really have any interest in deciding whether schools in Maryland begin after Labor Day or before, or whether Florida chooses to teach cursive writing? On the other hand, states should be able to join forces when they so choose. Common Core is an example of a state initiative to establish uniform curriculum guidelines, but then the Feds got involved by encouraging states to adopt Common Core, and the US Department of Education funded two companies to develop tests for measuring student achievement of the Common Core standards. The result, both educationally and politically, is a mess. A better result might be achieved by removing the federal government from primary and secondary education entirely while allowing states who so choose to form an association to set common standards, achieve common goals, conduct educational research, and compete for funding opportunities.

- Today most Americans agree that traffic regulations belong at the state level. Are you old enough to remember the 55 mph national speed limit? The US Department of Transportation even ran a national ad campaign, with the slogan "Stay Alive – Drive 55". As a partial response to the Arab oil embargo in 1973, the 55 mph National Maximum Speed Limit was passed in 1974 and signed by President Nixon as a way of both conserving fuel and saving lives. Congress amended the law to 65 mph in 1987 and repealed it altogether in 1995 – one of the most popular acts of the new Republican Congress elected in 1994. So why didn't the national speed limit work? The law was both ineffective and unenforceable. Too many people and too many states simply did not buy it for one simple reason: By no stretch of the imagination do drivers in New York or policy wonks in Washington have an interest in how fast trucks are permitted to drive in Montana. Period, end of story.

- Our current laws recognize that alcohol should be controlled at the state and local level. We experimented with a national prohibition on alcohol, adopted by the 18th Amendment to the Constitution in 1919, then repealed by the 21st Amendment in 1933. Yet today, having learned absolutely nothing from our failed experiment with Prohibition, we treat other intoxicants differently. We have an abundance of conflicting state and federal laws dealing with medical marijuana, recreational marijuana, and other drugs. It's hard to see why I as a resident of Maryland should give a hoot as to whether the folks attending a Super Bowl party in Denver are getting high on pot rather than Coors Beer. If this is a matter of concern for the citizens of Denver or the state of Colorado, they can deal with it – but please leave me out of that discussion.

Most common crimes are committed locally, with local perpetrators and local victims. Therefore, in our federal system of government, most criminal laws are state laws and local ordinances. The federal government has no discernible interest in those matters. For the most part, federal crimes involve multiple state jurisdictions or international actors, such as bank fraud or smuggling or kidnapping.

Attitudes of ideologues and of party activists have long argued over states' rights versus federal prerogatives, and it's interesting to see historically how the tides and attitudes have shifted over time. In the early days of the republic, for example, slave states wanted the federal government to enforce their property rights in non-slave states by forcing those states to return fugitive slaves to their slave-state owners, while anti-slave states believed that their states had the right to prevent such extraditions. Later, as the abolitionist movement grew, the slave states became advocates for states' rights, and abolitionists thought the federal government should have the right to outlaw slavery everywhere. Though of less import than slavery in the 19th century, the same argument has occurred in our own time concerning undocumented aliens, sanctuary cities, voting rights, marijuana laws, abortion rights, gun control, and same-sex marriage. In each of these cases and many others, advocates for one side or the other have alternately claimed that federal jurisdiction should be paramount over state statutes, or that states' rights should be protected against federal intrusion – all depending on who then controls the federal government versus who controls a state government.

The federal government has an obligation to enforce the rights and privileges of all American citizens enumerated in the Constitution, including the laws Congress has passed to implement those rights. Over and above that, the question should be on the locus of control, effect, and payment: Who is in a position to control an activity, who is affected by that activity, and who must pay for it? Air traffic control, for example, must be a federal matter, since most flights go over state boundaries and conflicting state laws would be a complete mess as well as dangerous. Regulations on food and on pharmaceuticals must be national since these products inevitably involve interstate commerce. But states can handle purely local matters, such as setting standards for locally-grown and sold vegetables, high school graduation requirements, highway speed limits, and local building codes.

One challenge that always arises in these discussions is the uneven wealth among the 50 states. A solution to that challenge, occasionally employed by Congress, is federal block grants. We do some of this with Medicaid, disaster relief, and Interstate Highway System projects. But do we have enough of this type of creative funding and federal-state partnerships? Congress can set minimal guidelines that states must follow to qualify for block grants, with the dollar amount of such grants based on the unique needs of each state; but the actual regulations and procedures are left to the states. Perhaps the Constitution should spell out the authority of Congress and of the several states to act in consonance on funding solutions.

The challenge going forward will be to reconsider federal laws and regulations with a view to relegating local matters back to the states, as is mandated in principle in Amendment 10 to the Constitution, to wit: "The powers not delegated to the United States by the Constitution, nor prohibited by it to the states, are reserved to the states respectively, or to the people."

The related fix in Constitution II appears in Article I, Section 4 Bill of Rights of States.

Power of States to Secede

Some will say that we tried this once in 1861, and it did not turn out well.

In response, I would ask this question: Why should the decisions of 13 state conventions in the 1780's bind all the states and all the citizens of all those states forever? First, none of us were alive when the Articles of Confederation were adopted (which is where the notion of a "Perpetual Union" of the states was articulated). Second, 37 of the 50 states now in existence did not exist when the Constitution was adopted. Third, this perpetual union idea appears nowhere in the Constitution.

Let me repeat that: The idea that no state can secede from the Union is NOT in our Constitution.

However, this idea IS in the Articles of Confederation from 1781, written and adopted before the Revolutionary War was over. In fact, the complete title of that agreement is "Articles of Confederation and perpetual Union between the states of New Hampshire, Massachusetts-bay, Rhode Island and Providence Plantations, Connecticut, New York, New Jersey, Pennsylvania, Delaware, Maryland, Virginia, North Carolina, South Carolina, and Georgia."

I would also posit (though I cannot demonstrate this) that leaving this "perpetual union" clause out of the Constitution was not an accident. The Constitution's Framers went over the "Articles of Confederation and perpetual Union" meticulously and retained those provisions which seemed to work well and discarded or replaced others. So why was it not included in the Constitution? Did the Framers realize that future generations might want to rethink their commitment to the Union?

This idea that the "Perpetual Union of the states" need not be perpetual has not been seriously debated since the Civil War, which for most Americans settled that matter once and for all. However, if we think about a system of empowering the people and the states, then the notion that a state might choose to opt out does have merit. The question is this: Why should the commitment to a perpetual union, made by a small, wealthy, privileged group of white men in the thirteen original states bordering the Atlantic Ocean, over two centuries ago, forever bind the people living in, for example, Texas or California (which at that time belonged to Spain), Louisiana and all the states that derived from the Louisiana Purchase of 1803 (which belonged then to France), Hawaii (which was an independent monarchy), or Alaska (which belonged to Russia)? Why should that 18th-century decision be binding on anyone in the 21st century?

Let me also interpose this thought: Once admitted to the Union, a state is vested in that Union; by the same token, the Union is vested in each state. Hence both entities, the state and the Union, must acquiesce in its dissolution.

Although we may not foresee the circumstances today that would propel the citizens of a state to make such a choice, is it fair to preclude that choice for now and forever more?

We exist as a single nation, and we function as a single entity. Among other results of our Civil War, the term "United States" became a singular noun rather than a plural noun. Clearly the ties that bind us together are strong. We depend on each other for so much, from a common military to a common currency and financial system to a fully integrated economy, transportation system, energy industry, and commercial sector.

Nevertheless, if some state or states among us conclude that they would be better off as a separate nation, then ought we not have a procedure short of civil war of allowing them to accomplish that? Secession should be difficult, much more than a passing fancy, and chosen deliberately over some period of years; and it should require acquiescence from the country as a whole as well as adequate notice to the other states to adjust – but it should be possible.

The related fix in Constitution II appears in Article I, Section 4, ¶ 4.2.

Power of the People to Initiate and Repeal Laws and to Amend the Constitution

Most states require that the citizenry approve state constitutional amendments at the ballot box, often by a super-majority. 24 states permit citizens to initiate new state laws or repeal existing laws through petitions followed by a popular referendum. We need to adopt similar measures at the federal level. Voters should approve any change to the U.S. Constitution, and citizens or states should also be able to create or repeal laws when Congress fails to act. Citizens should be able to call for a constitutional convention. The rules governing the exercise of such citizen power should make it difficult but not impossible for the citizens, through direct action, to modify our constitution or laws. We should not tinker with the Constitution or statutes on a whim, but citizens in a democracy should be able to effect change for good reason and upon due reflection.

Empowering the people to amend the Constitution will be an immense and historic step in realizing the promise of democracy. Amending our Constitution will not be easy; but if the people demand changes in the Constitution, they should have the means of achieving that result.

The political process known as "Initiative" gives citizens of a state the constitutional right to propose a state statute (and in some cases an amendment to the state constitution) through a petition, bypassing the state legislature. After a certain percentage of registered voters have signed a petition, the proposed law or constitutional amendment appears on the next general election ballot, where voters can accept or reject it. (Some states provide for an intermediate step, in which the proposal is submitted first to the legislature, where the lawmakers can deal with it, and only if the legislature ignores or rejects the proposal does it then go the voters.) Beginning with South Dakota in 1898, 24 states now include some form of Initiative in their state constitutions. The most recent state to adopt the Right of Initiative was Mississippi in 1992.

The term "referendum" simply means a ballot measure. All state constitutions include a "legislative referendum", which is a ballot measure submitted to the voters by the legislature. Typically, state constitutions require certain measures to be approved by the voters, such as constitutional amendments, bond issues, or tax increases. Some state constitutions also provide for discretionary items, in which the lawmakers just decide to punt on an issue and let the voters decide.

But a legislative referendum is not the type of referendum we are talking about here. Rather, we want to discuss another type, which could be called a "citizen referendum". Like the Initiative, a citizen referendum gives citizens the ability to circulate a petition to repeal an act of the legislature. In the typical procedure, after the legislature passes a new law, people who disapprove of that law have a limited amount of time (usually 90 days) in which they can "petition the bill to referendum". If they gain sufficient signatures on their petition, then the new law goes to the voters for an up-or-down vote at the next election, and in the meanwhile, the new law does not go into effect. 24 states have the citizen "Referendum" in their state constitutions – mostly the same states that have the "Initiative".

In sum, roughly half the states have Initiative and Referendum. States began experimenting with this more than a century ago, and nothing terrible has happened as a result. Therefore, isn't it time that we incorporate these tools of citizen empowerment into the US Constitution? We can use the rules for "Initiative and Referendum" in those states that already have such rights, encourage all states to adopt such rights, and fall back on state legislatures in those states that do not yet have such rights.

A constitutional amendment to empower citizens should replace Article V of the 1787 Constitution. This article would state:

- Citizens and states have the right to propose a federal statute, repeal a federal statute, propose a constitutional amendment, and convene a constitutional convention.

- Congress has the right to propose a constitutional amendment.

- Voters have the final decision: Voters will decide whether to enact or repeal a law brought to them through the Initiative or Referendum process; voters will ratify or reject all proposed constitutional amendments; and voters will decide whether or not to convene a constitutional convention and ratify or reject any amendments or new constitution proposed by said convention.

The Amendment on Amendments (Big Fix 3 in Part II above) gives citizens and states the power to propose constitutional amendments and gives citizens the final say in amending the Constitution. Constitution II goes further, expanding citizen participation in the enactment and repeal of federal statutes.

The related fix in Constitution II appears in Article VII: Citizen Empowerment; Constitutional Amendments.

Convening the Constitution II Convention

To adopt a new constitution, we need to convene a constitutional convention for the purpose of creating a new constitution. We will refer to this body as the *Constitution II Convention*. The Constitution II Convention will draft the new constitution, *Constitution II*, and the **people** in each state (not the **legislatures** of each state) will then ratify it.

Two approaches to convening the Constitution II Convention present themselves. The first approach is to follow the procedures in the current Constitution. The second follows the precedent established by the Framers of the current Constitution. Each approach can succeed only with a great deal of active citizen involvement and broad public support.

First Approach

The first approach uses the procedures in Article V of the Constitution to amend the Constitution, specifically, to replace *Article V – Amendments* with *the Amendment on Amendments*, detailed in Big Fix 3. The Amendment on Amendments gives citizens the exclusive power to approve all constitutional amendments and to propose a constitutional convention.

Article V of the Constitution spells out two procedures for proposing a constitutional amendment or constitutional convention: a) Two-thirds of the state legislatures ask Congress to call for a convention for the purpose of proposing amendments; or b) Congress itself, by a two-thirds vote in each chamber, proposes an amendment. When Congress submits a proposed constitutional amendment to the states, Congress can specify whether the amendment will be ratified by the state legislatures or by state conventions.

The American people could demand that our state legislatures petition Congress to convene a constitutional convention for the purpose of proposing the Amendment on Amendments. Or we could demand that Congress propose the Amendment on Amendments. We could further demand that Congress specify that state conventions (rather than state legislatures) will endorse the will of the people in each state, based on a ballot referendum on the Amendment on Amendments.

Under either procedure, the Amendment on Amendments is then submitted to the 50 states, where 38 states ratify it, making it part of the Constitution.

After we adopt the Amendment on Amendments, half of the states with at least half of the US population can call for a constitutional convention to rewrite the constitution.

We can expect a challenge to the constitutionality of the Amendment on Amendments since it removes the guarantee that no state will be denied its equal representation in the Senate without its consent. The counter-argument is that of James Madison: we have the authority to change our government.

If this first approach is successful, then the path will be clear to submit a rewritten constitution to the states for approval by the people, in accordance with the procedure in the Amendment on Amendments.

Second Approach

We should try the first approach first. It's clean and straightforward, and it will garner support from those who insist on following the letter of the law.

But what if it doesn't work? What if political obstructionism prevents us from replacing Article V with the will of the people, and yet public opinion polls demonstrate overwhelming public support for convening the Constitution II Convention?

In that case, we may need to follow the precedent of the guys who wrote the 1787 Constitution. That is, ignore the rules in the existing document for amending it because those rules are so prejudiced in favor of the existing power structure that we can never expect them to relinquish that power voluntarily. Instead, convene a new constitutional convention of the people, and campaign for widespread public support.

Here are specific suggested steps for convening the Constitution II Convention using the second approach:

1. The process begins with a petition, organized and circulated through any of the national civic organizations with a continuing interest in these matters, demanding a national convention for the purpose of creating a new constitution.

2. Then an existing non-partisan civic organization with a focus on politics agrees to take the lead in organizing discussions on Constitution II or helps form a new organization with this mission. The League of Women Voters, FairVote.org, Harvard University's John F. Kennedy School of Government (especially the Roy and Lila Ash Center for Democratic Governance and Innovation), the University of Virginia Center for Politics, the Brennan Center for Justice, and probably a dozen other entities would be candidates for this role. One or more state or national political leaders might see the merit in this effort and lend it credibility.

3. When citizen support for this endeavor becomes sufficiently widespread and vocal, the sponsoring organization will call together a core group of scribes to write and edit and vet the document.

4. As was the case before the 1787 Constitutional Convention, all states will be invited to participate in the process of drafting Constitution II; but this time around, direct citizen action must drive the process, rather than allowing politicians to exercise control over the process or veto power over the result.

5. The Constitution II Convention, charged with the task of drafting Constitution II, will hold its first official meeting when 60% of the states call for same and agree to send representatives to it. A state can join the Constitution II Convention by either an action of the state legislature or by a plebiscite of its citizens.

6. And, *voila!*, the Constitution II Convention is underway. Additional states can join the process throughout the Constitution II Convention whenever they see fit to do so.

If this second approach to convening the Constitution II Convention is followed, we can expect an intense national conversation and debate about the proper method to follow for ratification.

Constitution II Convention Procedures

Technology will facilitate the participation of a wide swath of citizens in the drafting and editing process.

State governments can designate representatives if they so choose, as can Congress and the federal judiciary; all representatives can participate either electronically or in person. The Constitution II Convention can begin meeting officially when it has representatives from at least 60% of the states. Citizen opinion polls and online voting schemes can be employed to ensure citizen support for each article, section, paragraph, sentence, and clause of Constitution II. I envision a lively, months-long, highly participatory civics lesson, at the end of which the American public will be much better informed concerning their government, their constitution, and democracy – and much more supportive of all three.

When the whole document is complete, sponsors will ask each state to submit it to their voters in a public referendum. This will happen, of course, only if citizens demand it, loudly and consistently over a long period of time.

If Americans follow the first approach to convening the Constitution II Convention, then the ratification procedure will be straightforward, following the procedure in the Amendment on Amendments. Voters in two general elections (separated by at least one general election and inauguration of a new President) will accept or reject Constitution II, and if they vote twice to accept it, then this will become the new constitution and the law of the land in all 50 states.

If Americans follow the second approach to convening the Constitution II Convention, then the path to ratification is less clear. Public demands for a plebiscite in every state will be necessary to force a vote. One can hope that, if several states approve Constitution II, more states will follow, and the effort will gain momentum. Though the last few states might be a challenge, 30 states will ultimately ratify. At that point, the other 20 states will need to decide whether to join in or else lose out entirely, and hopefully all will join.

This scenario is not as far-fetched as it might seem at first glance. In any case, working to achieve it or something like it is far better than simply wringing our hands and complaining bitterly how the system is rigged against us, or how Big Money always wins, or how the entrenched politicians will remain forever entrenched and there is nothing we can do about it.

Consent of 60% of Us

Today, of course, we want our Government to be far more democratic, far more representative of the people, than the Framers of the 1787 Constitution would ever have dared dream. Therefore, this new Constitution II will come into effect only after it has been adopted (or "ratified") by a majority of voters in at least 60% of the states, including states that constitute at least 60% of the US population according to the most recent census.

The suggested 60% threshold for ratification (for both states and population) is arbitrary. Any number can be argued, both pro and con.

At one extreme, we could put the new Constitution II into effect among the states that have approved it when ratified by just nine states, making up just a majority of the US population. We could argue for this suggestion for two reasons: 1) Precedent, since that is the number of states needed to ratify the 1787 Constitution and put it into effect; and 2) Conveniently, the nine most populous states comprise 51% of the US population.

At the other extreme, we could require unanimous approval by a plebiscite in every state, perhaps with a super-majority in every state. But that would be like trying to amend the Articles of Confederation by unanimous approval of all state legislatures or trying to reconstitute the US Senate under the strictures of the existing Article V. That simply was not going to happen in 1787, and it sure ain't gonna happen now.

So 60% seems a reasonable compromise. If a majority of the voters in 60% of the states containing 60% of the nation's population think it's time for a constitutional overhaul, then perhaps we ought to just go ahead with it, and trust that the rest of the states will buy into it in due course.

Formatting Notes in Constitution II

- Most of the provisions of Constitution II are unchanged from the Constitution of 1787 as amended, which Constitution II replaces. Some provisions have been reworded or modernized without changing the original meaning. Provisions copied or modernized from the 1787 Constitution appear in normal type along with a footnote indicating the source.

- New provisions appear in Italics. As needed, footnotes explain the new wording.
- In all cases, spelling, punctuation, and capitalization have been updated to reflect modern usage.

Finally, let me end with this: I suffer no illusion that this Constitution II is the be-all and end-all. It is merely one man's proposal and a starting point for discussions, which need to be wide-ranging, deep, extended over time, and inclusive.

And now for my *piece de resistance*, Constitution II. Read on!

Constitution II for the United States of America

Preamble

We the people of the United States, in order to form a more perfect union, establish Justice, ensure domestic tranquility, provide for the common defense, promote the general welfare, and secure the blessings of liberty to ourselves and our posterity, do ordain and establish this Constitution *II*[33] for the United States of America.[34]

This Constitution II replaces the United States Constitution of 1787, as amended.

---

[33] The revised constitution is referred to as "this Constitution II" throughout.

[34] The Preamble is copied from the 1787 Constitution, Preamble.

Stipulations

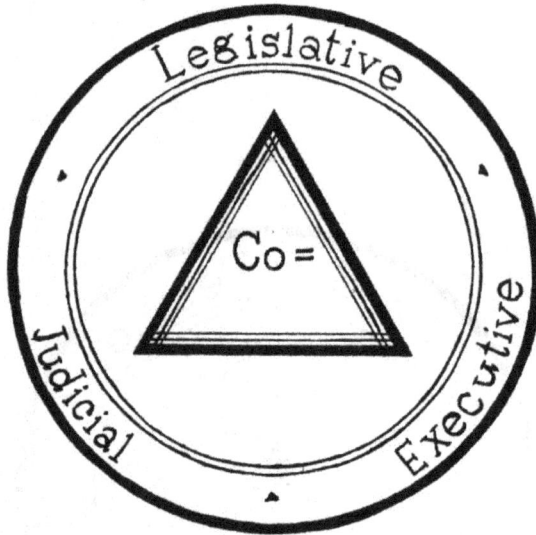

1. *All laws, treaties, responsibilities, regulations, debts, and other obligations of the United States, undertaken under the Constitution of 1787 as amended, continue in full force and effect, except where specifically contravened by this Constitution II.*[35],[36]
2. *This Constitution II establishes a federal government consisting of three co-equal branches: the Legislative Branch, the Executive Branch, and the Judicial Branch.*[37]

---

[35] The Stipulations need to be stated at the outset, though the ideas themselves are not new and in fact exist (with different wording) in the 1787 Constitution.

[36] Adapted from the 1787 Constitution, Article VI, first paragraph.

[37] While we have always talked about the three co-equal branches of the federal government, the 1787 Constitution does not explicitly state this. Perhaps it is a good idea to stipulate that this Constitution II prescribes three co-equal branches.

3. *Each of the 50 states existing at the time of the creation of this Constitution II is invited to conduct a plebiscite to ratify this Constitution II within ten years of its submission to the states. This Constitution II will become effective in those states ratifying same, provided it has been ratified by a plebiscite in 30 or more states, whose total population constitutes at least 60% of the population of the United States according to the most recent decennial census.*[38]

4. *The first elections conducted under this Constitution II will take place in the first Presidential election year that begins following ratification.*[39] *This first election will include the President, Senate, and House of Representatives. (The existing President, Vice President, and Congress will continue to serve until those newly elected under this Constitution II begin their terms of office.) The existing Vice President will serve as Chancellor until the first Chancellor election under Constitution II.*

5. *As provided by this Constitution II, federal judges serve for 16 years. Accordingly, when Constitution II has been ratified, all existing federal judges begin a new 16-year term of office.*

---

[38] The procedure for ratifying the 1787 Constitution appeared in Article VII. Interestingly, the framers simply ignored the procedure for amending the Articles of Confederation, which required unanimous consent of all thirteen original states.

[39] That is, a year evenly divisible by 4.

Article I: Bill of Rights

Section 1: Introduction to the Bill of Rights

1.1 This U.S. Constitution II establishes rights of natural persons, of citizens, and of states.[40] The federal government and the several states may also recognize rights of other legal entities, such as corporations, partnerships, trusts, charities, and benevolent associations; but such rights are not constitutionally guaranteed.[41]

---

[40] Before the Constitution of 1787 was adopted, citizens in many states stipulated that their agreement to this Constitution was dependent upon the adoption of a Bill of Rights, which became the first 10 Amendments to the Constitution. In Constitution II, these rights are built into Constitution II itself. Further, certain other rights of all persons, of American citizens, and of states deserve to be spelled out before Constitution II is adopted. Due to the preeminent importance of these constitutional protections, it makes sense to state them in Article I.

[41] This provision clarifies that Constitution II guarantees the rights of persons, citizens, and states, but not of corporations or other legal entities – whose rights may be recognized by

1.2 The federal government may delegate any of its powers to the several states. A collection of states may delegate any of their powers to the federal government. A collection of states may also create a public agency to jointly execute certain state powers and may request the federal government to participate or support such public agencies, but without ceding those powers to the federal government.[42]

1.3 The enumeration in this Constitution II of certain rights shall not be construed to deny or disparage others retained by the people. [43]

1.4 The powers not delegated to the United States by this Constitution II, nor prohibited by it to the states, are reserved to the states respectively or to the people.[44]

Section 2: Bill of Rights of Natural Persons

2.1 Equality of All Natural Persons[45]

All natural persons are created equal, and are born with certain inalienable rights, and among these rights are life, liberty, and the pursuit of happiness.

2.2 Freedom of Religion, Press, and Expression[46]

Congress shall make no law respecting an establishment of religion or prohibiting the free exercise thereof; or abridging the freedom of speech or of the press; or the right of the people peaceably to assemble and to petition the Government for a redress of grievances.

---

law, but are not guaranteed by this Constitution II. (By the way, the 1787 Constitution also does not mention corporations, free markets, or capitalism. It mentions private property only once: This occurs in Amendment 5 in the clause concerning eminent domain.)

[42] This notion of federalism has existed in practice for many years; this provision makes it explicit in this Constitution II.

[43] Copied from the 1787 Constitution, Amendment 9.

[44] Copied from the 1787 Constitution, Amendment 10.

[45] This fundamental idea, taken from the American Declaration of Independence (1776) and also incorporated in the Universal Declaration of Human Rights (1948), deserves to be a bedrock principle of Constitution II.

[46] Copied from the 1787 Constitution, Amendment 1.

2.3 Freedom from Discrimination[47]

Discrimination against any person on the basis of sex, race, ethnicity, religion, or sexual orientation is prohibited.

Discrimination against any person on the basis of age, between ages 40 and 70, is prohibited.[48]

2.4 Prohibition of Slavery[49]

Neither slavery nor involuntary servitude shall exist within the United States or any place subject to *its[50]* jurisdiction.

2.5 Prohibition of Cruel and Unusual Punishments *and of Torture*

Excessive bail shall not be required, nor excessive fines imposed, nor cruel and unusual punishments inflicted.[51] *The United States does not practice or tolerate the use of torture.[52]*

---

[47] This paragraph enshrines in Constitution II the basic civil liberties of the last 50 years of civil rights legislation and judicial decisions.

[48] Certain laws may require a minimum age for performing certain activities, such as signing a contract, driving a car or boat or airplane, getting married, and holding public office. Other laws may mandate a retirement age. But any laws dealing with age must not discriminate between the ages of 40 and 70.

[49] Copied from the 1787 Constitution, Amendment 13.

[50] The 1787 Constitution used the word "their" rather than "its" because, up until the Civil War, "United States" was a plural noun; since Reconstruction, "United States" became a singular noun. The United States is treated as a singular noun in Constitution II.

[51] Copied from the 1787 Constitution, Amendment 8.

[52] Based on all available medical and scientific evidence, torture is ineffective in producing operational intelligence, and its use as punishment has long been outlawed by the 1787 Constitution. This provision incorporates into Constitution II both American law and international conventions on the absolute prohibition of the use of torture, especially the Geneva Conventions of 1949 and Additional Protocols of 1977, treaties to which the U.S. is a signatory.

Section 3: Bill of Rights of Citizens

3.1 Definition of Citizens[53],[54]

The United States recognizes two categories of American citizens: a natural-born citizen and a naturalized citizen:

- *A natural-born citizen is any person*
  - *Who was born within the United States, its territories, or possessions, or*
  - *Whose biological mother or father was an American citizen at the time of the child's birth. To retain natural-born citizenship under this provision after one's 21st birthday, a citizen must notify the Secretary of State of the United States, between his/her 18th and 21st birthdays, of his/her intent to remain an American citizen.*
- *A naturalized citizen is any person who becomes an American citizen in accordance with the federal law regulating the naturalization process.*
- *With the sole exception of eligibility to hold the office of President of the United States, which requires the President to be a natural-born citizen, no distinction shall be made between natural-born and naturalized citizens.*
- *No government has the power to take American citizenship away from any American citizen.*

3.2 Right to Bear Arms[55]

---

[53] American citizens enjoy certain rights, over and above the rights of all persons who come under American jurisdiction. This section spells out those additional rights, starting with a definition of American citizenship.

[54] American citizenship was not explicitly defined in the 1787 Constitution. Article I Section 3.1 of this Constitution II provides clarity on this matter.

[55] Adapted from the 1787 Constitution, Amendment 2. This version of the Second Amendment ensures that an individual citizen may own a weapon but may be prohibited by law from owning a nuclear weapon, warship, fighter jet, fully automatic machine gun,

For reasons of personal safety, hunting, and/or recreation, a citizen has the right to keep and bear personal weapons, including firearms appropriate to such purposes. Possession of military-grade weapons by civilians is prohibited. States have the power to regulate firearms, unless Congress enacts superseding law.

3.3 Quartering of Soldiers[56]

No Soldier shall be quartered in any house in time of peace without the consent of the owner, nor in time of war but in a manner to be prescribed by law.

3.4 Search and Seizure[57]

The right of the people to be secure in their persons, houses, papers, and effects against unreasonable searches and seizures shall not be violated; and no warrants shall issue but upon probable cause, supported by oath or affirmation, and particularly describing the place to be searched and the persons or things to be seized. *This provision includes the right to privacy.*[58]

3.5 Trial and Punishment; Compensation for Takings[59]

No person shall be held to answer for a capital or otherwise infamous crime unless on a presentment or indictment of a grand jury, except in cases arising in the land or naval forces, or in the militia when in actual service in time of war or public danger; nor shall any person be subject for the same offense to be twice put in jeopardy of life or limb; nor shall any person be compelled in any criminal case to be a witness against himself, nor be deprived of life, liberty, or property, without due process of law; nor shall private property be taken for public use without just compensation. *No citizen shall be forced to surrender private property for private gain; the principle and legal process of eminent domain shall only be used to serve*

---

and other military-grade weapons.

[56] Copied from the 1787 Constitution, Amendment 3.

[57] Copied from the 1787 Constitution, Amendment 4, except for the final sentence, in italics.

[58] A right to privacy is inferred by the 1787 Constitution, Amendment 4, and has been so interpreted by the Supreme Court. Adding it to this provision in Constitution II makes this right explicit rather than implicit.

[59] Copied from Amendment 5, except for the final sentence, in italics.

a demonstrated public need, and any private property gained through eminent domain shall become public property in perpetuity.[60]

3.6 Right to Speedy Trial; Confrontation of Witnesses; Assistance of Counsel[61]

In all criminal prosecutions, the accused shall enjoy the right to a speedy and public trial by an impartial jury of the state and district wherein the crime shall have been committed, which district shall have been previously ascertained by law. The accused shall enjoy the right to be informed of the nature and cause of the accusation, to be confronted with the witnesses against him, to have compulsory process for obtaining witnesses in his favor, and to have the assistance of counsel for his defense.

3.7 Trial by Jury in Civil Cases[62]

In suits at common law, where the value in controversy shall exceed $1000, the right of trial by jury shall be preserved; and no fact tried by a jury shall be otherwise reexamined in any court of the United States other than according to the rules of the common law.

3.8 Healthcare, Education, and Necessities of Life[63]

Citizens of all ages have a right to basic healthcare, including physicians, hospitals, medicines, medical devices, reproductive services, dental and vision services, and mental health services.

---

[60] Both conservatives and liberals, from time to time, have condemned the abuse of eminent domain. This provision states clearly that eminent domain may only be used to acquire or protect a public benefit.

[61] Copied from the 1787 Constitution, Amendment 6.

[62] Copied from the 1787 Constitution, Amendment 7. However, the amount has been raised from $20 to $1000.

[63] Article I Section 3.8 guarantees to every citizen the most basic necessities of life. It enshrines in Constitution II the actual, concrete meaning of the Declaration of Independence statement about everyone's inalienable right to life, liberty, and the pursuit of happiness. It also provides a constitutional basis for all of our social support programs – Social Security, Medicare, Medicaid, veterans' healthcare, and ACA (or whatever replaces it).

Citizens have a right to tax-supported public education.

Citizens have a right to the basic necessities of life – food, clothing, and shelter – sufficient to prevent death from starvation and exposure to the elements.

While the citizen rights in Section 3.8 are guaranteed by this Constitution II, implementation of the necessary services is a joint responsibility of the federal government and of the state in which each citizen resides.

3.9 Equal Protection of the Laws[64]

No state shall make or enforce any law which shall abridge the privileges or immunities of citizens of the United States; nor shall any state deprive any person of life, liberty, or property, without due process of law; nor deny to any person within its jurisdiction the equal protection of the laws.

3.10 Voting rights[65]

All citizens who have attained the age of 18 are eligible to vote in all federal and state elections and in the state in which they reside. Citizens who reside outside the jurisdiction of any state are eligible to vote in the Non-State Election District.

Section 4: Bill of Rights of States

4.1 Voluntary Union of states

- *The United States of America is a voluntary union of those states which have ratified this Constitution II and have therefore agreed to join the Union and be subject to its jurisdiction.[66]*
- *In addition to the 50 states in the Union under the 1787 Constitution, the District of Columbia and the Territory of Puerto Rico also each have the right to voluntarily join the Union as states under this Constitution II, if*

---

[64] Copied from the 1787 Constitution, Amendment 14.

[65] Voting rights are adapted from the 1787 Constitution, Amendments 1, 15, 24 and 26. Prohibitions of discrimination on the basis of ethnicity and of sexual orientation are based on Supreme Court decisions that in turn depended on those constitutional provisions.

[66] The idea of a voluntary union is implied by the 1787 Constitution; this provision makes it explicit.

approved by a majority vote of their citizens, held within 10 years following adoption of this Constitution II.[67]

- New states may be admitted by the Congress into this Union. However, no new states shall be formed or erected within the jurisdiction of any other state, nor any state be formed by the junction of two or more states or parts of states, without the consent of the *voters and* legislatures of the states concerned as well as of Congress.[68]

4.2 Secession

A state may secede from the Union by following these steps:

1) *Any state may, by a two-thirds vote of its citizens and its legislature, give notice of its intention to secede from the Union.*

2) *At the next Presidential general election held at least two years after a state's initial vote to secede, all voters in the United States will decide whether to permit that state to secede. Permission to secede requires approval from a majority of all voters in the United States, which must include a majority of voters in each of the states bordering the state planning to secede.*

3) *If approved by two-thirds of the voters in the secessionist state in a second plebiscite, held not less than three nor more than five years after permission to secede was granted by the voters of the United States, that state shall notify the Secretary of State of the United States of its decision to secede. That state and the United States will then have three years in which to negotiate the terms and conditions of their separation, after which that state will no longer be a part of the Union.*

---

[67] This new provision is another attempt to empower citizens of the USA – in this case, citizens of two jurisdictions who have been treated as second-class citizens for many decades. Under Constitution II, DC will lose its three Electoral Votes unless it chooses to become a state, and both DC and Puerto Rico can claim their full rights as states if they so choose. By the way, there is some precedent for including this type of provision in our foundational document: The Articles of Confederation included a provision allowing Canada to join the Confederation if it wanted to do so.

[68] Copied from the 1787 Constitution, Article IV Section 3, with the addition of a voice for voters (in italics).

4.3 Each State to Honor All Others[69]

Full faith and credit shall be given in each state to the public acts, records, and judicial proceedings of every other state. Congress may by general laws prescribe the manner in which such acts, records, and proceedings shall be proved, and the effect thereof.

4.4 State Citizens, Extradition[70]

The citizens of each state shall be entitled to all privileges and immunities of citizens in the several states.

A person charged in any state with treason, felony, or other crime, who shall flee from justice and be found in another state, shall on demand of the executive authority of the state from which he fled, be delivered up, to be removed to the state having jurisdiction of the crime.

4.5 Republican Government[71]

The United States shall guarantee to every state in this Union a republican form of government and shall protect each of them against invasion and, on application of the legislature or of the executive (when the legislature cannot be convened), against domestic violence.

4.6 National Guard[72]

Every state has the right and obligation to maintain a well-regulated National Guard, according to the discipline established by Congress.

4.7 State Legislative Preference[73]

---

[69] Copied from the 1787 Constitution, Article IV.

[70] Copied from the 1787 Constitution, Article IV.

[71] Copied from the 1787 Constitution, Article IV.

[72] Adapted from the 1787 Constitution, Amendment 2. Many constitutional scholars believe that this was the original intent of the Framers of the 1787 Constitution.

[73] Advocates for states rights often argue that some federal laws and regulations improperly infringe on state prerogatives. This provision would allow a state, in certain circumstances and with the concurrence of two-thirds of its citizens, to adopt a state law that supersedes a federal law.

A state statute takes precedence over a federal statute within that state, provided that the state statute

- *Does not conflict with this Constitution II,*
- *Addresses matters wholly within the state's jurisdiction,*
- *Does not adversely affect other states or citizens of other states, and*
- *Is approved by a two-thirds majority of that state's voters in a referendum on that statute, which includes the assertion that the state statute is in conflict with a federal statute but complies with all elements of this provision.*

Article II: The Legislative Branch

Section 1: The Legislature

All legislative powers herein granted shall be vested in a Congress of the United States, which shall consist of a *lower chamber, known as the House of Representatives, and an upper chamber, known as the Senate.*[74],[75] *Members of both chambers shall be chosen by voters in accordance with the provisions of Article VI – Elections.*

---

[74] The 1787 Constitution is often confusing when using the term "House(s)", which sometimes refers to the House of Representatives and sometimes refers to either the House or the Senate, or to both of them together. To avoid that confusion in Constitution II, the term "House" always refers to the House of Representatives, the term "Senate" refers to the Senate, and the terms "body" or "chamber" refer to either or both the House of Representatives and the Senate.

[75] Slightly reworded from the 1787 Constitution, Article I Section 1.

Section 2: The House of Representatives

2.1 Composition

The House of Representatives shall be composed of *501* Members chosen every second year. Congress may modify the number of members by law.

500 Seats in the House of Representatives shall be apportioned among the states during the first year of each new decade, based on the average number of voters who voted in each state in the two most recent Presidential general elections; but each state shall have at least one Representative, and *each Representative shall have one vote.*

American citizens who do not reside in any state do reside, for election purposes, in the Non-State Election District (NSED). The NSED shall elect 1 seat in the House.

2.2 Eligibility[76]

When he/she takes office, a Representative must be

- At least 25 years old;
- At least 7 years a citizen of the United States;
- *Less than 19 years a Member of the House of Representatives;*[77] *and*
- A resident of the state from which he/she shall have been chosen.

2.4 Officers

The House of Representatives shall choose their Speaker and other officers. The Speaker shall have no vote unless the House be equally divided.

Section 3: The Senate

3.1 Composition[78]

---

[76] Except for the term limit clause in italics, these provisions are adapted from the 1787 Constitution, Article I Section 2.

[77] This provision implements term limits for the House. Ten 2-year terms is specified as the maximum amount of time a member may remain in the House.

Bob Spear

The Senate of the United States shall be composed of Senators from each state, chosen by the voters for a six-year term of office; and each Senator shall have one vote. The number of Senators from each state is determined automatically by the number of Representatives apportioned to each state, according to this table:[79]

Representatives	Senators
1 to 5	1
6 to 10	2
11 to 15	3
16 to 20	4
21 to 25	5
26+	6

The NSED shall elect one Senator.

Seats in the Senate shall be divided as equally as they may be into three classes (Class I, Class II, and Class III). For any state, the number of seats assigned to each Class shall be the same, as nearly as possible. One Class shall be elected every two years. Thus one-third of the total Senate, and one-third of the Senate

---

[78] One of the fundamental improvements of Constitution II over the 1787 Constitution is replacing the unrepresentative Original Senate with the population-based New Senate.

[79] That is, a state with 1 to 5 House seats will have one Senator; a state with 6 to 10 House seats will have two Senators; a state with 11 to 15 House seats will have three Senators; and so on. This provision mandates that every state shall have from one to six Senators. This scheme still gives more power to states with small populations than is strictly justified based on population alone, but it is vastly fairer than the current scheme of two Senators per state regardless of population, and it is much easier to implement than a scheme based only on population, which would require election districts that cross state boundaries.

212

seats from each state, shall be elected every two years.[80] *Whenever a state elects more than one Senator in a given election cycle, a separate election shall be held for each Senate seat.*

Voters will elect senators to Class I Senate seats in 2024 and every 6 years thereafter; to Class II Senate seats in 2026 and every 6 years thereafter; and to Class III Senate seats in 2022 and every 6 years thereafter.[81]

When, due to the decennial Congressional reapportionment, the number of Senators for any state is decreased, the next Senator from that state whose term of office is expiring shall not be replaced after his term expires. When the number of Senators from any state is increased, a new Senator from that state shall be elected at the next election, and that seat will be assigned to Class I, II, or III, so that, as far as possible, one third of the Senate remains elected every two years, and one third of the Senators from each state remains elected every two years.

The first election cycle following reapportionment will include separate primary and general elections for all three Senate classes. This will include elections for 6-year terms for all the seats in the class normally scheduled for elections that year, as well as elections for 4-year terms and for 2-year terms for those seats in the other two classes which do not have an incumbent.

3.2 Eligibility[82]

When he/she takes office, a Senator must be

- At least 30 years old;
- At least 9 years a citizen of the United States;
- *Less than 17 years a Senator;*[83] and

---

[80] This paragraph mirrors the 1787 Constitution, Article I Section 3, except for the clause dealing with the equal distribution of Senate seats from each state across the three Senate Classes.

[81] This continues the Senate Class assignments under the 1787 Constitution.

[82] Except for the term limit clause in italics, these provisions are adapted from the 1787 Constitution, Article I Section 3.

[83] This provision implements term limits for the Senate. Three 6-year terms is specified as the maximum amount of time a member may remain as a Senator.

- A resident of the state from which he/she shall have been chosen.

3.3 Chancellor

In accordance with Article VI – Elections, voters shall elect a Chancellor to a four-year term of office in even-numbered years not evenly divisible by four. The Chancellor shall preside over the Senate. The Chancellor shall have no vote unless the Senate be equally divided.

The Chancellor must meet the same eligibility requirements as the President of the United States. A person may be elected to the office of Chancellor a maximum of two times. Whenever there is a vacancy in the office of Chancellor, the President shall nominate a Chancellor who shall take office upon confirmation by a majority vote in both chambers of Congress; this nominee must meet the eligibility requirements to become Chancellor and must also be a Member of Congress.

The Chancellor shall appoint a Chancellor Pro Tempore, with the concurrence of the Senate. The Chancellor Pro Tempore shall preside over the Senate in the absence of the Chancellor, or when the Chancellor is serving as Acting President.

3.4 Judicial Nominations and Appointments

The Chancellor[84] (but not the Chancellor Pro Tempore) shall have power to nominate and, by and with the advice and consent of the Senate, shall appoint Associate Justices of the Supreme Court and federal judges of inferior courts. The Chancellor may appoint no more than three Associate Justices in any one year and no more than eight Associate Justices during the Chancellor's four-year term of office.

3.5 Senate's Authority

In all cases of Chancellor judicial nominations and Presidential executive branch nominations, if the Senate fails to approve or disapprove a nomination within 60 calendar days after the Chancellor/President has made the nomination, unanimous consent of the Senate shall be recorded.

Section 4 - Meetings

Wednesdays through Sundays from 4 pm to 10 pm, except federal holidays, are designated as legislative days. When Congress is in session, it shall meet on

---

[84] An important change in Constitution II is that the Chancellor, rather than the President, makes all judicial appointments.

designated legislative days, unless Congress adopts a different schedule.[85] Either chamber, when it does not meet with a quorum of members present for three consecutive legislative days, shall be deemed to be in recess.[86]

Section 5 - Membership, Rules, Journals, and Adjournment

Each chamber shall be the judge of the elections, returns, and qualifications of its own members, and a majority of each shall constitute a quorum to do business; but a smaller number may adjourn from day to day and may be authorized to compel the attendance of absent members, in such manner and under such penalties as each chamber may provide.[87]

All decisions taken within each chamber shall be by majority vote of members present, except for those specific items in this Constitution II requiring a two-thirds or a three-fifths vote.

Any member may make a motion to call a bill, a resolution, or a Presidential or Chancellor appointment to the floor for a vote; and, if a majority of members present concur, that bill, resolution, or appointment shall become the first order of business in that chamber on the next legislative day; and at that time, such bill, resolution, or appointment will, by majority vote, be either approved, disapproved, or tabled for later consideration.[88]

Each chamber may determine the rules of its proceedings, punish its members for disorderly behavior, and, with the concurrence of two-thirds, expel a member.

---

[85] Important Congressional debates should occur in prime time and on weekends, when many more Americans could pay attention.

[86] This provision requires each chamber to be either in session or in recess. It cannot use an artificial device of meeting briefly with only a few members in order to pretend that it is still in session.

[87] Except for the two paragraphs in italics, Section 5 is copied from the 1787 Constitution, Article I Section 5.

[88] This provision allows either chamber to vote on items that a majority of the members want to vote on.

Each chamber shall keep a Journal of its proceedings and from time to time publish the same, excepting such parts as may in their judgment require secrecy; and the yeas and nays of the members of either chamber on any question shall, at the desire of one fifth of those present, be entered on the journal.

Neither chamber, during the session of Congress, shall, without the consent of the other, adjourn for more than three days, nor to any other place than that in which the two chambers shall be sitting.

No member, during the session of Congress, shall engage in any fundraising activity.

In even-numbered years (that is, election years), Congress shall adjourn sine die no later than July 4. Unless called back into session by the President of the United States due to a national emergency, Congress shall not reconvene until the convening of the new Congress following that year's election.

Section 6 - Compensation

All Members of Congress *and the Chancellor* shall receive compensation for their services, to be ascertained by law, and paid out of the Treasury of the United States. However, no law varying the compensation for the services of the Senators, Representatives, *or Chancellor* shall take effect until an election of Representatives shall have intervened. [89]

No Senator or Representative shall, during the time for which he was elected, hold any additional civil or military office under the United States or any state.[90]

Senators and Representatives shall in all cases, except treason, felony and breach of the peace, be privileged from arrest during their attendance at the session of their respective chambers, and in going to and returning from the same; and for any speech or debate in either chamber, they shall not be questioned in any other place.

---

[89] This section is adapted from the 1787 Constitution, Article I Section 6, and Amendment 27.

[90] The purpose of these changes is to prohibit Senators and Representatives from holding military (as well as civil) appointments while they serve in Congress, including the Armed Forces of the United States as well as any state militia.

Section 7 - Revenue Bills, Legislative Process, and Presidential Veto

All bills for raising revenue shall originate in the House of Representatives, but the Senate may propose or concur with amendments as on other bills.[91]

The earliest effective date of any bill, when enacted by Congress, shall be July 1st following the next Congressional election after passage of the bill. An earlier effective date can only be enacted if (1) the sole purpose of the bill is to repeal a bill which has not yet gone into effect, or (2) each chamber, upon final passage of the bill, adopts an earlier date, with the concurrence of three-fifths of members present and voting.[92]

Every Bill which shall have passed the House and the Senate, shall, before it becomes a law, be presented to the President of the United States. If he approves the bill, he shall sign it, but if not he shall return it, with his objections to that chamber in which it shall have originated, who shall enter the objections at large on their journal, and proceed to reconsider it. If after such reconsideration two-thirds of that chamber shall agree to pass the bill, it shall be sent, together with the objections, to the other chamber, by which it shall likewise be reconsidered, and if approved by two-thirds of that chamber, it shall become a law. But in all such cases the votes of both chambers shall be determined by yeas and nays, and the names of the persons voting for and against the bill shall be entered on the journal of each chamber respectively. If any bill shall not be returned by the President within ten days (Sundays excepted) after it shall have been presented to him, the same shall be a law, in like manner as if he had signed it, unless the Congress by their adjournment prevent its return, in which case it shall not be a law.

Every order, resolution, or vote to which the concurrence of the Senate and House may be necessary (except on a question of adjournment) shall be presented to the President of the United States; and before the same shall take effect, shall be

[91] Except for the paragraph in italics, this section is copied from the 1787 Constitution, Article I Section 7.

[92] This provision eliminates the need for a filibuster to delay action on a bill until "the people exercise their right to weigh in". It also extends to both chambers the same privilege to pass emergency legislation with a super majority, but to enact normal legislation by a simple majority vote.

approved by him, or being disapproved by him, shall be repassed by two thirds of the Senate and of the House of Representatives, according to the rules and limitations prescribed in the case of a bill.

Section 8 - Powers of Congress

The Congress shall have power as follows:[93]

To lay and collect taxes, duties, imposts, and excises, to pay the debts and provide for the common defense and general welfare of the United States; but all duties, imposts, and excises shall be uniform throughout the United States;

To lay and collect taxes on incomes, from whatever source derived, without apportionment among the several states, and without regard to any census or enumeration;[94]

To borrow money on the credit of the United States;

To regulate commerce with foreign nations, and among the several states, and with the Indian Tribes;

To establish a uniform rule of naturalization and uniform laws on the subject of bankruptcies throughout the United States;

To coin money, regulate the value thereof, and of foreign coin, and fix the standard of weights and measures;

To provide for the punishment of counterfeiting the securities and current coin of the United States;

To establish post offices;

To conduct a census or enumeration of the United States and to maintain estimated census figures at all times. The actual enumeration shall be made within three years after the first meeting of the Congress of the United States *under this Constitution II, and subsequently during every year evenly divisible by 10,* in such manner as they shall by law direct;[95]

---

[93] Except for the clauses in italics, and except also for the clauses noted individually, this entire section is adapted from the 1787 Constitution, Article I Section 8.

[94] Copied from the 1787 Constitution, Amendment 16.

[95] The first sentence of this provision is adapted from the 1787 Constitution, Article I,

To promote the progress of science and useful arts *by conducting and sponsoring scientific research and cultural and artistic endeavors;*[96]

To secure for limited times to authors and inventors the exclusive right to their respective writings and discoveries, *provided, however, that copyright protection shall not exceed 50 years, and patent protection shall not exceed 25 years;*[97]

To constitute tribunals inferior to the Supreme Court;

To define and punish piracies and felonies committed on the high seas, and offenses against the Law of Nations;

To declare war, *authorize privateers and other military proxies,*[98] and make rules concerning captures wherever they may occur;

To raise and support the *Armed Forces*[99] of the United States *(on land, on and under the sea, in the air, and in cyberspace)*;

Section 2. The second sentence is copied from the 1787 Constitution, Article I, Section 2. The italicized clause clarifies the requirement for a decennial census.

[96] This clause makes the federal role in science and the arts more explicit.

[97] This new limitation on Congressional power is a response to Congress' abuse of that power in recent decades.

[98] The 1787 Constitution used the now-obsolete phrase "grant letters of marques and reprisal". In the 18th century, governments sometimes issued "letters of marques and reprisal", which authorized a private vessel (privateer or pirate ship) to seize and confiscate enemy ships. Constitution II substitutes the phrase "privateers and other military proxies", meaning essentially the same thing but employing modern terminology. The significance of this passage is that Congress – not the President or any sort of king – has this power.

[99] Constitution II refers to the Armed Forces of the United States rather than to just the Army and the Navy. It addresses all American forces, wherever they may be – on land, on sea, in the air, or in cyberspace. The term "Armed Forces" is preferable to naming the service branches (Army, Navy, Air Force, Marine Corps, Coast Guard), since a number of proposals have been made to merge all of the service branches into one, or to restructure them in some other way. The single term "Armed Forces" covers all of our federal military forces, no matter how they are organized in the future.

To make rules for the government and regulation of the Armed Forces;

To provide for calling forth state National Guards to execute the laws of the Union, suppress insurrections, and repel invasions;

To provide for organizing, arming, and disciplining the state National Guards, and for governing such part of them as may be employed in the service of the United States, reserving to the states respectively the appointment of the officers and the authority of training their National Guards according to the discipline prescribed by Congress;

To protect the environment, and to provide for public health and safety by ensuring access to clean and safe water, air, energy, medicines, and the food supply;[100]

To provide financial assistance to the several states, based on the unique needs of each state, for infrastructure projects, for emergency relief from natural disasters, for fulfillment of each state's obligations under Article I Section 3.8, and for such other purposes as Congress may deem appropriate and necessary;[101]

To provide public financing for federal elections and election campaigns, to regulate and limit campaign contributions, and to mandate full disclosure of the sources and amounts of campaign contributions and expenditures;[102]

To regulate all federal elections in accordance with Article VI, provided that the actual conduct of the elections is left to the states; and to modify by law any of the provisions of Article VI, provided two-thirds of members present in each chamber agree.[103]

To dispose of and make all needful rules and regulations respecting the territory or other property belonging to the United States, and nothing in this Constitution II

---

[100] This provision ensures that Congress has the constitutional authority to pass environmental regulations.

[101] This provision ensures that Congress can issue block grants to the states to help states meet their financial obligations, taking into account the differing needs of each state.

[102] This provision ensures that Congress has the constitutional authority to fund federal elections and to regulate election finances, Specifically, it overturns the Supreme Court's decision in the *Citizens United v Federal Elections Commission* case.

[103] Since the specific procedures of Article VI are new, it is wise to provide a mechanism to alter them without the more challenging procedure of amending Constitution II.

shall be so construed as to prejudice any claims of the United States or of any particular state;[104]

To exercise exclusive legislation in all cases whatsoever over the District of Columbia *(unless the District of Columbia chooses to become a state, in accordance with Article I Section 4}*, and to exercise like authority over all places purchased by the consent of the legislature of the state in which the same shall be, for the erection of forts, magazines, arsenals, dockyards, and other needful buildings;[105] And

To make all laws which shall be necessary and proper for carrying into execution the foregoing powers, and all other powers vested by this Constitution II in the Government of the United States, or in any department or officer thereof.

Section 9 - Limits on Congress

The privilege[106] of the writ of habeas corpus[107] shall not be suspended, unless when in cases of rebellion or invasion the public safety may require it.

No bill of attainder[108] or ex post facto[109] law shall be passed.

---

[104] Copied from the 1787 Constitution, Article IV, Section 3.

[105] Copied from the 1787 Constitution, Article II Section 8, with additional wording in italics concerning Washington, DC, should it choose to become a state.

[106] Except for the clauses on liquor and other drugs, Section 9 is copied from the 1787 Constitution, Article I Section 9, although several provisions of that Section are omitted from Constitution II.

[107] A writ of *habeas corpus* is a demand issued by a court to an executive over whom the court has jurisdiction, demanding that the executive bring to the court someone whom the executive is holding in confinement, and requiring the executive to explain to the court the legal justification for continuing to confine that person. This provision, including the suspension of the privilege during a rebellion or invasion, is lifted directly from British Common Law. It is included verbatim in the 1787 Constitution, Article I, Section 9.

[108] A bill of attainder makes a person or group guilty of treason or other capital offense without a trial, and also takes away the civil rights, property, and titles of the person "attainted".

No tax or duty shall be laid on articles exported from any state.

No preference shall be given by any regulation of commerce or revenue to the ports of one state over those of another: nor shall vessels bound to, or from, one state, be obliged to enter, clear, or pay duties in another.

The transportation or importation into any state, territory, or possession of the United States for delivery or use therein of intoxicating liquors, *marijuana, cocaine, or any other mood-altering substances,* in violation of the laws thereof, is hereby prohibited. *In states where such substances are permitted by state law, Congress shall not prohibit them. Congress shall make no national law regarding the manufacture, import, export, possession, or use of such substances.*[110]

No money shall be drawn from the Treasury but in consequence of appropriations made by law; and a regular statement and account of the receipts and expenditures of all public money shall be published from time to time.

No title of nobility shall be granted by the United States: And no person holding any office of profit or trust under them shall, without the consent of the Congress, accept any present, emolument, office, title, or *payment*, of any kind whatever, from any king, prince, foreign state, or *other public or private foreign entity.*[111]

Section 10 - Powers Prohibited of States

No state[112] shall enter into any treaty, alliance, or confederation; *authorize privateers or other military proxies for the state*[113]; print or coin money; emit bills

---

[109] An *ex post facto* law is a law that criminalizes behavior that occurred before the law was passed.

[110] The provisions concerning intoxicating liquors are copied from the 1787 Constitution, Amendment 21. Marijuana and other drugs have been added to Constitution II. This provision ensures that the use of alcohol, marijuana, and other mind-altering substances is entirely a state matter. The federal government will neither compel nor prohibit state action in this realm.

[111] Corporations and other private commercial entities were not typically instruments of monarchical power when the 1787 Constitution was written. The added words make it clear that all such foreign payments, from whatever source, public or private, are prohibited.

of credit; pass any bill of attainder, ex post facto law, or law impairing the obligation of contracts; or grant any title of nobility.

No state shall, without the consent of Congress, lay any imposts or duties on imports or exports, except what may be absolutely necessary for executing its inspection laws: and the net produce of all duties and imposts, laid by any state on imports or exports, shall be for the use of the Treasury of the United States; and all such laws shall be subject to the revision and control of Congress.

No state shall, without the consent of Congress, lay any duty of tonnage, keep troops, or ships of war in time of peace, enter into any agreement or compact with another state, or with a foreign power, or engage in war, unless actually invaded, or in such imminent danger as will not admit of delay.

Section 11 - Transition from the 1787 Constitution to this Constitution II

The first Presidential and Congressional elections under this Constitution II will take place in the first year evenly divisible by 4 which begins after this Constitution II is adopted. The first elections for Chancellor will occur two years later. Beginning in January of the first Presidential election year, the last Vice President under the 1787 Constitution will become the Interim Chancellor and will continue to serve in that capacity until replaced by the first elected Chancellor. The Interim Chancellor will arrange for an orderly transition from the Congress under the 1787 Constitution to the Congress under this Constitution II.

The Chancellor will oversee the apportionment of seats in the House of Representatives in accordance with Article II, Section 2.1. After the apportionment of seats in the House, apportionment of seats in the Senate is automatic.

All incumbent Senators will complete their six year terms. Those Senate seats which will continue to exist in the New Senate retain their current Class assignments. The Chancellor will assign each additional seat in the New Senate to Class I, II, or III, in accordance with Article II, Section3.1.

---

[112] Section 10 is copied entirely from the 1787 Constitution, Article I Section 10,

[113] The 1787 constitution used the phrase "grant letters of marques and reprisal". The phrase "authorize privateers and other proxies for the state" is the modern equivalent.

The first elections for the New Senate will follow the rules for elections following reapportionment, in accordance with Article II, Section 3.1.

All incumbent Supreme Court Justices will complete their 15 year terms. Those Justices who have served for more than 15 years on the Supreme Court will continue to serve only until the Interim Chancellor nominates and the Senate confirms their replacements.

Article III: The Executive Branch

Section 1 - The President

1.1 The executive power shall be vested in a President of the United States of America.[114] *He/she shall hold office for a four-year term. Voters shall choose the President in years evenly divisible by four. Presidential elections shall be conducted in accordance with Article VI – Elections.[115]*

1.2 Eligibility for the office of President:[116] Upon taking office, the President must be

---

[114] Copied from the 1787 Constitution, Article II, Section1.

[115] All election procedures in Constitution II appear in Article VI.

[116] Adapted from the 1787 Constitution, Article II Section 1 and Amendment 12. Since the office of Vice President has been eliminated in Constitution II. the requirement that the

- At least 35 years old,
- A natural-born citizen of the United States,
- At least 14 years a resident within the United States, and
- Less than 6 years the President of the United States.

1.3 Lack of a qualified President-elect: If, at the time fixed for the beginning of the term of the President, the President-elect shall have died, the *Chancellor* shall become President. If a President shall not have been chosen before the time fixed for the beginning of his term, or if the President-elect shall have failed to qualify, then the *Chancellor* shall act as President until a President shall have qualified.[117] *And the first duty of the Acting President shall be to arrange for new Presidential elections as soon as practicable or to pursue whatever actions are necessary to qualify the President-elect; but the Acting President shall also carry out all the duties of the President until a properly-elected President shall have qualified.*[118]

1.4 Vacancy in the office of President:[119]

1.   In case of the removal of the President from office or of his death or resignation, the *Chancellor* shall become President.

2.   Whenever the President transmits to the *Chancellor of the Senate* and the Speaker of the House of Representatives his written declaration that he is unable to discharge the powers and duties of his office, and until he transmits to them a written declaration to the contrary, such powers and duties shall be discharged by the *Chancellor* as Acting President.

3.   Whenever the *Chancellor* and a majority of the *Justices of the Supreme Court* transmit to the *Chancellor Pro Tempore* of the Senate and the Speaker of the House of Representatives their written declaration that the President is

---

President and the Vice President reside in different states has been deleted.

[117] Copied from the 1787 Constitution, Amendment 20.

[118] This is a new provision, which provides an elected official with a national mandate (the Speaker of the House) as a caretaker President, until a properly-elected President can assume the office.

[119] The remainder of this section is copied from the 1787 Constitution, Amendment 25.

unable to discharge the powers and duties of his office, the *Chancellor* shall immediately assume the powers and duties of the office as Acting President.

Thereafter, when the President transmits to the *Chancellor Pro Tempore* of the Senate and the Speaker of the House of Representatives his written declaration that no inability exists, he shall resume the powers and duties of his office unless the *Chancellor* and a majority of the *Justices of the Supreme Court* transmit within four days to the *Chancellor Pro Tempore* and the Speaker their written declaration that the President is unable to discharge the powers and duties of his office. Thereupon Congress shall decide the issue, assembling within forty-eight hours for that purpose if not in session. If the Congress, within twenty-one days after receipt of the latter written declaration, or, if Congress is not in session, within twenty-one days after Congress is required to assemble, determines by two thirds vote of both chambers that the President is unable to discharge the powers and duties of his office, the *Chancellor* shall continue to discharge the same as Acting President; otherwise, the President shall resume the powers and duties of his office.

1.5 Compensation: At stated times the President shall receive for his/her services a compensation, which shall neither be increased nor diminished during the period for which he/she shall have been elected, and he/she shall not receive within that period any other emolument, *either directly or indirectly,* from the United States or any of them.[120]

1.6 Oath of Office[121]: Before the President enters on the execution of his office, he shall take the following oath or affirmation:

"I do solemnly swear (or affirm) that I will faithfully execute the office of President of the United States, and will to the best of my ability, preserve, protect and defend this Constitution II of the United States."

Section 2 - Civilian Power over Military; the Cabinet, Pardon Power, and Appointments

The President shall be Commander in Chief of the Armed Forces of the United States, and of the militia of the several states, when called into the actual service of

---

[120] Copied from the 1787 Constitution, Article II Section 1.

[121] Copied from the 1787 Constitution, Article II Section 1.

the United States; he may require the opinion, in writing, of the principal officer in each of the executive departments, upon any subject relating to the duties of their respective offices, and he shall have power to grant reprieves and pardons for offenses against the United States, except in cases of impeachment[122] *or of alleged offenses by the President or the Chancellor.*[123]

As Commander in Chief, the President may order the use of military force in a war properly declared by Congress in accordance with Article II Section 8. In the absence of a declaration of war, the President may employ military force to defend the United States or its allies, or for such other purposes as the President deems necessary in the national interest of the United States, *provided that the President notifies Congress within 48 hours of the beginning of such a military operation, and provided also that Congress approves of such use within 60 days after such a military operation commences. Without a declaration of war, the President may continue a military operation into a new calendar year only if Congress, by a law enacted no more than six months before the calendar year, authorizes the continued use of military force.*[124]

The President shall have Power, by and with the advice and consent of the Senate, to make treaties; and he shall nominate, and by and with the advice and consent of the Senate, shall appoint ambassadors, other public ministers and consuls, and all other officers *in the Executive Branch* of the United States *Government*, whose appointments are not herein otherwise provided for, and which shall be established by law: but Congress may by law vest the appointment of such inferior officers, as they think proper, in the President alone or in the heads of departments.[125]

Failure by the Senate to approve or disapprove a nomination within 60 calendar days after the President has made the nomination results in automatic Senate confirmation by unanimous consent.

---

[122] This provision is copied from the 1787 Constitution, Article II Section 2.

[123] The President cannot absolve himself or those around him from alleged wrongdoing.

[124] This provision codifies and strengthens the Authorized Use of Military Force doctrine within Constitution II. It insures that any continuing military operation not supported by a Declaration of War will have Congressional authorization at least once every year.

[125] Except for the clause in italics, this provision is copied from the 1787 Constitution, Article II Section 2.

The President shall have power to fill up all vacancies that may happen during the recess *or adjournment* of the Senate, by granting commissions which shall expire *when the next Congress convenes.*[126]

For any position appointed by the President with Senate confirmation, that position must have a permanent deputy which must be a Civil-Service position. Whenever the Presidentially-appointed position becomes vacant, the Civil Service deputy becomes the Acting official, and remains in that capacity until a replacement is confirmed by the Senate.[127]

Section 3 - State of the Union, Convening Congress, and Executive Orders

Each February, the President shall give to the Congress information on the State of the Union, and recommend for their consideration such measures as he shall judge necessary and expedient; he may, on extraordinary occasions, convene both chambers, or either of them, and in case of disagreement between them with respect to the time of adjournment, he may adjourn them to such time as he shall think proper; he shall receive ambassadors and other public ministers; he shall take care that the laws be faithfully executed, and shall commission all the *military* officers of the United States.[128]

In carrying out his responsibility to "take care that the laws be faithfully executed", the President may issue Executive Orders which have the same effect as the law upon which the Executive Order is based, provided that any Executive Order will have an effective date not less than thirty days from its issuance, and provided further that either chamber by majority vote taken during that 30-day waiting period may prevent any Executive Order from coming into effect.[129]

---

[126] This provision is adapted from the 1787 Constitution, Article II Section 2. The words "or adjournment" were added. The expiration date for temporary appointments has been modified.

[127] This provision, based on a British model, replaces the existing rules for succession. It ensures that the President cannot replace Executive Department officials without Congressional input, and it greatly assists the transition between Administrations.

[128] Adapted from the 1787 Constitution, Article II Section 3.

---

[129] This provision gives Congress a role in the issuance of Executive Orders (which have the force of law but are not actually laws). It ensures that Congress has at least some measure of buy-in to E.O.s issued by the President.

Article IV: The Judicial Branch

Section 1 – The Judiciary

The judicial power of the United States shall be vested in one Supreme Court and in such inferior courts as the Congress may from time to time ordain and establish. *The Supreme Court shall consist of a Chief Justice of the United States and not more than 16 Associate Justices.* The judges, both of the Supreme Court and inferior courts, *shall serve for 16 years beginning at the time of their appointment. However, federal judges appointed to office under the 1787 Constitution shall begin a new 16-year term under Constitution II. All federal judges* shall, at stated times, receive for their services a compensation which shall not be diminished during their continuance in office.[130]

Any current or former federal judge is eligible to be nominated to serve as an Associate Justice of the Supreme Court. When the position of Chief Justice of the

---

[130] Copied from the 1787 Constitution, Article III Section 1, except for the new clause in parentheses.

United States becomes vacant, the sitting Associate Justices shall select one of their own number as the next Chief Justice.[131] The newly-selected Chief Justice will then begin a 16-year term of office.

Section 2 – Judicial Power, Original Jurisdiction, and Jury Trials

2.1 Judicial Review. The judicial power extends to judicial review of acts of the Legislative branch, in order to judge whether such acts are in conformance with this Constitution II, and the federal courts shall have the power to invalidate any law, or any part of any law, found by the courts not to be in compliance with this Constitution II. The judicial power also extends to judicial review of all acts of the Executive branch, in order to judge whether such acts are in conformance with this Constitution II and with laws duly enacted by Congress, and the federal courts shall have the power to invalidate any such acts or parts of such acts, found by the courts not to be in compliance with this Constitution II or the laws of the United States. In conducting judicial reviews of both the Legislative and the Executive branches, federal courts may consider both the inscribed provisions of this Constitution II and laws enacted by Congress, as well as their intent. [132]

2.2 Judicial Power. The judicial power shall extend to all cases, in law and equity, arising under this Constitution II, the laws of the United States and treaties made, or which shall be made, under their authority; to all cases affecting ambassadors, other public ministers and consuls; to all cases of admiralty and maritime jurisdiction; to controversies to which the United States shall be a party; to controversies between two or more states; between a state and citizens of another state; between citizens of different states; between citizens of the same state claiming lands under grants of different states, and between a state, or the citizens thereof, and foreign states, citizens or subjects.[133]

---

[131] The purpose of this provision is to encourage comity among the Justices. They will be more likely to work well together if their leader is chosen by them.

[132] This provision incorporates into this Constitution II the principle of judicial review, which has been practiced and followed under the 1787 Constitution ever since the Marbury v. Madison decision in 1803.

[133] Copied from the 1787 Constitution, Article III Section 2.

The Judicial power of the United States shall not be construed to extend to any suit in law or equity, commenced or prosecuted against one of the United States by citizens of another state, or by citizens or subjects of any foreign state.[134]

2.3 Original Jurisdiction. In all cases affecting ambassadors, other public ministers and consuls, and those in which a state shall be party, the Supreme Court shall have original jurisdiction. In all the other cases before mentioned, the Supreme Court shall have appellate jurisdiction, both as to law and fact, with such exceptions and under such regulations as the Congress shall make.[135]

2.4 Jury Trials. The trial of all crimes, except in cases of Impeachment, shall be by jury; and such trial shall be held in the state where the said crimes shall have been committed; but when not committed within any state, the trial shall be at such place or places as the Congress may by law have directed.[136]

Section 3 - Treason

Treason[137] against the United States shall consist only in levying war against the United States or in adhering to the enemies of the United States, giving them aid and comfort. No person shall be convicted of treason unless on the testimony of two witnesses to the same overt act or on confession in open court. The Congress shall have power to declare the punishment of treason.

Section 4 – Misconduct by Public Officials

The President, *the Chancellor,* and all civil officers of the United States shall be removed from office on impeachment for, and conviction of, treason, bribery, or other high crimes and misdemeanors. [138]

---

[134] Copied from the 1787 Constitution, Amendment 11.

[135] Copied from the 1787 Constitution, Article III Section 2.

[136] Copied from the 1787 Constitution, Article III Section 2.

[137] Copied from the 1787 Constitution, Article III Section 3.

[138] Copied from the 1787 Constitution, Article II, Section 4, except that the word "Chancellor "replaces "Vice President".

No person or office is above the law, and no individual is indispensable. Accordingly, a person holding a public office, even while continuing to hold that office, shall nevertheless be liable and subject to indictment, trial, judgment, and punishment, according to law.[139] *Any federal official indicted for a felony or impeached by the House is suspended from office until the matter is resolved through conviction or acquittal.[140] If convicted following impeachment or indictment, the official shall be immediately removed from office and disqualified to hold and enjoy any office of honor, trust or profit under the United States: if acquitted, the person shall resume the duties of the office.*

When alleged misconduct by the President warrants an investigation, the Chancellor shall appoint a Special Counsel to conduct that investigation. When alleged misconduct by the Chancellor warrants an investigation, the Attorney General shall appoint a Special Counsel to conduct that investigation. The Special Counsel will submit a report of his findings to the Chancellor, the Speaker, the Attorney General, and the public.[141]

The House of Representatives, *by majority vote,* shall have the sole power of impeachment.[142]

The Senate shall have the sole power to try all impeachments. When sitting for that purpose, they shall be on oath or affirmation. When the President of the United States *or the Chancellor of the Senate*[143] is tried, the Chief Justice shall preside: And no person shall be convicted without the concurrence of two-thirds of the members present. [144]

Article V: Debts, Supremacy, and Oaths

[139] Holding a high public office does not shield the incumbent from prosecution for any crime.

[140] Defending oneself in a criminal proceeding or impeachment trial is so time-consuming and onerous that an official in that situation cannot give proper attention to his official duties. Therefore, the public interest demands that such an official temporarily step aside until the matter is resolved.

[141] A high public official such as a President or a Chancellor should not investigate himself.

[142] Copied from the 1787 Constitution, Article I, Section 2. The phrase "by majority vote" is added for clarity.

[143] The Chancellor, were he/she impeached by the House, should not preside over his/her own trial. Therefore, the Chief Justice should carry that responsibility.

[144] This entire paragraph, except for the phrase in italics, is copied from the 1787 Constitution, Article I, Section 3.

All debts contracted and engagements entered into before the adoption of this Constitution II shall be as valid against the United States under this Constitution II as under the 1787 Constitution.[145],[146]

The notion of a "national debt ceiling" has no meaning or merit whatsoever. When Congress legislates expenditures from the United States Treasury and the Treasury borrows money to make those expenditures, then the resulting debts are a sovereign debt of this nation and must be repaid.[147]

---

[145] The first two paragraphs of this article are new; the last two paragraphs are copied from the 1787 Constitution, Article VI.

[146] The 1787 Constitution contained basically the same idea in the first paragraph of Article VI, but in that case it referred to the validity of debts of the United States entered into under the Articles of Confederation.

[147] This provision simply makes it clear that, when the United States borrows money, the debt must be repaid.

This Constitution II and the laws of the United States which shall be made in pursuance thereof and all treaties made or which shall be made under the authority of the United States shall be the supreme law of the land; and the judges in every state shall be bound thereby, anything in the constitution or laws of any state to the contrary notwithstanding.

The Senators and Representatives before mentioned, and the members of the several state legislatures, and all executive and judicial officers, both of the United States and of the several states, shall be bound by oath or affirmation, to support this Constitution II; but no religious test shall ever be required as a qualification to any office or public trust under the United States.

Article VI: Elections

Section 1. General Provisions

1.1 Introduction

Article VI[148] governs the elections for all elected federal offices, namely, President, Chancellor, Representative, and Senator. Congress may refine these procedures by law.

---

[148] Article VI is entirely new.

1.2 Voter Eligibility

All citizens who have attained the age of 18 are eligible to vote in all federal and state elections and in the state in which they reside.[149] Citizens who reside outside the jurisdiction of any state are eligible to vote in the Non-State Election District.

1.3 Automatic Voter Registration

Congress shall establish a National Voter Registration Authority, which will

- *create a national database of registered voters, to be shared with all jurisdictions that conduct elections,*
- *prevent the national database of registered voters from unauthorized disclosure or access from unauthorized entities,*
- *ensure that the national database of registered voters is used for no other purpose than voter registration, authentication, and authorization,*
- *assign to each voter a unique Voter Identifier which remains with that voter for life,*
- *maintain for each voter both their legal (voting) address and current contact information,*
- *accept and process voter registration applications from all eligible citizens,*
- *automatically register each citizen to vote upon their 18th birthday,*
- *automatically register each citizen to vote, or verify his/her earlier registration, whenever a citizen interacts with a state or federal government entity,*
- *remove a voter who has deceased, and*
- *establish appropriate means of voter authentication and authorization to vote.*

1.4 Ranked Choice Voting

Ranked Choice Voting (RCV) is mandatory for all federal elections.

---

[149] Adapted from the 1787 Constitution, Amendment 26

VOTING: For primary elections, for each office being contested, voters will be able to rank their choices, selecting a 1st choice, a 2nd choice, and a 3rd choice. For general elections, with only three names on the ballot, voters will be able to select a 1st choice and a 2nd choice.

COUNTING BALLOTS:

- *For each primary election, follow this procedure to determine the three primary winners who qualify for the general election.:*

    1. *Count the 1st choice votes for each candidate, and rank order the results. Repeat steps 2 through 4 until only three candidates remain or until three candidates each exceed 25% of the 1st choice votes.[150]*

    2. *Eliminate the candidate with the fewest votes.*

    3. *Reassign each vote for the eliminated candidate to each voter's next highest choice for a candidate not yet eliminated.*

    4. *If a ballot for the eliminated candidate contains no choice for a candidate not yet eliminated, then that ballot is exhausted and is no longer counted as part of the total vote.*

- *For a general election, follow this procedure to determine the winner:*

    1. *Count the 1st choice votes for each candidate, and rank order the results. If the leading candidate has less than a majority, then eliminate the candidate that came in third, and reassign each vote for the eliminated candidate to each voter's 2nd choice*

    2. *If a ballot for the eliminated candidate contains no 2nd choice, then that ballot is exhausted and is no longer counted as part of the total vote.*

---

[150] It is mathematically impossible for more than three candidates to each exceed 25% of the vote.

[151] The procedure on vacancies is adapted from the 1787 Constitution, Amendment 17. However, that Amendment gave the governor the power to make temporary appointments to fill vacancies. This Constitution II stipulates that vacancies will be filled by an election and is exactly the same for both chambers.

1.5 Voting Procedures

Regular elections: All regular elections for federal offices occur in even-numbered years. The National Primary Election takes place in October, and the National General Election takes place in December.

Special elections: When a vacancy occurs in any state's representation in the Senate or the House, the executive authority of that state shall issue a Writ of Special Election to fill that vacancy.[151]

States conduct all elections[152] but the Secretary of State shall conduct elections in the one Non-State Election District. A secret ballot is guaranteed. Voters record their votes on paper ballots, which states must retain for ten years. Voters submit completed ballots either by mail or by delivering them to ballot collection boxes. By law, Congress may authorize other methods of voting.

The "voting window" – the period when received ballots are processed and counted – lasts for fifteen days in every election. For the National Primary Election, the voting window is from October 1 to 15; for the National General Election, the voting window is from December 1 to 15; for Special Elections, the Writ for Special Election shall specify both fifteen-day voting windows. Votes must be received by the last day of the voting window.

Election officials shall announce the first-choice results of every election each day during the last five days of the voting window. After the voting window closes, election officials shall apply Ranked Choice Voting procedures to each election and shall then announce and certify election results as soon as they are known.

Open primaries are mandatory for all federal elections. Any eligible candidate may compete in any primary, subject to state rules for qualifying for the ballot. The party affiliation of a candidate, if any, will be indicated on the ballot. Each primary has three winners, and these are the only candidates that appear on the general election ballot. A primary winner may withdraw within one week after being certified to appear on the general election ballot.

No candidate for a federal office may personally engage in fundraising nor appear at a fundraising event while Congress is in session.

To appear on a primary ballot, a candidate must authorize the US Treasury to release, two weeks after the National Primary, the five most recent tax returns of

---

[152] The current, well-established system gives the responsibility for conducting elections to the states. There is no compelling reason to change this.

that candidate and his or her spouse, if that candidate qualifies for the general election, and if that candidate does not withdraw as a candidate before such tax returns are released. To appear on a general election ballot, each candidate must also release, on the same schedule, a statement of net worth, showing his/her complete assets and liabilities and those of his/her spouse, including details concerning creditors, investors, and customers.[153]

1.6 Consolidated Election Schedule

- *In even-numbered years, Congress adjourns sine die before July 4.*
- *September 15: States mail primary ballots to all registered voters.*
- *October 1 – 15: Voting window for National Primary Election.*
- *November 15: States mail general election ballots to all registered voters.*
- *December 1 – 15: Voting window for National General Election.*
- *Noon on the 1st Sunday in January: Congress convenes. Inauguration of the newly elected chancellor*
- *Noon on the 2nd Sunday in January: Inauguration of the newly elected president.*

Section 2. Elections for President and for Chancellor

The President and the Chancellor shall be elected directly by the voters. The President shall be elected for a four-year term of office in years evenly divisible by 4. The Chancellor shall be elected for a four-year term of office in even-numbered years not evenly divisible by 4.

Any candidate who withdraws as a Presidential or Chancellor candidate by September 1 may become a candidate for the Senate or for the House in the same election cycle. A person can be a candidate for only one federal office at a time.

Congress shall establish a National Vote Tabulation Authority, whose responsibility is to collect from the states the 1st choice results of the primary and general elections for President and for Chancellor, to apply RCV counting

---

[153] This provision requires all general election candidates to be completely transparent with respect to their personal finances.

procedures on a nationwide basis, to collect updated 1st choice results from the states as candidates are eliminated, to tabulate and summarize the results, and to announce the winners.

Section 3. Elections for Members of Congress

3.1 Election Districts

Following apportionment of seats in the House of Representatives to each state, each state will be redistricted into the appropriate number of Congressional Districts (CDs). Each CD will elect one Representative.

The objectives in drawing CDs are:

- *Equalize populations among districts within a state,*
- *Keep neighbors together, and*
- *Ignore all other considerations*

3.2 Redistricting Principles

The redistricting procedure must satisfy these principles:

- *Avoid human decisions concerning any particular CD boundary.*

- *Adopt a completely rule-governed process.*

- *Follow the same process in every state,*

- *Make the process transparent to and replicable by anyone so interested.*

- *Equalize the population of each CD within a state. (Each CD's population must fall within 5% (plus or minus) of the average population per seat in that state.)*

- *Without violating the 5% rule, assign an entire county to the same CD. When necessary to complete a CD while meeting the population criterion, partition one county into Zip Code Tabulation Areas (ZCTAs).*

- *A CD should consist of an entirely contiguous landmass. This is a desirable but not mandatory criterion.*

- *When redistricting for any state is complete, redistricting for that state will not be repeated until the redistricting required following the next decennial census.*

3.3 Redistricting Procedure Summary

Repeat the following steps to create each CD:

1. *Select the Starting Point for drawing the current CD.*

2. *Assign to the current CD whole counties closest to the Starting Point.*

3. *When necessary, partition LAST COUNTY into ZCTAs in order to reach the population target for a CD.*

3.4 Redistricting Procedure Details

Congress shall legislate a procedure to implement subsections 3.2 and 3.3 of this section, including special cases and anomalies.[154]

Section 4. Continuance in Office

To continue in office, all federal elected officials, by October 1 of each year, must authorize the US Treasury to release the five most recent tax returns of that official and his or her spouse. Each official must also release, on the same schedule, a statement of net worth, showing his/her complete assets and liabilities and those of his/her spouse.

Every federal elected official is prohibited from hiring, nominating, or appointing any member of his/her immediate family to any position within the federal government.

---

[154] The detailed procedure appears in Appendix 1.

Article VII: Citizen Empowerment; Constitutional Amendments

Section 1. Enacting and Repealing Federal Statutes

Any citizen or state may initiate a proposal to adopt a new federal statute or repeal an existing federal statute.[155] Each of the several states may endorse the proposal either through ordinary state legislation or through its own state procedures for initiative and voter-approved referendum. When half of the states comprising half of the population have endorsed the proposal, the proposal will appear on the ballot throughout the United States at the next general election.

---

[155] Section 1 extends citizens' power of Initiative and Referendum, currently available in 24 states with respect to state statutes, to the citizens of the United States with respect to Federal statutes.

Adoption of the proposal requires the approval of 1) a majority of all votes cast, and 2) a majority of votes cast in 50% of the states containing 50% of the population.

Section 2. Proposing an Amendment

This section prescribes two methods for proposing an amendment to this Constitution II:

- ***Method 1.** The Congress, whenever a majority of both chambers shall deem it necessary, shall propose an amendment to this Constitution II.*[156]

- ***Method 2.** Each of the several states may propose a constitutional amendment by approving the amendment according to the procedures of each state for amending their own state constitutions. When at least half of the states comprising at least half of the US population propose such an amendment, then this amendment becomes a proposed constitutional amendment.*

When an amendment to this Constitution II has been proposed according to either method specified in this Section, that amendment shall be valid to all intents and purposes as part of this Constitution II, when ratified by the people as specified in Section 4.

Section 3. Constitutional Convention

This section prescribes two methods for calling a Constitutional Convention charged with the task of drafting a New Constitution:

- ***Method 1.** On the application of the legislatures of two-thirds of the several states, Congress shall call a Constitutional Convention.*

- ***Method 2.** Each of the several states may propose a Constitutional Convention by approving the call for a Constitutional Convention according to the procedures of each state for amending their own state*

---

[156] Article VII grants citizens the exclusive power to approve all constitutional amendments. It seems unreasonable to allow one-third of the House or Senate the power to block an amendment desired by a majority. Hence in Constitution II a mere majority (rather than 2/3) of each chamber is necessary for the Congress to propose a constitutional amendment.

constitutions. When at least half of the states comprising at least half of the US population propose a Constitutional Convention in this manner, Congress shall call a Constitutional Convention.

When states have called for a Constitutional Convention according to either method specified in this Section, Congress shall convene said convention. The product of said convention shall be the Proposed New Constitution, which shall be valid and will replace this Constitution II when ratified by the people as specified in Section 4.

Section 4. Ratification

The power to amend or replace this Constitution II rests solely with the people of the United States. This section prescribes the only method for ratification of a proposed constitutional amendment or a proposed New Constitution.

- ***Two General Elections.*** *Ratification requires the approval of voters in two general elections. Between these two general elections, at least one other general election must have taken place and a new person must hold the office of President.*

- ***Ratification Threshold.*** *In both of these two general elections, ratification requires the approval of 1) a majority of all votes cast and 2) a majority of votes cast in 60% of the states containing 60% of the population.*

APPENDICES

Appendix 1. Detailed Redistricting Procedure

If my proposed redistricting scheme is adopted as a constitutional amendment or as part of a new constitution, the general redistricting principles and rules will be in the Constitution itself, but Congress will need to legislate the details. This appendix provides the details.

If my proposed redistricting scheme is adopted through national or state-level legislation, the general redistricting principles and summary of the rules will appear in that legislation. Again, this appendix provides the necessary details.

Obtain the state's source data:

- Obtain the state's total population (STATEPOP) according to the most recent census. Throughout the redistricting process, STATEPOP is divided between ASSIGNED, that is, the land area and population that has already been assigned to a CD, and UNASSIGNED, that is, the land area and population that has not yet been assigned to a CD.

- Find the Number (N) of seats apportioned to this state. CDs will be numbered consecutively as CD 1, CD 2, CD 3, …, CD (N-1), CD N.

- Calculate the Average population per seat (AVG), that is, STATEPOP divided by N, rounded to a whole number.

- Calculate Maximum Variation (MAXVAR), that is, the maximum variation (plus or minus) from the TARGET permitted for any CD. MAXVAR is defined as 5% of AVG, rounded to a whole number. TARGET will be defined for each CD and is the total state population which should be assigned when the current CD is completed, that is, the CD # x AVG.

- Download a map of all counties in the state and a map of all ZCTAs in the state. The term "county" in this context means the first level of political subdivision of a state, whatever word is used to describe such a jurisdiction –examples include county, borough, parish, and city.

- Download a spreadsheet of all county populations and of all ZCTA populations within each county.

Follow this procedure to build each CD from CD 1 to CD (N-1):

Preliminarily:

CD #: Increment the CD #. The first CD is CD 1, followed by CD 2, and so on, up to and including CD (N-1).

TARGET: Calculate the TARGET for the current CD, that is, the CD # * AVG. This is the total state population which should be assigned to all CDs drawn so far.[157]

CONTIGUITY: The UNASSIGNED AREA (**UA**) must always remain a contiguous land area. This means that the creation of any CD must not leave an isolated pocket disconnected from the rest of UA (with the obvious exception of islands).

Determine the STARTING POINT (S):

1. If the width (east-west extent) of UA >= height (north-south extent) of UA, then the STARTING POINT (S) for drawing the current CD is the westernmost point of UA; provided that, if multiple pointes in UA are tied as westernmost (such as in the case of a vertical western border), then S is the northernmost of those westernmost points.
2. If the height of UA > the width, then S is the northernmost point of UA; provided that, if multiple points in UA are tied as northernmost (such as in

---

[157] This definition is preferable to simply defining target as AVG (the average population per seat in the state). By defining target to include all CDs constructed so far, the excess or shortage of population in each CD will be self-corrected in subsequent CDs. If we use AVG as the target for each CD, then, in a given state, every CD from CD 1 to CD N-1 might end up a little over (or they all might end up a a little under) AVG, meaning that the final CD in the state might miss AVG by an unacceptably large amount.

[158] The choice of western (rather than eastern) and northern (rather than southern) seems natural, in that we read a page in English from left to right and from top to bottom.

the case of a horizontal northern border), then S is the westernmost of those northernmost points.[158]

Build the Congressional District

1. Draw an ever-widening arc around S, adding counties to the current CD, including any remaining portion of a county previously partitioned. When the arc crosses into a county, add the entire county to the CD. Keep adding counties until the addition of one more county (termed LAST COUNTY (LC)) would cause the total population assigned to all CDs so far to exceed TARGET.

2. Decide whether LC must be omitted from the current CD, included in the current CD, or partitioned, as follows:

   a. If the CD population without LC is under TARGET by less than MAX-VAR, then the CD is complete without adding LC. Skip to Step 5.

   b. If the CD population with LC added is over TARGET by less than MAX-VAR, then complete the CD by adding LC. Skip to Step 5.

   c. If both (a) and (b) are true, then either add or do not add LC to the CD, depending on which of these actions brings the running state total (ASSIGNED) closer to TARGET. Skip to Step 5.

   d. If both (a) and (b) are not true, then partition LC into ZCTAs, following Steps 3-4. Then continue with Step 5.

3. Continue drawing the same ever-widening arc through LC around S, adding ZCTAs to the current CD.[159] When the arc crosses into a ZCTA, add the entire ZCTA to the CD. Keep adding ZCTAs until the addition of one more ZCTA (termed LAST ZCTA (LZ)) would cause the total population assigned to all CDs so far to exceed TARGET.

---

[159] In lieu of Steps 3 and 4, you can use this shortcut to draw a very rough approximation of the location of the arc within LAST COUNTY: Calculate the percentage of the LC population needed to reach TARGET; then draw the arc assigning the same percentage of land area in LC to the current CD. Of course, in reality, the population of a county may not be evenly distributed across the county, but that is why this is a rough approximation. Also in reality, ZCTA boundaries are a jigsaw pattern, not an even arc – which again means that the arc shape is an approximation.

4. Decide whether LZ must be omitted from the current CD, included in the current CD, or partitioned, as follows:

   a. If the CD population without LZ is under TARGET by less than MAX-VAR, then the CD is complete without adding LZ.

   b. If the CD population with LZ added is over TARGET by less than MAX-VAR, then complete the CD by adding LZ.

   c. If both (a) and (b) are true, then either add or do not add LZ to the CD, depending on which of these actions brings the running state total (ASSIGNED) closer to TARGET.

   d. If both (a) and (b) are not true, then partition LZ into census tracts (which are ~4000 people each). Continue drawing the same ever-widening arc through LZ around S, adding census tracts until TARGET is reached.

5. While adding counties, ZCTAs, and census tracts, do not allow an "island" to develop, that is, a section of land unconnected to the rest of the unassigned portion of the state. Also, when a county is partitioned, ensure that the remaining unassigned part of the county is a single contiguous area. If necessary to achieve this, add the smaller remaining area to the current CD and enlarge the larger unassigned area. See the discussion of anomalies below.

6. Could the LAST ZCTA Be Too Large? Before deciding that the current CD is complete, we must check the CD's population to ensure that it falls within 5% of the average population for a CD in this state. Though technically possible, exceeding this ±5% criterion is most unlikely, based on the following logic:

   a. Based on the 2020 Census figures, there were 761,952 residents per House member (that is, total US population divided by 435). 5% of this average is 38,098. We either add or do not add LAST ZCTA to complete a CD, depending on whether or not the addition of LAST ZCTA brings the CD population closer to the average or not. Hence to exceed the 5% threshold, LAST ZCTA would have to have more than 76,195 residents, and the breakpoint would have to be such that the smaller portion would have to exceed 38,098. (To apply this principle to any particular state, we calculate 5% of the average population per House seat in that state. This amount is the allowable variance when deciding whether or not to partition LAST ZCTA.)

b. Of the 33,092 ZCTAs in the United States in 2010, only 126 had a population over 76K. (The average population per ZCTA was 9330.)

c. The greatest population ZCTA in the country (ZCTA 60629, near Chicago's Midway Airport) had 113,916 residents in 2010. If that ZCTA happens to be the last ZCTA added or not added to complete a congressional district, and if the target was exactly in the middle of that ZCTA, then that CD would miss Target by a maximum of that ZCTAs population divided by 2, or 56,958, which is about 9% of AVG for Illinois. Technically possible, but not likely.

In short, when following the procedure for assigning LAST ZCTA, the likelihood of creating a congressional district whose population is too small or too large is tiny. But if such an event were to occur, we can split LAST ZCTA into two parts by census tracts, which contain ~4000 people per tract. Just use the same Scan Line to scan the census tracts within LAST ZCTA, and stop adding census tracts when Target is reached.

Last CD in a State (CD-N)

When all CDs except the last one have been drawn, then everything left over at that point necessarily belongs to the last CD, that is, CD-N.

ANOMALIES and a STATE DISTRICT BOUNDARY RESOLUTION COMMISSION:

Should any anomalies remain, such as an island far removed from the main landmass, or an isolated pocket of territory not assigned to any CD, or a non-contiguous portion of any CD, then a non-partisan commission should be empowered by the state to resolve such anomalies (but not empowered to redraw the maps generally). The governor will appoint a citizen volunteer, who must be registered as an Independent, as the non-voting Chairman of the State District Boundary Resolution Commission. The Chairman will organize and administer the Commission. The Chairman will ask for citizens to volunteer to serve on the Commission and will ensure that all volunteers are registered voters qualified to serve. The Chairman will divide the qualified volunteers into three groups: registered Republicans, registered Democrats, and registered Independents or 3rd party members. From the pool of qualified volunteers in each of the three groups, the Chairman will select three commissioners by lot. The final maps adopted by the nine-member Commission must be approved by a majority of each of the three groups of commissioners.

Appendix 2. Maryland Redistricting

Let's apply this scheme to Maryland as our test case. I chose Maryland as my sample state for three reasons:

1) With eight House seats, Maryland's population is about average (the 50 state average is 8.7seats per state).

2) Maryland has two major metro areas (Baltimore and the Maryland suburbs of Washington, DC) and two large rural areas (Western Maryland and the Eastern Shore, the area east of the Chesapeake Bay). Maryland is one of the most weirdly shaped states in the nation. Hence, a redistricting scheme that can work for this oddly-shaped and unevenly-populated state might well work for them all.

3) I live here! So I'm partial to my home state. In addition, Democrats have gerrymandered Maryland for years, and even though I myself am a Democrat, I consider our own gerrymandering regrettable, so I'd like to come up with a scheme to fix this.

As explained in Appendix 1, the proposed scheme depends on a detailed map showing all the counties and all the Zip Code Tabulation Areas (ZCTAs) in a state. Here is an overall map of Maryland's ZCTAs from the 2010 Census:

You can see that this map has nowhere near enough detail for the purpose of drawing exact Congressional District boundaries, especially in the densely populated areas near Washington, DC, and in Baltimore. Maryland had 546 ZCTAs in 2010, and this map cannot show that level of detail.

I was able to find detailed Maryland ZCTA boundary maps from the 2000 census. Here are two samples for Montgomery and Garrett counties:

2000 CENSUS ZCTA BOUNDARIES FOR MONTGOMERY COUNTY

Source: U.S. Census Bureau
Prepared by the Maryland Department of Planning, Planning Data Services, August 2001.

2000 CENSUS ZCTA BOUNDARIES FOR GARRETT COUNTY

From the maps above, you can also see that any partitioned county will have a jagged boundary between the partitions, not a smooth and even arc.

To keep this project manageable and easily understandable, I chose to create approximate boundaries for partitioned counties, using county population figures as a rough guide. I estimate the location of the CD boundary line roughly where it would occur if I had more detailed and complete input data. Consider the result a proof of concept rather than a definitive solution.

So we begin with a map of Maryland's 23 counties plus Baltimore City, along with the population of each jurisdiction:

County	Population
Allegany MD	68106
Anne Arundel MD	588261
Baltimore City MD	585708
Baltimore County MD	854535
Calvert MD	92783
Caroline MD	33293
Carroll MD	172891
Cecil MD	103725
Charles MD	166617
Dorchester MD	32531
Frederick MD	271717

Garrett MD	28806
Harford MD	260924
Howard MD	332317
Kent MD	19198
Montgomery MD	1062061
Prince Georges MD	967201
Queen Annes MD	49874
Somerset MD	24620
St. Marys MD	113777
Talbot MD	37526
Washington MD	154705
Wicomico MD	103588
Worcester MD	52460

Significant data points for drawing Congressional Districts based on the 2020 Census include the following:

- Total state population
- Number of House seats apportioned to the state
- Average population per CD (AVG), that is, total population divided by the number of House seats
- Maximum Variation (MAX-VAR), that is, the maximum population by which a CD's population can differ from TARGET. The MAX-VAR for a state is defined as 5% of AVG. TARGET is defined as AVG multiplied by CD#.

Statewide Data	
State	Maryland
State Population	6177224
House Seats	8
AVG	772153
MAXVAR	38608

Maryland Congressional District 1

Next, let us create Maryland's 1st congressional district. Since the state's width exceeds its height, the Starting Point (S) is the westernmost point in the state. Since the western border of the state is a vertical line, multiple westernmost points exist, so we choose the northernmost of those westernmost points.

The counties nearest S are Garrett, Allegany, Washington, Frederick, and Carroll. These five counties are wholly included in CD 1. The LAST COUNTY (L) is Montgomery, which must provide 7% of its population to complete CD 1.

We cannot omit Montgomery County, because 7% of its population exceeds Maryland's MAXVAR.

Master Congressional District Table - Maryland									
		County Population				Running Aggregates			
					Left	State		Total	
CD#	County	Avail	This CD	%	Over	Total	This CD	Target	Diff
1	Previous State Total and New Target for This CD					0	0	772153	772153
1	Garrett	28806	28806	100%	0	28806	28806	772153	743347
1	Allegany	68106	68106	100%	0	96912	96912	772153	675241
1	Washington	154705	154705	100%	0	251617	251617	772153	520536
1	Frederick	271717	271717	100%	0	523334	523334	772153	248819
1	Carroll	172891	172891	100%	0	696225	696225	772153	75928
1	Montgomery	1062061	75928	7%	986133	772153	772153	772153	0

Note on Partitioning Montgomery County

For purposes of the demos in this paper, I did not obtain the detailed maps of the ZCTAs in each partitioned county. However, since ZCTAs are simply zip codes with boundaries, and since every zip code defines a collection of mail delivery routes, we can expect each ZCTA to contain a relatively compact and contiguous land area. Therefore, we know that we can scan LAST COUNTY on the edge of a CD and add ZCTAs as we encounter them until the requisite population for the CD is attained. The partitions in these demos are based on the portion of each county needed to complete the current CD.

With more complete and detailed source data, we would scan the partial counties, using the map of ZCTAs for those counties, along with population data for those ZCTAs. We would then add ZCTAs to the current CD until the addition of one more ZCTA would cause the target population to be exceeded. We then add or do not add this LAST ZCTA to the current CD depending on whether the addition of LAST ZCTA would or would not bring the aggregate population closer to Target.

Maryland Congressional District 2

After drawing CD 1, the height of the remaining UNASSIGNED AREA (UA) is greater than its width, so S for CD 2 is the northernmost point in UA. Since we have multiple northernmost points (Maryland's northern border, which is the Mason-Dixon Line), S becomes the westernmost of those northernmost points, to wit, the northwest corner of Baltimore County.

Baltimore County's population exceeds the population of a CD in Maryland. Hance Baltimore County is also LC. We need 90% of LC to meet TARGET. The arc of the partition line passes through the southeast corner of Baltimore County, leaving 10% for inclusion in a later CD.

		County Population				Running Aggregates			
CD#	County	Available	Assigned to this CD	%	Left Over	State Total	This CD	Total Target	Diff
2	Previous State Total and New Target for This CD					772153	0	1544306	772153
2	Baltimore County	854535	772153	90%	82382	1544306	772153	1544306	0

Master Congressional District Table

Maryland Congressional District 3

For CD 3, UA is still higher than wide, so S is the northernmost point in UA. The Mason-Dixon Line is still the northern border of UA, providing multiple northernmost points. Hence we select S as the westernmost of those tied northernmost points, that is, the northwest corner of Harford County.

As we begin to build CD 3, we add Harford and Cecil counties, and the next jurisdiction the arc encounters is Baltimore City. 70% of the city would complete CD 3. However, CD 3 would not be a contiguous land mass, violating one of our ground rules. Therefore, we must skip Baltimore City for CD 3. We then pick up the UA portion of Baltimore County and then Kent County. The arc then enters Anne Arundel County, but we cannot add Anne Arundel, because that would leave Baltimore City as an isolated UA. So instead we move on down the Eastern Shore of Maryland, adding Queen Anne's, Talbot, Caroline, Dorchester, Wicomico, and Somerset counties. At this point the arc enters Worcester, which becomes CD 3's LC.

We need 25K people to complete CD 3, which is less than MAXVAR, so Worcester could be skipped. We could also include all of Worcester, since CD 3 would then have just 28K people too many, which again is less than MAXVAR.

But omitting LC would leave Worcester as an isolated pocket of UA, violating a rule on contiguity. Therefore we will include Worcester in CD 3.

		County Population				Running Aggregates			
CD#	County	Available	Assigned to this CD	%	Left Over	State Total	This CD	Total Target	Diff
3	Previous State Total and New Target for This CD					1544306	0	2316459	772153
3	Harford	260924	260924	100%	0	1805230	260924	2316459	511229
3	Cecil	103725	103725	100%	0	1908955	364649	2316459	407504
3	Baltimore County	82382	82382	10%	0	1991337	447031	2316459	325122
3	Kent	19198	19198	100%	0	2010535	466229	2316459	305924
3	Queen Anne's	49874	49874	100%	0	2060409	516103	2316459	256050
3	Talbot	37526	37526	100%	0	2097935	553629	2316459	218524
3	Caroline	33293	33293	100%	0	2131228	586922	2316459	185231
3	Dorchester	32531	32531	100%	0	2163759	619453	2316459	152700
3	Wicomico	103588	103588	100%	0	2267347	723041	2316459	49112
3	Somerset	24620	24620	100%	0	2291967	747661	2316459	24492
3	Worcester	52460	52460	100%	0	2344427	800121	2316459	-27968

Master Congressional District Table

Maryland Congressional District 4

For CD 4, UA is taller than wide. So S is the northernmost point, which means the east-west northern boundary of Baltimore City. We select the westernmost point along the northern border of the city as S. CD 4 consists of all of the city plus 27% of Anne Arundel County.

		County Population				Running Aggregates			
		Available	Assigned to this CD	%	Left Over	State Total	This CD	Total Target	Diff
CD#	County								
4	Previous State Total and New Target for This CD					2344427	0	3088612	744185
4	Baltimore City	585708	585708	100%	0	2930135	585708	3088612	158477
4	Anne Arundel	588261	158477	27%	429784	3088612	744185	3088612	0

Master Congressional District Table

Maryland Congressional District 5

For CD 5, UA is taller than wide, so S is the northernmost point in UA. CD 5 contains all of Howard County plus 41% of Montgomery.

		County Population				Running Aggregates			
			Assigned		Left	State		Total	
CD#	County	Available	to this CD	%	Over	Total	This CD	Target	Diff
5	Previous State Total and New Target for This CD					3088612	0	3860765	772153
5	Howard	332317	332317	100%	0	3420929	332317	3860765	439836
5	Montgomery	986133	439836	41%	546297	3860765	772153	3860765	0

Master Congressional District Table

Maryland Congressional District 6

S is again the northernmost point in UA. The arc covers the remainder of Montgomery and 23% of Prince George's.

		County Population			Running Aggregates			
			Assigned		Left	State		Total	
CD#	County	Available	to this CD	%	Over	Total	This CD	Target	Diff
6	Previous State Total and New Target for This CD					3860765	0	4632918	772153
6	Montgomery	546297	546297	51%	0	4407062	546297	4632918	225856
6	Prince George's	967201	225856	23%	741345	4632918	772153	4632918	0

Master Congressional District Table

Maryland Congressional District 7

For CD 7, S is the northernmost point in Anne Arundel's UA. CD 7 consists of the remaining 73% of Anne Arundel plus the next 35% of Prince George's.

		County Population				Running Aggregates			
			Assigned		Left	State		Total	
CD#	County	Available	to this CD	%	Over	Total	This CD	Target	Diff
7	Previous State Total and New Target for This CD					4632918	0	5405071	772153
7	Anne Arundel	429784	429784	73%	0	5062702	429784	5405071	342369
7	Prince George's	741345	342369	35%	398976	5405071	772153	5405071	0

Master Congressional District Table

268

Maryland Congressional District 8

After drawing all but one of the CDs in a state, the last CD must necessarily contain all of the remaining UA. For the last CD, we do not need to define S, draw an arc, or determine LC.

We were careful to avoid leaving any isolated pockets while drawing CDs 1 through 7. Thus both by design and through happenstance, the remaining area in Maryland's CD 8 is one contiguous land mass. If this turns out not to be true in some other state, it may be necessary to make some final adjustments

		Master Congressional District Table							
		County Population				Running Aggregates			
			Assigned		Left	State		Total	
CD#	County	Available	to this CD	%	Over	Total	This CD	Target	Diff
8	Previous State Total and New Target for This CD					5405071	0	6177224	772153
8	Prince George's	398976	398976	41%	0	5804047	398976	6177224	373177
8	St. Mary's	113777	113777		0	5917824	512753	6177224	259400
8	Calvert	92783	92783		0	6010607	605536	6177224	166617
8	Charles	166617	166617		0	6177224	772153	6177224	0

Summary of Maryland Congressional Districts

The proposed method as applied to Maryland results in only four partitioned counties (Montgomery, Prince George's, Baltimore County, and Anne Arundel), although two of these (Montgomery and Prince George's) are divided into three parts. The populations of all eight CDs are within MAXVAR.

Appendix 3. North Carolina Redistricting

Again reminding you that this is a proof of concept demonstration and not a definitive plan, I developed this North Carolina redistricting solution using data from 2021 population estimates from the Census Bureau's annual American Community Survey. The datapoints are approximately the same but slightly higher than the 2020 US Census as the North Carolina population continues to grow slowly.

This is the map of North Carolina counties and the 2021 county population data:

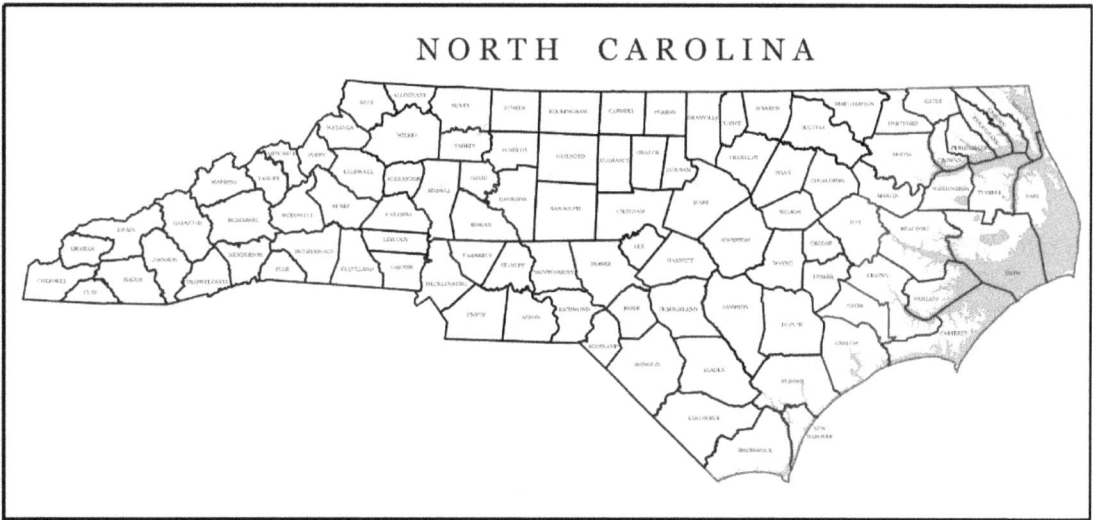

Name	2021 Population	Name	2021 Population
Alamance County	175499	Brunswick County	154700
Alexander County	37829	Buncombe County	265055
Alleghany County	11,135	Burke County	90645
Anson County	24,398	Cabarrus County	226165
Ashe County	27,411	Caldwell County	82482

Name	2021 Population	Name	2021 Population
Avery County	17615	Camden County	11249
Beaufort County	46870	Carteret County	69543
Bertie County	18629	Caswell County	22544
Bladen County	31864	Catawba County	161279
Chatham County	77156	Iredell County	188754
Cherokee County	29098	Jackson County	44614
Chowan County	13699	Johnston County	222633
Clay County	11445	Jones County	9031
Cleveland County	98803	Lee County	62921
Columbus County	54886	Lenoir County	55867
Craven County	101741	Lincoln County	90149
Cumberland County	339667	Macon County	37026
Currituck County	29257	Madison County	21935
Dare County	37813	Martin County	22000
Davidson County	170111	McDowell County	46338
Davie County	43412	Mecklenburg County	1143570
Duplin County	58241	Mitchell County	14900
Durham County	330506	Montgomery County	27365

Edgecombe County	50448	Moore County	105030
Forsyth County	388453	Nash County	94706
Franklin County	73805	New Hanover County	238907
Gaston County	228327	Northampton County	19053
Gates County	11560	Onslow County	199984
Graham County	8401	Orange County	149468
Granville County	61371	Pamlico County	12912
Greene County	20995	Pasquotank County	40306
Guilford County	546308	Pender County	65146
Halifax County	48762	Perquimans County	13627
Harnett County	139256	Person County	39598
Haywood County	63171	Pitt County	183076
Henderson County	119251	Polk County	20836
Hertford County	23275	Randolph County	144503
Hoke County	56312	Richmond County	44711
Hyde County	4759	Robeson County	128107

Name	2021 Population	Name	2021 Population
Rockingham County	91796	Union County	247917

273

Rowan County	144008	Vance County	44335
Rutherford County	67537	Wake County	1152740
Sampson County	63903	Warren County	19555
Scotland County	34967	Washington County	11202
Stanly County	64058	Watauga County	56463
Stokes County	45751	Wayne County	122919
Surry County	71431	Wilkes County	68110
Swain County	14315	Wilson County	82619
Transylvania County	34809	Yadkin County	38039
Tyrrell County	3818	Yancey County	18461

This table provides the statewide data needed for drawing CDs:

Statewide Data (2021 population)	
State	North Carolina
State Population	10701027
House Seats	14
AVG21	764359
MAXVAR	38217

The following pages display North Carolina's14 CDs, drawn according to the scheme detailed in Appendix 1. On each map, S is the Starting Point for drawing an ever-widening arc touching counties that comprise the CD. The arc stops expanding when it touches LAST COUNTY, which may be included, omitted, or partitioned. Below the map is a list of the counties wholly or partially in the CD. Where a county is only partially included in a CD, the list displays the percentage of the county's population that lies within the CD.

North Carolina Congressional District 1

Starting Point: Westernmost point in the Unassigned Area

LAST COUNTY: McDowell (omitted from CD 1)

Cherokee
County

Clay County

Graham
County

Swain

Macon

Jackson

Haywood

Transylvania

Madison

Buncombe

Henderson

Polk

Rutherford

Yancy

Bob Spear

North Carolina Congressional District 2

Starting Point: Westernmost point in the Unassigned Area

LAST COUNTY: Gaston (50 % included in CD 2)

McDowell

Mitchell

Avery

Burke

Cleveland

Watauga

Caldwell

Catawba

Lincoln

Gaston (50%)

278

North Carolina Congressional District 3

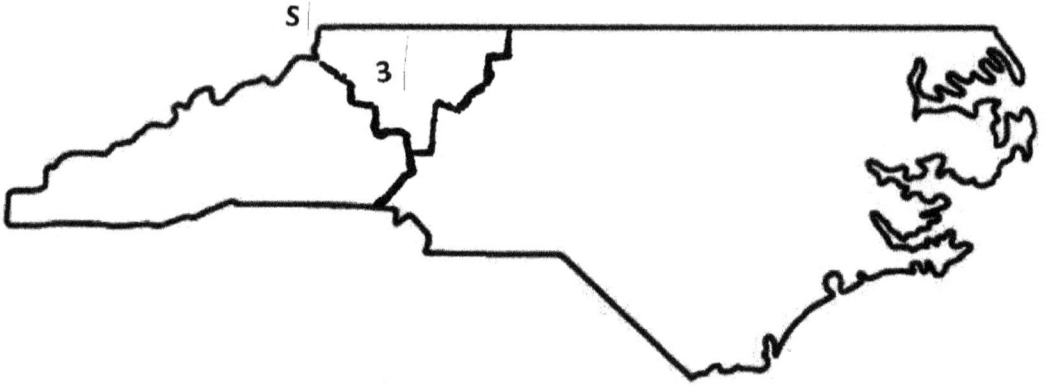

Starting Point: Westernmost point in the Unassigned Area

LAST COUNTY: Forsyth (60% in CD 3)

Ashe

Wilkes

Alleghany

Alexander

Surry

Yadkin

Irredell

Davie

Stokes

Forsyth (60%)

Bob Spear

North Carolina Congressional District 4

Starting Point: Westernmost point in the Unassigned Area

LAST COUNTY: Mecklenburg (57% in CD 4)

Gaston (50% left over from CD 2)

Mecklenburg (57%)

North Carolina Congressional District 5

Starting Point: Westernmost point in the Unassigned Area

LAST COUNTY: Cabarrus (omitted from CD 5)

Mecklenburg (43% left over from CD 4)

Union

North Carolina Congressional District 6

Starting Point: Westernmost point in the Unassigned Area

LAST COUNTY: Randolph (91 % in CD 6)

Cabarrus

Rowan

Stanly

Davidson

Anson

Montgomery

Randolph (91%)

North Carolina Congressional District 7

S

tarting Point: Westernmost point in the Unassigned Area

LAST COUNTY: Rockingham (included in CD 7)

Forsyth (40% left over from CD 3)

Guilford

Rockingham

Bob Spear

North Carolina Congressional District 8

Starting Point: Westernmost point in the Unassigned Area

LAST COUNTY: Cumberland (22% in CD 8)

Richmond

Moore

Scotland

Hoke

Randolph (9% left over from CD 6)

Chatham

Robeson

Lee

286

Harnett

Cumberland (22%)

North Carolina Congressional District 9

Starting Point: Westernmost point in the Unassigned Area

LAST COUNTY: Granville (included in CD 9)

Caswell

Alamance

Orange

Person

Durham

Granville

North Carolina Congressional District 10

The widening arc for constructing CD 10 appears to touch Pender County before it touches New Hanover. However, adding Pender County to CD 10 would leave New Hanover County as an island, unconnected to the remaining Unassigned Area. For this reason, Pender is skipped, and New Hanover is included in CD 10 instead.

Starting Point: Westernmost point in the Unassigned Area0
LAST COUNTY: New Hanover (75% included in CD 10

Columbus

Bladen

Brunswick

Bob Spear

Cumberland (78% left over from CD 8)

Sampson

New Hanover (75%)

North Carolina Congressional District 11

Starting Point: Westernmost point in the Unassigned Area

LAST COUNTY: Wake (66% included in CD 11)

Wake (66%)

North Carolina Congressional District 12

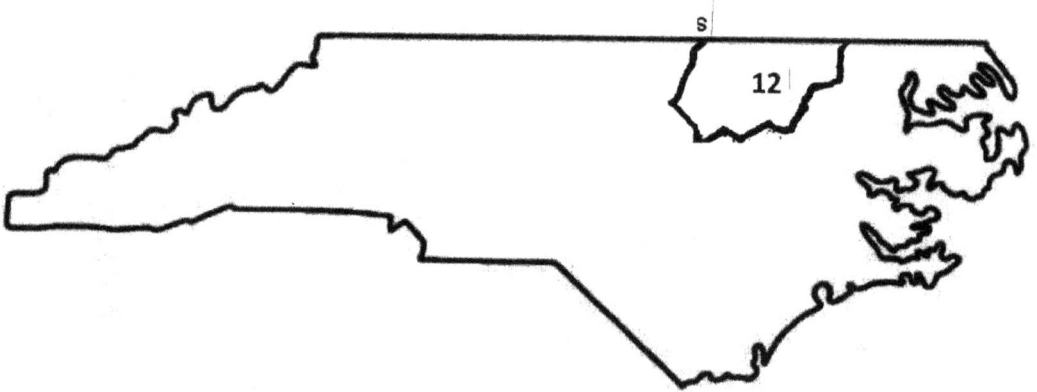

Starting Point: Northernmost point in the Unassigned Area

LAST COUNTY: Johnston (omitted from CD 12)

Vance

Warren

Northampton

Halifax

Franklin

Nash

Wake (34% left over from CD 11)

Edgecombe

North Carolina Congressional District 13

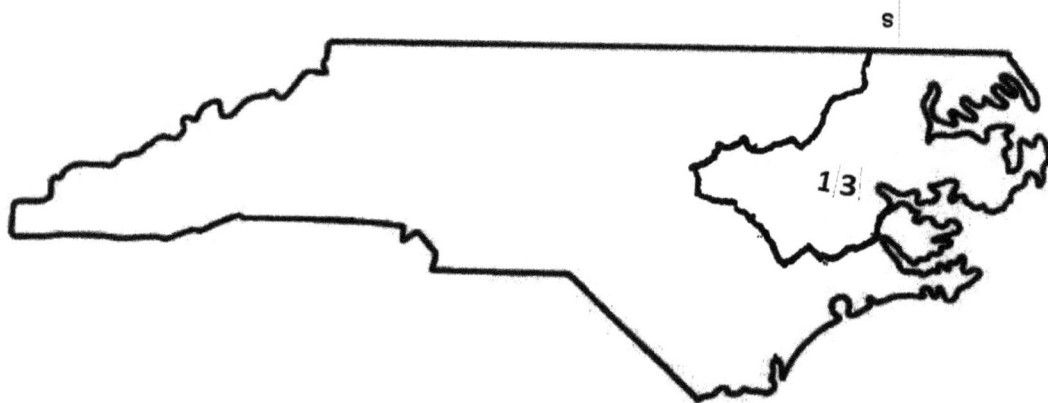

Starting Point: Northernmost point in the Unassigned Area

LAST COUNTY: Pamlico (omitted from CD 13)

Hertford

Gates

Camden

Currituck

Bertie

Chowan

Perquimans

Pasquotank

Washington

Martin

Beaufort

Pitt

Hyde

Tyrell

Greene

Wayne

Dare

Lenoir

Craven

North Carolina Congressional District 14

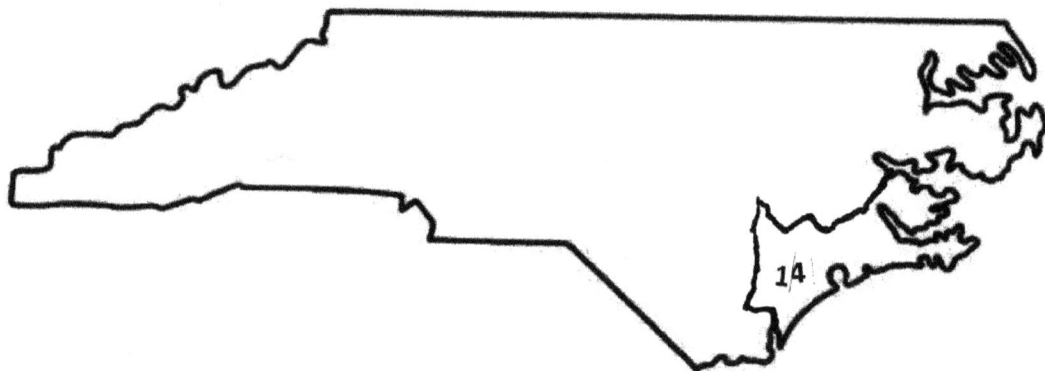

The last CD in any state does not need a procedure for drawing its boundaries. Rather, it consists of all of the remaining Unassigned Area aft completing all the other CDs.

Carteret

Duplin

Johnston

Jones

New Hanover (25% left over from CD 10)

Onslow

Pamlico

Pender

Wilson

North Carolina -- All 14 Congressional Districts

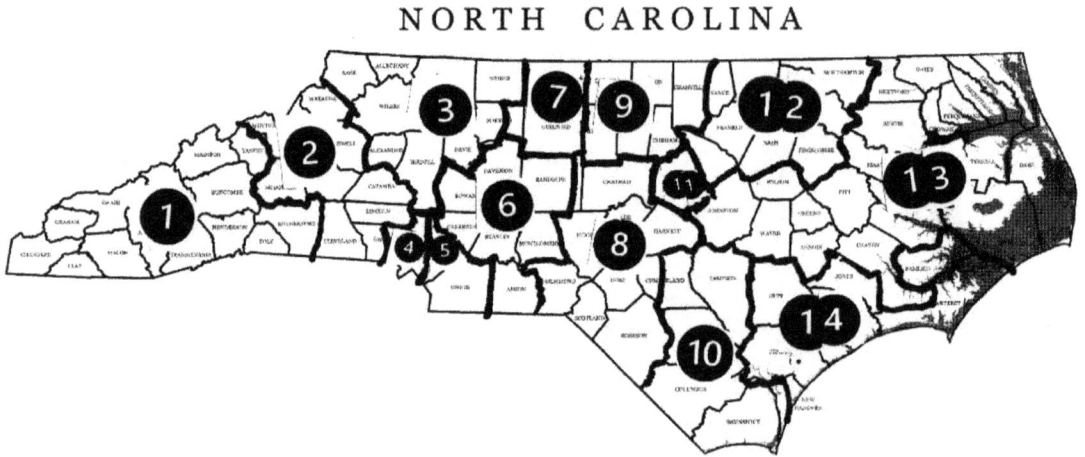

NORTH CAROLINA

Sources/Citations

Articles of Confederation (1781). Downloaded from https://www.govinfo.gov/content/pkg/SMAN-107/pdf/SMAN-107-pg935.pdf

Ballotpedia (2019). Multiple articles containing election results. https://ballotpedia.org/Main_Page

Baltimore Sun (2016). "Senator proposes two-state solution on redistricting reform" (February 6). https://www.baltimoresun.com/news/maryland/politics/blog/bal-senator-proposes-twostate-solution-on-redistricting-reform-20160209-story.html [accessed on May 10, 2019].

Brennan Center for Justice (2019). "The National Popular Vote, Explained". https://www.brennancenter.org/blog/national-popular-vote-explained [accessed on May 10, 2019].

Common Cause (http://www.commoncause.org/issues/money-in-politics/)

Common Cause (http://www.commoncause.org/issues/voting-and-elections/)

Constitution of the United States (1787); aka "1787 Constitution". Downloaded from https://www.govinfo.gov/content/pkg/CDOC-110hdoc50/pdf/CDOC-110hdoc50.pdf

Curiel, J. and T. Steelman, "How to measure the impact of partisan gerrymandering". Paper presentation at *Reason, Reform & Redistricting Conference*, Duke University, January 2019.

Daniller, A. (2020). "A majority of Americans continue to favor replacing the Electoral College with a nationwide popular vote". Pew Research Center (March 13). [Available online at https://www.pewresearch.org/fact-tank/2020/03/13/a-majority-of-americans-continue-to-favor-replacing-electoral-college-with-a-nationwide-popular-vote/, accessed on 2/5/2022.]

End Citizens United (http://endcitizensunited.org/)

EveryVoice.org (http://everyvoice.org/)

FairVote (2017). "Why James Madison wanted to change the way we vote for President". http://www.fairvote.org/why-james-madison-wanted-to-change-the-way-we-vote-for-President. [Accessed on June 16, 2017.]

FairVote. https://www.fairvote.org/

Gallup (Nov 2020 to Jan 2022). "Party Affiliation" (public opinion poll). https://news.gallup.com/poll/15370/party-affiliation.aspx [accessed on Feb 5, 2022].

Koza, J.R., B. Fadem, M. Grueskin, M. Mandell, R. Richie, and J. Zimmerman (2013). Every Vote Equal: A State-Based Plan for Electing the President by National Popular Vote. (4th edition). National Popular Vote Press.

League of Women Voters (http://lwv.org/issues/protecting-voters)

League of Women Voters (https://www.lwv.org/voting-rights/money-politics)

Louisiana Secretary of State: Voting and Elections (2019). https://www.sos.la.gov/ElectionsAndVoting/Pages/default.aspx

Machiavelli, N. (1513). *The Prince.* Downloaded from the Maryland Digital eLibrary Consortium. https://maryland.overdrive.com/media/283602?utm_campaign=searchfeed &utm_source=google [accessed on May 10, 2019].

Madison, J (1793). "Helvidius No. 3" (September 7). https://founders.archives.gov/documents/Madison/01-15-02-0066 [accessed on May 10, 2019].

Maryland State Board of Elections (2019). https://elections.maryland.gov/

MAYDAY.US (https://mayday.us/)

Minnesota Secretary of State: Elections and Voting (2019), https://www.sos.state.mn.us/elections-voting/

Missouri Census Data Center (2019). "Geocorr 2014: Geographic Correspondence engine. http://mcdc.missouri.edu/applications/geocorr2014.html [accessed on May 2, 2019].

MoveToAmend.org (https://movetoamend.org/)

New Republic (Nov. 8, 2012). "Welcome to America's Most Gerrymandered District". https://newrepublic.com/article/109938/marylands-3rd-district-americas-most-gerrymandered-congressional-district [accessed on May 9, 2019].

New York Times (August 1, 2016). "Only 9% of America Chose Trump and Clinton as the Nominees". https://www.nytimes.com/interactive/2016/08/01/us/elections/nine-percent-of-america-selected-trump-and-clinton.html?_r=0 [accessed on June 15, 2017].

North Carolina State Board of elections (2019). https://www.ncsbe.gov/index.html

Paine, T. (1776). *Common Sense*. Downloaded from https://archive.org/details/commonsense00painrich

Pennsylvania Department of State, Bureau of Commissions, Elections, and Legislation (2019). https://www.dos.pa.gov/VotingElections/Pages/default.aspx

Roosevelt, F. (1932). Commencement Address at Oglethorpe University, May 22, 1932. *The Atlanta Constitution*, May 23, 1932.

Singh, R.S. (2019). *In Defense of the United States Constitution*. Routledge (New York).

Supreme Court of the United States (June 2019). "Rucho et al. v. Common Cause et al." Downloaded from https://www.supremecourt.gov/opinions/18pdf/18-422_9ol1.pdf on October 27, 2019.

Tweed, W (n.d.). "Top 6 Quotes from Boss Tweed", *AZ Quotes*, http://www.azquotes.com/author/14885-Boss_Tweed [accessed on June 15, 2017].

US News & World Report (https://www.usnews.com/news/articles/2015/12/01/redistricting-reform-gains-steam) [accessed on July 1, 2019].

Wikipedia (2017). "United States Presidential Election, 1788-89." https://en.wikipedia.org/wiki/United_States_Presidential_election,_1788-89 [accessed on June 6, 2017].

Wikipedia (2019). "Electoral system of Australia". https://en.wikipedia.org/wiki/Electoral_system_of_Australia [accessed on May 10, 2019].

Wikipedia (2019). "Instant-runoff voting". https://en.wikipedia.org/wiki/Instant-runoff_voting [accessed on May 10, 2019].

Wolf-PAC (http://www.wolf-pac.com/)